Thorns Lust and Glory

THORNS LUST AND GLORY

The Betrayal of ANNE BOLEYN

ESTELLE PARANQUE

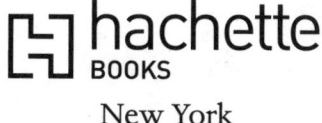

New York

Copyright © 2024 by Estelle Paranque

Cover design by ClarkevanMeurs Design
Cover image © Getty Images
Cover copyright © 2024 by Hachette Book Group, Inc.

Hachette Book Group supports the right to free expression and the value of copyright. The purpose of copyright is to encourage writers and artists to produce the creative works that enrich our culture.

The scanning, uploading, and distribution of this book without permission is a theft of the author's intellectual property. If you would like permission to use material from the book (other than for review purposes), please contact permissions@hbgusa.com. Thank you for your support of the author's rights.

Hachette Books
Hachette Book Group
1290 Avenue of the Americas
New York, NY 10104
HachetteBooks.com
Twitter.com/HachetteBooks
Instagram.com/HachetteBooks

First US Edition: November 2024
Originally published in the UK by Ebury Press in May 2024

Published by Hachette Books, an imprint of Hachette Book Group, Inc. The Hachette Books name and logo is a trademark of the Hachette Book Group.

The Hachette Speakers Bureau provides a wide range of authors for speaking events. To find out more, go to hachettespeakersbureau.com or email HachetteSpeakers@hbgusa.com.

Books by Hachette Books may be purchased in bulk for business, educational, or promotional use. For information, please contact your local bookseller or Hachette Book Group Special Markets Department at special.markets@hbgusa.com.

The publisher is not responsible for websites (or their content) that are not owned by the publisher.

Library of Congress Control Number: 2024939643

ISBNs: 9780306835933 (hardcover); 9780306835957 (ebook)

Printed in the United States of America

LSC-C

Printing 1, 2024

To ma lumière de vie, *my son,* Zachary Aurélien Gill

Contents

Author's Note ix

Prologue: A Rose Between a Lion and a Salamander, Calais, October 25–27, 1532 xi

Part 1:
In the Shadow of the Court of Fleur-de-Lys, 1514–1526

Chapter 1: Games of Court 3
Chapter 2: The Rise of a Magnificent King and His Ladies 19
Chapter 3: Witnessing the Pursuit of Grandeur 39
Chapter 4: Troubled Waters 59

Part 2:
The Pursuit of a Crown, 1527–1532

Chapter 5: Struggle to Power 81
Chapter 6: Ainsi Sera, Groigne Qui Groigne 101
Chapter 7: Every Rose Has Its Thorn 123
Chapter 8: "The Most Happy" 139

Part 3:
The Pitfalls of Glory, 1533–1536

Chapter 9: A Tudor Rose Cannot Replace a Lion Cub — 159
Chapter 10: An Impossible Mission — 177
Chapter 11: The Tide Has Turned — 195
Chapter 12: The Inconceivable — 217

Epilogue: *À Jamais* Remembered — 243

Notes — 249
Bibliography — 261
Acknowledgments — 267
Index — 271

Author's Note

As with *Blood, Fire and Gold*, my aim with this book is to provide an account of history that is accurate, but also relatable and immersible. For that reason, some dialogue has been re-created from primary sources and perhaps I have also allowed myself more speculative claims that again are based on primary evidence, but rely evidently on my own judgment and appreciation of them.

Writing about the enigmatic and charismatic Anne Boleyn and her life and tragic death has not been easy—her voice has been for the most part erased from history. But it has deeply reinforced my strong belief in elevating, promoting, fighting for, protecting, and amplifying women's voices and experiences. I will therefore keep writing about them.

Estelle Paranque, Colchester, 2023

Prologue

A Rose Between a Lion and a Salamander, Calais, October 25–27, 1532

She hadn't seen Francis I of France for over ten years.

Her mounting excitement was palpable, as was her anxiety.

During the time she'd spent at his court in her younger years, the king had taught her a great deal about the games of power, and now she would need to play them herself.

Would he recognize her? Would he support her and Henry as she so desperately needed him to?

In her heart she carried so many questions, so much hope and—dare one say it—vaulting ambition.

★

Henry VIII had ensured that he looked magnificent for the coming event. Today, he was receiving his "brother," the monarch—King Francis—at Calais, the last English stronghold on the continent.

Wearing a golden robe adorned with diamonds and rubies, Henry was accompanied by his bastard son, Henry Fitzroy, and by the boy's mother, Elizabeth Blount. Following them were several English bishops and secular lords; they had all traveled two or three miles outside of Calais to welcome the French king, who had organized splendid receptions and other events to greet Henry and his men in Boulogne-sur-Mer.

The two kings embraced each other.

"My good brother, welcome to Calais!"[1] Henry exclaimed.

In noisy celebration of their arrival, three cannons were fired from the ramparts of the city's fortifications, and there were cheering crowds as people celebrated in the streets. It was, after all, an extremely rare sight to see two great rulers together in one place.

Once they had entered the city walls, two lines of people formed: the servants and the guards of the English king. The servants were in red hats and fawn-colored clothing while the guards wore blue and red uniforms, holding halberds in their right hands. Henry VIII was proud of the welcome he had orchestrated for his longest rival and friend, and he guided Francis to his accommodation—known as "The Staple" or the "Hostel of Guises"—before taking his leave. A square house with a high tower at its center, it was big enough, and believed to be prestigious enough, to receive a king.

The king's mistress, Anne Boleyn, had not taken part in the brief welcoming party. As soon as Henry had taken his guest to his house, he made his way to her, where she was staying with a dozen ladies-in-waiting, all patiently anticipating the role they would play in this royal encounter. After all, the two lovebirds had made the journey to France with only one real purpose: to obtain Francis's support and allyship for their union.

That evening a dinner was to be held, one which needed to follow the diplomatic protocols. Francis, however, never liked abiding by these rules. He often had his own agenda, and this occasion was no exception.

As soon as he arrived, instead of sitting down in the appointed position, he ordered his Provost of Paris, Jean de la Barre—who was acting as his right-hand man—to find Anne, who was sitting opposite the French contingent. Jean was to offer her the present

Francis had brought from Paris—a magnificent diamond, estimated to cost between 10,000 and 15,000 crowns.

De la Barre executed the king's order, and as he bowed to present Anne with the gift, he said, "From my master, the King of France, who finds you as exquisite as ever."[2]

One can imagine Anne blushing, both at this unexpected gift and the compliment. She certainly must have been relieved; after all these years, Francis had not forgotten her. Even more importantly, she still remained in his good graces—meaning she had a strong chance of getting the support she so desperately needed.

No one has recorded Henry VIII's reaction to this moment, though a mix of emotions must surely have been running through his mind: another man, another king, though not just any other king; a king who had spent seven years at the French court with Anne, who was now offering a prestigious gift to his concubine. And not just any gift, but a diamond that could be perceived as more than a simple token of affection.

Henry had to put all these thoughts to rest, however, as he was there to seek the support of Francis I. After all, his gift to Anne was also a token of the French king's good disposition toward England.

Perhaps more than that, it was hopefully a sign of approval—and even a promise to vouch for Henry's union with Anne to the Pope. There was so much at stake with this meeting. Henry could not afford to let his ego, or his jealousy, ruin it all.

And he didn't.

★

The next day, the two kings went to the Church of Notre-Dame, where they would attend the mass and discuss diplomatic matters with their councillors. They spent the whole day together while Anne remained with her ladies.

Then, on Sunday, October 27, Henry VIII organized a great

banquet in honor of his counterpart, serving 16 fat capons, 7 swans, 20 pheasants, 50 chickens, 40 partridges and several other birds. Other festivities were included as part of the entertainment, including mastiff, bull and bear fights. Everything was absolutely extravagant, to match the image of the English king.

Henry and Francis had never appeared to be so close—not even 12 years before at the Field of the Cloth of Gold, the summit that took place in June 1520 and that had forged a bond of friendship between the two kings and their nations. Laughing, drinking and enjoying themselves now, one could imagine that no prior rivalry had ever existed between the men, who both looked positively regal as they indulged in their mutual admiration.

Francis wore an embroidered doublet, adorned with diamonds that seemed to shine with exaggerated brightness, and were estimated to be worth 100,000 crowns.

Henry, too, looked striking, in a robe made of gold and royal purple along with a very heavy three-row necklace. On the first row, there were 14 rubies, almost the size of eggs, while brilliant pearls adorned the second row. The last row featured 14 impressive diamonds. The pendant he wore was an outstanding heraldic piece representing a precious stone—probably an antique garnet—from which emerged eight raises ending in fleurs-de-lys, the symbol of French royalty. People believed Henry's pendant was worth at least 4,000 crowns.

Undeniably, the two kings were the center of attention.

Anne had not been invited to the dinner, as was the custom, so when she made her entrance at the end of the feast with a group of masked ladies—including Lady Derby, Lady Mary (who some historians believed to be Mary Boleyn herself), Lady Fitzwater and Lady Wallop—everyone applauded to welcome them.

Francis I arose and went immediately to Anne. He offered her his hand, to be kissed, and—more importantly—to ask her for the first dance. Whereafter, the other French lords present invited the other English ladies to dance.

Henry kept his watchful gaze on Francis and Anne throughout. When the dance had finished, he ordered all the ladies to leave, including Anne. However, some court gossips reported that this was not actually what occurred.

Allegedly, Eustace Chapuys—known for his spicy dispatches to Charles V of Spain, the Holy Roman Emperor, and for having eyes and ears in all places (apparently even in France)—later reported that Anne chose not to follow her ladies and instead asked for a private audience with Francis I.

No one knows exactly what was said between the two during this audience, but Anne's detractors—who loved sharing scandalous gossip—believed that she used the moment to seduce Francis into supporting her cause. After all, they said, apparently she (or possibly her sister) had gained the nickname "the mule of the French king" during her time in France, implying that she had already consented to intimate favors.

While it is very hard to believe that Anne would have defied Henry, the man who was to be her future husband, in such a manner, it is certainly possible that she asked for an audience with the French king, not to flirt, but to discuss her future as queen of England—and as an ally to France. For such a conversation, she would need to have found the perfect moment to make him promise to give his blessing to what was surely to become the most scandalous marriage in Europe.

Francis I was a pragmatic man, and though he must have had—at least at this time—his own affectionate feelings for Anne, he would also let nothing jeopardize the future of his son, Henry, Duke of Orléans—or the future of France and its place in the whole of Christendom. In fact, he had recently been negotiating, on behalf of his son, the hand of the niece of Pope Clement VII, Catherine de Medici. This was his utmost priority, and he could not have that undermined by any potential scandal.

It is, however, possible that he agreed, at least implicitly, to help Anne and Henry be restored into the good graces of the

Pope. Advocating for them—as long as it was not too insistent, or persistent—was a small price to pay to have Anne as an agent of France, operating right at the center of the English court.

But no one will ever know what Francis actually promised, if indeed he promised anything. Other reports in fact claimed that he was certainly not supportive of Henry and Anne's union. Charles V of Spain's ambassador at the French court, the Count of Cifuentes, assured the Holy Roman Emperor that "the king of France had confessed to the Pope that, during his meeting with Henry VIII, he had tried to dissuade him from divorcing Catherine of Aragon, or at the very least, to wait some time until he was convinced this was the only possible outcome."[3]

While this might have been true, for Francis I, there were also several real advantages to having Anne as the new queen of England.

For one, it would truly infuriate his real enemy: Charles V, Holy Roman Emperor. Francis had not forgotten how the Spanish king had humiliated him and, later, his sons during their respective imprisonments in Spain. The divorce of Charles's aunt, Catherine of Aragon, from Henry VIII meant that Francis and his English counterpart would be able to forge an alliance against the emperor.

More straightforwardly, Anne had spent many years in France and was therefore a familiar ally. In a future marriage between her and the English king, she could serve the interests of the French monarchy. Indeed, with her upbringing and her sense of style, she might almost be mistaken for a French noblewoman, or even a princess.

Of course, this did not mean that Francis would risk falling out of favor with the Pope, and many others all over Europe—French, Venetian, Spanish and English—knew this. The future of France, and his own legacy, was at stake.

The French–English encounter in Calais lasted for two more days, and for the most part Francis had more pressing diplomatic priorities on his mind than his support, or otherwise, of Henry's marriage to Anne. The monarchs, however, departed on good terms, and Anne was full of hope for what would come next—optimism that was to prove misguided. Regardless, fate was following its course and the young woman who had been raised at the French court would soon become queen of England.

During her time at the French court, Anne had undeniably been influenced by many powerful characters, mostly women: Louise of Savoy, Francis I's mother, and Claude of France, his wife and consort. More significantly, perhaps, she was influenced by the king's sister, Marguerite of Angoulême, later queen of Navarre, who had shown great interest in ideas of religious reformation during the first half of the sixteenth century, which would go on to interest the new queen. And then, obviously, there was Francis I himself, whose charisma and kingship must have made a great impression on the young Anne.

To understand Anne Boleyn's experience in the English court, and her hope of an alliance with France, one needs to know the stories of these influential individuals, and how they operated during Anne's time at the French court. And to understand her fascination with France, one also has to reveal the lives and motivation of the men who were Francis's mouthpieces later, at the English court.

In the end, was Anne right to trust that they would support her in her ambitions? Or did she ultimately fool herself into thinking she had a key role to play in the stability and prosperity of the Anglo-French alliance? Would Anne Boleyn, queen of England, be betrayed?

PART I

In the Shadow of the Court
of Fleur-de-Lys

1514–1526

I

Games of Court

In the early hours of January 9, 1514, a dark and gloomy Monday, the flamboyant Anne of Brittany—who had twice been crowned queen of France through her two successive unions to French kings—died of a kidney-stone attack in the Castle of Blois, taking her last breath at around six o'clock. The queen had been suffering violent stomachaches for months, and had shown incredible strength despite the pain she'd endured.

This woman—who had brought harmony between Brittany and the kingdom of France, and who had married both French kings without providing a male heir—was now at peace on her royal bed.

Anne had been pregnant 14 times in 20 years, but the only babies who made it to adulthood were her daughters Claude and Renée. Claude was meant to continue her mother's legacy and secure the line of both her parents.

As the Venetian ambassador reported, Queen Anne's death touched everyone: "The whole court is wearing black and the king is so terribly sad that he is in bed with fever. No one mentions the war or the Italian affairs any more."[1]

Anne's death changed everything, potentially threatening France's stability. As there was no direct male heir, Louis XII knew that his first cousin once removed—the dashing and impetuous Francis of the house Valois-Angoulême—was next in line to the throne. For Louis, this was a far from pleasant thought; he feared that, even though Francis was his cousin, his legacy would be ruined by this new dynasty. He had to act, and quickly.

Anne's funeral was a way for relatives from the Angoulême branch to assert their legitimacy and proximity to the throne. Louis XII was not dead but, without a male heir, Francis was now dauphin of France.

At the end of January, Francis—alongside his mother, the pragmatic and charismatic Louise of Savoy, and his sister, Marguerite of Angoulême—arrived at court from Cognac. After several tumultuous negotiations over recent years, Francis had been promised to Claude. The truth was, Louis had to be convinced of this match; it was only due to the perseverance of both his late wife, Anne of Brittany, and Louise of Savoy that he had agreed to the union. Even though the marriage had not yet happened, Francis knew it would take place eventually—the sooner the better, to ensure that his right to the throne was unquestioned.

During Anne's funeral, Francis stood by Claude's side, next to Anne's coffin—a symbol of the continuity of her legacy. The betrothed couple were illustrating their unity to the whole court, and Louise of Savoy was not far behind, "wearing a very long crepe dress" like most noblewomen following the procession.[2] People from all over Europe came to pay their respects. The dashing and instantly recognizable John Stewart, Duke of Albany, could also be found in the midst of the crowd, standing near Marco Dandolo, ambassador of Venice.

Once the two ceremonies taking part in Brittany and Paris were complete, discussions commenced once again. Would Louis XII honor his promise and agree to the marriage of his eldest daughter and his cousin? Having initially protested against the match, Louis finally gave in and accepted the union. Louise of

Savoy agreed to the marriage, too—despite finding Claude "very small and strangely fat."[3]

Francis himself did not show great enthusiasm for the betrothal. He was, of course, keen to further assert his right to the crown, but Claude was far from his liking and he frequently showed interest in other women, both at court and beyond, whom he deemed more attractive. His behavior did not fail to go unnoticed by many, including his own mother and King Louis.

On May 18, 1514, Francis and Claude were nevertheless finally married at the chateau of Saint-Germain-en-Laye, though the atmosphere was somber; most people were still mourning the death of Anne of Brittany. Indeed, Francis complained that it was a ceremony "without the pomp due to a royal marriage even in mourning." Louis, the king, showed no interest at all, only displeasure, and the jugglers, comedians and other buffoons that were supposed to amuse the crowd were instead "thrown out" on his orders.[4] Francis was insulted and, in retaliation, decided to show no interest in his young wife. Instead, after the wedding, he went straight to Paris, "whoring, gambling, and drinking."[5] This did not necessarily do a great deal for his reputation, although later Pierre de Bourdeille, Seigneur de Brantôme and a contemporary of Francis's son, seemed to think that Francis was simply following the fashion of the times: "King Francis loved too wildly and too much; for being young and free, he became involved first with one and then with another, for in that time, a man was not considered much of a gallant unless he whored every place without distinction."[6]

Louis XII, however, raged when he heard the news and decided to take revenge upon his new son-in-law—an act of retaliation that Francis did not see coming and that would make his future, and his place on the throne, more complicated than ever.

For Louis had been persuaded that he needed a new wife.

And, ideally, a young one who could give him his lifelong wish: a male heir.

*

Across the Channel, an English courtier by the name of Thomas Boleyn had been rising in the Henrician court. Married to Elizabeth Howard, sister to the powerful Thomas Howard, Duke of Norfolk, the family was gaining in influence. In 1512, Thomas Boleyn was sent as a special envoy to Mechelen to discuss important diplomatic matters between Maximilian, the Holy Roman Emperor, and Henry VIII. There, he met Margaret of Austria, Duchess of Savoy, the emperor's daughter and governor of the Habsburg Netherlands. It was thanks to Thomas's friendly relationship with Margaret that "an alliance of powers dedicated to the destruction, dismemberment, and partition of France" was formed.[7]

Through his friendship with Margaret, Thomas managed to secure a position for his youngest daughter, Anne, at the duchess's court in Mechelen. Being a lady-in-waiting at any court was a real honor; being a lady-in-waiting to one of the most powerful women in Europe was a true blessing.

While ladies-in-waiting at court were often paid scant regard, apparently mere companions to their mistress, in reality they were much more than that, proving their importance. Not only did they get an invaluable education by being acquainted with the best tutors, thinkers and writers that inevitably gravitated to the courts of Europe, they were right at the center of court politics—and, if they chose to, could eavesdrop on the to-and-fro dealings of the great men and women whom they served. The value of what was in effect a political apprenticeship explains why the ambitious Thomas Boleyn wanted so much to secure it for his daughter. Ladies-in-waiting could lobby on behalf of a range of people, including their own families.[8] And they had the trust of their mistress, which made them influential at court and beyond.

By the summer of 1513, Anne was at the heart of Margaret's prestigious court, receiving a continental education. The governess of the Habsburg Netherlands herself showed great pleasure at this decision:

> I have received your letter by the Esquire [Claude] Bouton who has presented your daughter to me, who is very welcome, and I am confident of being able to deal with her in a way which will give you satisfaction, so that on your return the two of us will need no intermediary other than she. I find her so bright and pleasant for her young age that I am more beholden to you for sending her to me than you are to me.[9]

Anne's own feelings about being pulled away from England and Hever Castle, her family home, to be placed in a foreign country were not known. What we do know for sure is that Anne, whether excited or morose at the prospect, spent her early teenage years at a court where great thinkers and humanists—such as Desiderius Erasmus—were regularly received, making it a reputable place to receive a highly regarded education. It was the perfect place for Anne to start her schooling. Here, the young woman learned fashionable skills such as playing musical instruments, but crucially, she also mastered the French language.

While Anne settled into her new life, however, the political situation was far from stable. War against France was imminent, and conflict between the two nations seemed inevitable, with no reconciliation seeming possible. Even Thomas Boleyn was getting ready for war.

What Henry did not expect was that he would be betrayed by Maximilian and Margaret; good personal relationships, it seemed, did not necessarily equal prosperous political ones.

The Habsburgs had encouraged Henry to go to war against Louis XII, but instead of supporting him, they played both kings off against each other. Their ultimate goal was for England and France to deplete their military power until they were both in weak enough positions to discuss peace treaties—giving the upper hand to the Holy Roman Empire and Spain. The plan worked in the short term. However, once Henry realized his mistake, he restrategized with the help of his primary adviser, Cardinal Thomas Wolsey, the most powerful man in England after the king. They decided to pursue an alliance with France, and to do so urgently.

The French king desired a new bride and Henry had the perfect candidate: his youngest sister, Mary Tudor. Fifteen years old, beautiful, pious and allegedly obedient, she had all the attributes the 52-year-old Louis XII sought. France and England might have been going through a rough patch over the last decade, but once they realized they'd been played against each other, there was an unexpected chance for reconciliation.

There was, however, a stumbling block. Mary had already been promised to Charles of Austria, who was not only to become Charles V of Spain and Holy Roman Emperor, he was also nephew to Margaret of Austria and Catherine of Aragon, queen of England, as well as the grandson of Ferdinand of Aragon and Isabel of Castile. Charles's heritage was in the most powerful monarchs of Europe.

In April 1514, Margaret of Austria complained to her ambassador at the English court that she hoped Henry VIII had not forgotten about "the marriage between Charles of Austria and Mary of England," reminding him that it was too late "to take a step back" now.[10]

In a direct letter to Margaret, Henry did not offer reassurance on the matter. Instead, he promised that his ambassadors "will let her know of his attentions" regarding his sister's marriage.[11]

This was not promising at all for the Habsburgs, who feared

that a close alliance between England and France would be to their detriment. After all, they had tried very hard to divide and conquer. If the two countries were to become allies, they could counterbalance Spain and the Holy Roman Empire's power in Europe.

Charles Brandon, Duke of Suffolk, was responsible for assuring that good relations remained intact between the governor of the Habsburg Netherlands and the King of England. During one evening in Tournay, Brandon made the case for the alliance and marriage between the King of France and Princess Mary Tudor in order to secure this. Margaret was not foolish; she understood well how the diplomatic games were played in European politics. Indeed, she herself had been promised to men for whom she cared little.

"As you know, I have been unhappy in husbands,"[12] she confided in Brandon—referring to the loss of her spouses as well as, perhaps, how perilous it was for a young woman to be married to someone much older than her. Brandon was not sure how to answer this and instead chose to remain silent while the conversations continued on the subject of good relations between the European neighbors.

Dynastic alliances were all that mattered, and Margaret knew there was little she could do to prevent the marriage between Louis and Mary. Nor did she want to appear too hostile, as she could not afford to have both countries rallying against the Habsburgs.

Nothing—and, more importantly, no one—would stop this union.

★

In June 1514, Louis XII sent two special envoys to the Henrician court—Louis I of Orléans, Duke of Longueville, and the General of Normandy.

"I am so pleased that the king of England desires as much as myself the good peace, amity, and alliance between our realms and that he has agreed to the marriage of his sister."

Louis XII charged Longueville to conclude the union on his behalf. He expressed his surprise that Henry wished to marry off his sister without a dowry, but this did not seem to tarnish his enthusiasm for the match.[13]

Gérard de Plaines, Margaret's ambassador to Henry's court, praised Mary's perfection, though he also seemed to think that the match between Charles of Austria and Mary was still a possibility.

> I have never seen such a beautiful lady. Her deportment is exquisite both in conversation and in dancing, and she is very lively. She is very well brought up and appears to love the Prince [Charles] wonderfully. She has a very bad picture of him and is said to wish to see it ten times a day, and to take pleasure in hearing from him. She is not tall but is a better match in age and person for the Prince than he had heard say.[14]

Unfortunately for the Habsburgs, this could not be further from the truth. Mary was no longer promised to Charles; she would instead marry the French king to ensure that the (Peace) Treaty of London was respected and remained valid.

So, on July 30, 1514, in the royal manor of Wanstead and in the presence of Charles, Duke of Suffolk, the Bishop of Lincoln, the Bishop of Winchester, the Bishop of Durham and the Duke of Norfolk, among others, Mary publicly renounced her promise of marriage to Charles, Prince of Spain.

At first, this news greatly displeased Pope Leo X, but then he realized how beneficial it was for all of Christendom that France and England were at peace. The stability would provide an opportunity to pursue other ambitions. He encouraged Henry VIII, therefore, to pursue a crusade against the Turks.

So it was decided: the marriage between Mary and Louis would happen.

On August 13, 1514, at Greenwich Palace, in front of Henry VIII, his queen, Catherine of Aragon, the Archbishop of Canterbury, the dukes of Buckingham, Norfolk and Suffolk, and other gentlemen of the court, Princess Mary and the Duke of Longueville (representing Louis XII in the ceremony) were married.

Acting on Louis XII's behalf, Longueville took Mary's right hand in his and recited the king's words of espousal in French. She reciprocated—also in French. They then both signed the schedule that was proof of the ceremony.

So many thoughts must have raced through Mary's mind, having been forcibly obliged to agree to this union—a union to an old man whom she'd never met and who was over 35 years her elder. Even in his prime, Louis had not been described as a handsome and charming king; he had inherited the long nose and grave look of his father, Charles, Duke of Orléans.

In a letter she sent to the French king, Mary conceded, "I will love you as cordially as I can," which is far from a declaration of love.[15] There is no doubt: Mary wished that the marriage had never taken place.

For Louis, however, it was quite different. As he repeated to his special envoy, Longueville, he was extremely eager to meet his new, young wife.

On August 18, the marriage was declared consummated, again with Longueville representing his king; the bride undressed and went to bed in the presence of many witnesses, and Longueville, "in his doublet, with a pair of red hose, but with one leg naked from the middle of the thigh downwards, went into bed, and touched the Princess with his naked leg."[16] With this symbolic gesture, the union was sealed.

Louis rejoiced, writing the following to Cardinal Wolsey, one of the men who had helped secure the marriage:

I am so indebted to you, my good friend, for all your hard work strengthening a good and perfect alliance between the king, my brother, and myself and for arranging my union to my future wife, the queen, and ensuring that her apparel was *à la mode de France*.[17]

Wolsey replied to Louis:

I am so honored that you were pleased that I wrote privately to you and that you desired me to continue to do so just as if I were of your Privy Council. Therefore, I will inform you of the following matter. The King appointed Madame de Guildford [Joan Vaux, governess of Mary and Margaret Tudor] because of her experience and knowledge of the language, to accompany the queen, his sister, who, being young, and knowing none of the ladies there, might suffer in health for want of someone to confide in.

He continued, "You will find her wise and discreet."[18]

In September, the French king ordered that a tournament be organized in Paris to celebrate his wedding to Mary. Francis—his presumptive heir—participated, but he was not delighted to see such a young bride at his cousin's side. For him, the throne now seemed utterly out of reach.

Thomas Boleyn had been keeping a watchful eye on proceedings and had decided that this union was the perfect opportunity to change his own diplomatic strategy in order to accrue his own value at Henry VIII's court. In August 1514, he wrote to Margaret of Austria, asking that his daughter be sent back to England in order to join Mary Tudor's household in France. He explained that this was not his choice and that, instead, this was a request from above (a reference to Cardinal Wolsey) that he simply could not refuse.

"I humbly implore you to release my daughter from your service so she can leave your court with the people I sent for her."

He signed this appeal, "Your very humble servant, Sir Thomas Boleyn."[19]

Would Margaret accept this request, which was bold given the tensions between France and Austria and Spain? It would have been hard to refuse, though this was certainly a sign that the English would further favor the French over the Habsburgs. In many respects, what Maximilian and Margaret had tried to avoid was the very thing they achieved: An alliance against their empire was forming. Margaret might also have been disappointed in Thomas Boleyn's request and, while she could not refuse, she could delay Anne's arrival to France—which is exactly what she did.

As Mary Tudor got ready to leave her native country to be crowned queen of France, her household was being appointed. There was much to be arranged, including the shipment of 15 gowns in the French fashion, which were designed for her, alongside 6 in the Milan style and 7 after the English fashion. A cradle covered with scarlet was also packed in the hopes that it would be of use when she would go on to bear the next king of France.

The princess was now ready to meet her fate.

As soon as she arrived, however, Mary expressed her discontent. For one thing, all her ladies-in-waiting had been removed from her service, including Madame de Guildford.

"My chamberlain, with all other men servants, were discharged alongside my mother Guildeford, with my other women and maidens," she complained. "I wish to return to you, my brother the king."[20]

While the French wanted to place more of their people in the queen's household, they soon realized that removing her closest counselors was a mistake that needed to be rectified. No real detail can be found on how this was resolved, but the French king did eventually make a list of people to be retained in order to serve the queen.

On that list, "Madamoyselle Boleyne"[21] was mentioned, and on the French record of the same list, "Madamoyselle Marie Boullone" appeared.[22]

Anne was apparently still stuck in Mechelen, and Thomas Boleyn—who had been invited to the royal wedding—needed to ensure that her place at the French court remained secure. He brought his second daughter, Mary, with him for that very purpose.[23] The Boleyns continued to make significant progress on the European diplomatic scene.

*

In November 1514, Mary Tudor—escorted by various and notable gentlemen and gentlewomen—was ready to make her official entrance at the French court. While Anne did not witness Mary's coronation, once in France she had the opportunity to be right at the center of the court, among those who flocked around the king.

It was Sunday, November 5: the day had finally arrived. Mary Tudor, the youngest sister of Henry VIII of England, was crowned queen of France.

Surrounded by her ladies-in-waiting, including Anne's sister, the young woman arrived at the church—the exact name and location of which are now lost. Francis, heir to the French throne, alongside with Longueville, whom Mary already knew, welcomed her with great enthusiasm.

Mary was even more beautiful than Longueville had reported; her olive skin and dark auburn hair were deemed perfect, and were perhaps more to French taste than to that of England, where paleness held sway. Her lips were small and rosy, and she had dark, almond-shaped eyes that many women must have envied. Mary and Anne shared attributes that were deemed attractive during the sixteenth century; Anne in particular, who was good-looking but not the court's greatest classical beauty, had a certain je ne sais quoi, which elevated her.

As she knelt before the altar, Mary "was anointed by the

Cardinal of Pree as delivered her the scepter and put a ring on her finger and lastly set the crown upon her head."[24]

A high mass followed the coronation, and the congregation acclaimed the newly anointed queen of France.

A sumptuous dinner had been organized for after the ceremony to honor the young queen, and the most important gentlemen of France—alongside the English ambassadors and Mary's household—were all invited.

The next day, Mary—who with her companions had spent the night in a village two miles outside Paris—got ready to make her remarkable entry into the capital. Much had been prepared for the celebration, and pageants representing the alliance between France and England, as well as the grandeur of her royal house, could be seen all along the river that led to Paris.

Mary made her entrance with great solemnity as the procession headed through the Porte Saint-Denis on the *"pont levis."* On the side of the riverbank, she could hear cheerful French mariners singing: "Our noble lady, welcome to France where we live in pleasure and joy. Frenchmen and Englishmen live at their own pleasure and we praise God for all his goodwill toward us."

The crowd had already started drinking, and there was lively enthusiasm on display as the masses watched the former English princess making her way to their beloved city of Paris.

Paris, then as now, was one of the finest cities of Europe. On this day, great beauty could be seen all over the city: tapestries covering the walls of the town depicted the new alliance forged between France and England, and other celebratory images depicted the Queen of Sheba and King Solomon, symbols of Mary and Louis XII themselves. This was the ultimate representation of peace. "Queen Sheba" Mary was "our queen and mistress" who "brought to our magnanimous and courteous king the present of peace for the French and the English."[25]

The French people understood that this union symbolized the end of a long war between the two countries—or at least this was what they hoped for. Peace between France and England never lasted long during the sixteenth century.

Even so, Mary—being a young bride—gave the people hope that this alliance would bring heirs, and therefore stability, which would further strengthen the peace between the two realms. Indeed, Mary was everything the French people might have hoped for: young, fertile, beautiful and, they hoped, devoted to her more mature and experienced husband. As Mary journeyed down the river, an eloquent, unfortunately anonymous, orator shouted these words from one of the bridges that crossed La Seine: "Your most renowned and magnanimous princess, Paris bows and honors you!"

Between the bridge and the gate of the city, meanwhile, Mary was received by the Prevost of Merchants, the Echevins, Clerks, and Receiver of Paris. Here, a canopy was held over her head by the Echevins and principal burgesses, and public citizens took turns carrying the canopy.

Mary's procession continued to the Church of the Holy Innocents, where another scaffold had been erected. On it, there was a tent "in antique style painted gold color, called the throne of honor. Within was planted a lily in an orchard called the Orchard of France, surrounded by four Virtues: Pity and Truth on the right, and Fortitude and Mercy on the left."[26] These were symbols of great monarchs and dynastic alliance.

The day eventually ended at the Palais Royal, where a magnificent banquet had been prepared and where Louis XII had been impatiently waiting for his wife.

Mary's formidable entrance into Paris had been made solo, but if she had been nervous about the occasion, she certainly did not show it. Observers were united in their appreciation, as was recorded by Pierre Gringore, who dedicated a pamphlet to the queen herself. His words were circulated throughout all of France, so that soon everyone knew Mary's triumph in Paris and the peace it underlined.

A week later, a tournament took place to continue the festivities. Frenchmen and Englishmen alike participated in jousting competitions and other sports to indulge in some friendly rivalry.

While the tournament was mostly amicable, there were also a number of injuries and incidents reported by one of the special envoys sent to the French court. Thomas, Marquis of Dorset, wrote to Wolsey: "The tournament and course in the field began as roughly as ever I saw; for there was divers times both horses and man overthrown, horses slain, and one Frenchman hurt that is not likely to live." He admitted to briefly participating in the event, but he mostly kept his distance as he feared injuring himself. To justify his decision, he claimed that "the dauphin [future Francis I] himself was a little hurt on his hand."

This demonstration of masculinity continued and, although both sides were hurt in the process, Dorset recalled the tournament being enjoyed by both the English and the French participants, who appreciated the chance to demonstrate their virility.

Dorset ended his letter on the subject of what mattered most to Wolsey and, without a doubt, to Henry VIII himself: "The Queen continues her goodness and wisdom, and increases in the favor of her husband and the Privy Council."[27]

Indeed, Mary appeared to be the perfect bride—and the perfect pawn—for the English.

While Anne Boleyn had not been present at these glorious celebrations, welcoming parties and tournaments, she was still expected to arrive at the French court soon—her position having been secured by her sister, Mary. One can also imagine that the two sisters discussed the pageantry of the wedding together and that, indirectly, Anne experienced Mary Tudor's glory through her sister.

For now, both Mary Tudor and Anne were fulfilling their duties as daughters, meaning that one of their primary functions was to serve as vessels for advancing their male relatives' own political and diplomatic agendas. Nevertheless, Anne's life would continue to offer surprises. Her time at court might take her in many directions. Perhaps she would fall in love with a French nobleman and never return to England? Or maybe some other future awaited her.

2

The Rise of a Magnificent King and His Ladies

He had been suffering from gout for several months. Some were already saying that he would not last the winter. Others were adamant that he would get better soon. The truth was, the potential death of Louis XII of France—"father of the people"—pleased only a few: his young wife, Mary, who saw her marriage to the old man as a punishment and, of course, his heir, Francis of Angoulême, who, with his mother Louise of Savoy, had been waiting for this moment for as long as he could remember. It had certainly been a very long waiting game, but it was one that looked like it was finally coming to an end.

On January 1, 1515, the French king took the sacrament early in the morning. By the time evening came, he had breathed his last—passing the crown to his cousin and son-in-law, the dashing and charismatic Francis I.

It did not take long for Francis to show the whole court who was in charge now. During Louis XII's funeral, the Venetian ambassador reported that he refused to wear "the traditional mourning dress." Instead, the new king opted for "a purple mantle with a long train." The ambassador further remarked that "he resembled the Devil."[1] In his choice of clothing, Francis was undoubtedly making a name for himself among his people and beyond—a name that was rather ambivalent, though he was determined to make his own mark on history.

In the eyes of everyone around him—including the young Anne Boleyn, who had served as a lady-in-waiting and who "engage[d] all her wits to imitate them well"—the tone was set: Francis was a young and flamboyant king who would break from his ancestors' legacy to create his own.[2] The young Anne Boleyn was watching and continuing to learn the ways and rules of the French court—invaluable lessons she would, as we shall see, later come to rely on.

One important question, however, remained for England: What of the fate of Mary Tudor, who had only just married the late king?

Rumors were spreading that Francis was suspicious of Mary's behavior with the "special emissary"—Charles Brandon, Duke of Suffolk—and that Louise, his mother, had ordered Claude, one of Mary's ladies-in-waiting, never to leave her alone "unless the king was with her."[3]

Orders from England could not come fast enough as Wolsey instructed Mary: "Don't do anything without the advice of his grace."[4] The entire Anglo-French alliance depended on this marriage, after all.

Although Mary agreed that she would await further instructions, the truth was she had been enamored with Charles Brandon, Duke of Suffolk, for a long time, and the strange limbo afforded by the death of Louis XII offered them an opportunity to act on their feelings for each other.

In late January 1515, Suffolk—who was torn between his duties toward Henry VIII and his love and affection for Mary—wrote to the English king. He pleaded for Mary, who desired nothing more than to have a say in her next "husband," and claimed: "I never saw a woman so weep."[5]

Later, Suffolk met with Francis I and Louise of Savoy. The mother of the new French king had long been suspicious of

Suffolk and Mary and, during dinner, in the company of Claude and her sister Renée, said bluntly, "I agree that the [former] queen, Mary, the English king's sister, should come home as shortly as may be."[6]

There were too many queens at court, and Louise was determined to be the one who shone.

Meanwhile, there were demonstrations of good faith aplenty as those at court met the English ambassadors, Suffolk and Sir Richard Wingfield. In an audience that took place in the early afternoon of Saturday, January 27, 1515, Francis declared that "the marriage between the queen, the English king's sister, and the late king, my predecessor, was for a great cause that should endure."[7]

This did not, however, resolve the matter at hand. There were still three queens at the French court and one wished to leave and marry the man of her choice: the Duke of Suffolk.

In haste, and out of love and passion, the couple married in secret on March 3, 1515. Consumed with guilt, Suffolk wrote to Wolsey, "begging for your help in this difficult matter."[8] When Wolsey revealed that he had no other choice but to show the letter to the king, Henry VIII, both lovers hastily wrote to him, asking for forgiveness and acceptance.

Mary showed more courage than regret:

> I beg you to remember that I have sacrificed myself for the good of the Christendom when you dispatched me to marry Louis who was very aged and sickly. I did so on condition that if I survived him I would marry whom I like. Since my husband is dead, remembering the great virtue in my Lord of Suffolk to whom I have always been of good mind as you well know, I chose to marry him.[9]

Their secret marriage was technically an act of treason, as the couple should have requested the king's consent beforehand.

Indeed, some privy councillors urged Suffolk's arrest and execution. Instead, the king chose to fine the couple heavily, and the marriage remained. It was even legitimized by Pope Clement VII years later in 1528.

The couple returned to England, but one lady—according to her father's wishes—had to continue her education at the French court, in Queen Claude's household.

It is very unlikely that Anne had managed to attend Mary in France; in the French manuscript that lists Mary's household, there is no mention of her name.

Furthermore, Anne wrote to her father, stating:

> Sir, I understand from your letter that you desire me to be an entirely virtuous woman when I come to the court and you tell me that the queen [Queen Claude] will take the trouble to converse with me and it gives me great joy to think of talking with such a wise and virtuous person. This will make me all the keener to persevere in speaking French well...[10]

Francis I would likely have needed to give his consent to this, so must have gladly accepted the offer, even if he certainly had other, more important, matters on his mind than disputing the position of a lady-in-waiting in his wife's household.

So, it was decided. Anne remained and, soon, everyone agreed. They "would never have judged her to be English in her manners, but a natural-born Frenchwoman."[11]

As for Francis, his eyes were now turned to the Italian territories, with one specific goal in mind: recovering the duchy of Milan.

★

During this period, a good king was a warrior king, and Francis I had no time to waste in the pursuit of glory. In order to prove his worth as a true Renaissance ruler, therefore, he picked up where his predecessor left off: the military campaigns in Italy.

Due to Francis's recent military victories—most notably, the Battle of Marignano in September 1515—the mother of the king, Louise of Savoy, and his consort, Claude, were about to go on a royal progress in the south of France to receive him and congratulate him on his military exploits.

The queens and their courts, including Anne Boleyn, left Amboise on October 20, 1515. The goal was to be present when the king returned from Italy, as well as go on a pilgrimage to pray for good fortune. Never before had Anne embarked upon such a journey, and she never would again. Thousands of servants and other supplies were prepared for this complex undertaking.

Their first significant stop was in the city of Lyon, where they all stayed for a month. Many foreigners, notably Italian traders, had made Lyon—which had been built around two important rivers: the Rhône and the Saône—their home. Over the course of the sixteenth century, therefore, the city became more and more vibrant and cosmopolitan, with fairs and markets in abundance.

While Claude of France and Anne Boleyn were used to the court, they had spent much less time in cities. When Claude became queen of France, she and her household avoided the effervescence of big cities, such as Paris, to avoid disease and to give Claude some privacy during her numerous pregnancies. Residing as they did in the capital's peripheral castles of the Loire Valley—mostly Amboise, where Claude had given birth to her first daughter, Louise, on August 19, 1515—this was the first time that Anne fully witnessed the dynamism of such a highly populated city.

Lyon certainly did not disappoint.

Many fine festivities had been prepared for the royal households, with feasts and extraordinary spectacles, such as the show of beasts, organized to entertain the queens and their ladies.

During that time, Marguerite, Duchess of Angoulême—who was the sister of the king—joined the royal party. Almost certainly, it was then that she first met Anne Boleyn, who was by now one of Claude's shadows. Other members of the king's privy council were also part of the procession, such as Jacques de Beaune-Semblançay and Henry of Navarre, son of John III, King of Navarre.

Whether or not an "official" meeting took place between Marguerite and Anne remains unknown, but their presence in these cities at the same time was certainly recorded—albeit indirectly for Anne, as she was in Claude's service.

In mid-December, the queens and their people finally left the city of lights, making their way to the south. On December 20, they stopped at Montélimar and, by the following day, they were at Pont-Saint-Esprit. Their procession also visited Orange, Avignon and Tarascon, where they remained for the Christmas festivities; the queens and their households made their entrance via the river in the medieval town of Tarascon. To this day, the city is associated with fairy tales and legends and, for centuries, many pilgrims visited the town, its geographical and strategic location making it a very important city in the south.

The queens were gifted "twelve gold images representing Saint Marthe, accompanied by twelve gold rings," by the city, which had cost it a small fortune.[12] All this, even though the queens were just passing through.

Anne Boleyn witnessed all this glory and magnificence, an experience that likely never left her. The Provençal landscapes were not at their peak, as the procession took place during winter, but it was still very different from English flora and fauna. Undoubtedly, Anne was entranced by such beauty, as were all the women around her—including the queens.

On December 26, the procession entered Arles—a relatively poor town, which had made considerable efforts to receive the royal court at short notice of just one month. The queens and their households lodged at the house of Mr. Arlatan, Sieur de Beaumont.

For three days, the queens and their ladies-in-waiting prayed at the Church of Saint-Honorat, where holy relics such as "the arms of the Maries of Notre-Dame-de-la-Mer" were preserved and revered, as well as visiting the old Roman theater of Arles.

On December 30, the court arrived at Aix-en-Provence, where it would then disperse to visit several different towns, which were all more or less prepared for such visitors: Saint-Maximin, Sainte-Baume and Aubagne. Their final destination was the fabulous and strategically significant port of Marseille.

Here, they would wait for the king to return.

The city was well prepared for the queens; myrtle covered the walls in many streets, and tapestries from Saint Victor had been commissioned in honor of the royal family. As myrtle was a symbol of military success, these decorations acted as a tribute to Louise's son, the king.

On January 3, 1516, Louise of Savoy, Claude of France and their households finally arrived at the coastal city. Cannons rang out in the port to salute their arrival, which was set out in spectacular style.

With the feasts, spectacles and dances that accompanied their arrival, Anne Boleyn, part of the retinue, was experiencing French royal grandeur in all its forms—something she would surely recall later in life when she started pursuing her own ambitions. More importantly, she may have been fascinated to observe that these festivities were taking place without the presence of the king and that, instead, the guests of honor were mostly women—even the lords who accompanied them were not the centers of attention. Francis was ruling as a powerful Renaissance king but, at the heart of his court, three important female figures emerged—the women who would also benefit from his glory. And as Claude's shadow, wherever the young queen went, Anne Boleyn followed.

On Saturday, January 5, Claude was invited to dine with the lords of Saint Victor. After that, she and her household made their way to Notre-Dame de la Garde—one of the largest basilicas ever built. Anne must have felt she was living in a dream; witnessing the beauty of the French southern landscape, and its extraordinary architecture, would have been an entirely new experience for a young woman more used to life in the confines of court.

They were even lucky with the weather, though they were technically in the depths of winter; there were no records of heavy rain, and indeed there were even reports of clear blue skies during the time of their travels. Anne would also have seen the Mediterranean Sea for the first time, which, with its blue far superior to the English Channel or the North Sea, was another view altogether. By now, gray and rainy England was no more than a faraway memory. Anne was instead rejoicing in the Provençal landscapes and their perfumes.

The procession paused in Provence for a few weeks, before Francis made his way back from Marignano. By this time, it had been decided: the reunion of the champion and his family would take place in Marseille. The city's people were ready to receive their victorious king.

*

On a sunny Tuesday, January 22, the good people of Marseille flooded the streets on their way to meet the king and his queens, who were now arriving on the road from Aubagne.

Two thousand children, all dressed in white, were at the head of the welcoming procession. They were followed by the men of Marseille, wearing armor and holding crossbows or arquebuses in honor of the king's victory in Italy.

Wearing his silver velvet coat, Francis I was followed by his mother, Louise, his wife, Claude, and his sister, Marguerite. Behind them were the nobles of the realm and Francis's closest advisers.

"Welcome to our magnificent city, my lord," said one of the magistrates of Marseille.[13]

Francis bowed and, beneath the sound of cannons firing up through the air, entered the city with his noble procession. For the ladies-in-waiting accompanying the queens, this was surely the most impressive reception yet.

The city put on a fine pageant for the royal visitors, with actors playing the roles of Mars and Vulcan, the two powerful martial heroes of ancient Greece. As they welcomed the king, both actors were said to have been overcome by their emotions, finding themselves, according to the source, lost for words. The king noted "they seem confused" and continued on his journey into the city.

The people who could not find a place on the busy streets instead stood at their windows, shouting greetings to their king as he passed. The atmosphere was joyful, for here was a king who was truly admired by his people. Anne would not have failed to notice this.

The queens and the king's sister, alongside their households, played a central part in these climactic festivities. Provençal dances, such as "the dance of Olivettes," "the Moresque" and "La pellegrina," were performed in front of the king and his ladies.[14] The celebrations spilled into the evening, culminating in a glorious feast.

Francis must have welcomed the festivities, but for him this was a visit of both business and pleasure, particularly as he was a king who reveled in the business of politics. In the following days, he went on to discuss the important business of the realm with magistrates of the southern cities, visiting Arles, Tarascon, Aix and Salon.

Claude and her household, including Anne, meanwhile, were taken aside by the nuns. They wanted the queen and her ladies-in-waiting to go with them in procession to Notre-Dame de la Garde. There, prayers were made for the queen's longevity and prosperity, and among these wishes were that, with God's mercy, she would give a son and heir to the French crown. While the royal couple were clearly popular, nothing was more important than securing the dynastic line of Francis I if that was to continue. Anne would have witnessed these prayers for Claude's fertility, and they may have made an impression on her, given they were close in age. She would have quickly learned what was expected of a queen.

Fortunately for Claude, these prayers would be answered. Although it was a daughter, Charlotte, to which Claude first gave birth on October 23, 1516, she would eventually fulfill her role as a queen and wife, giving France a dauphin heir. The message was clear: above all was the need to put the good of the dynasty first, providing a male offspring to the crown. The significance of this was understood by all of the queen's entourage.

Finally, after this concluding journey to the south of France, in the spring the royal procession made its way back to the Parisian court and its various peripheral castles. This had been Anne Boleyn's first royal tour, and her first real experience of the grandeur of the royal spectacle. The women at its heart may have been given a great welcome and afforded solemn respect even without their king, but it was clear that there were duties to fulfill in order to retain it.

★

While, like his predecessors, Francis I had been crowned in 1515 at the Cathedral of Reims, Claude—who had suffered from illness in her first pregnancy—was only crowned queen of France two years later on May 10, 1517, at the Basilica of Saint-Denis.

The ceremony was both solemn and grandiose. Claude was, after all, the daughter of the late king, Louis XII, and of Anne of Bretagne, who had been twice crowned queen of France. She, too, had her power, and, bearing the arms of both Brittany and

France, Claude reminded everyone of her powerful and regal lineage. Coiffed with white satin, cloth of gold and a surcoat of ermine, she entered the basilica flanked by her sister-in-law, Marguerite of Angoulême, and Françoise d'Alençon, Duchess of Vendôme, who were both wearing "velvet robes encrusted with rare gems."[15]

After being anointed, three dukes held the priceless Crown of Charlemagne over Claude's head. She was also presented with the "scepter and the hand of justice"—symbols of royal authority.[16] Her ladies-in-waiting and other important noblewomen were present, as was the king himself, who stood next to his mother.

It is unlikely that Anne would have missed this important event, now that she was at the heart of Claude's court. The chances are that she saw the occasion in all its splendor. In truth, Claude would only experience a glimmer of glory: after multiple pregnancies that compromised her health, Claude would die at the age of 27. But, on this day, the young queen was celebrated in all her splendor. Anne would also have noted the presence of Marguerite of Angoulême, who was by the queen's side at the coronation—demonstrating her own value at the French court and her own role within Francis's government. This was another woman for Anne to observe, and to learn from.

While Claude was revered, she was not celebrated for her appearance. In fact, Antonio de Beatis—an Italian courtier who traveled through Europe between 1517 and 1518—remarked that Claude was "small in stature, plain, and badly lame in both hips"—though he added that she was also "said to be very cultivated, generous, and pious."[17] Certainly, the latter were important qualities for a queen to possess, and they were what Claude would be remembered and loved for by her people—even if her husband was to prove unfaithful in their marriage. While it was through this discreet and pious consort that Anne was able to experience life at the Court of the Fleur-de-Lys, she would also have noticed the rise of Francis's mistresses, notably the charismatic Françoise de Foix, Countess of Châteaubriant. There were, Anne realized, several ways to succeed as a woman in a royal court.

Claude's popularity was underscored two days after her coronation when she joyfully entered Paris with a procession of 16 ladies wearing "gold hats fashioned like crowns."[18] She herself wore an even grander crown—it was her time to shine, and even Francis would not have had it any other way.

The magistrates of Paris, along with several noblemen and members of the bourgeoisie, welcomed Claude as she made her entrance at the head of "twenty four bowmen and sixty crossbowmen."[19] Other guards walked in front of the queen's carriage while, behind her, people could see the princes of blood and the realm's most noted noblemen, followed by Louise of Savoy in her own carriage. Toward the end of the procession there were three carriages, and in one of these were Claude's ladies-in-waiting, where Anne Boleyn would have been seated. Anne, therefore, had a front-row seat to this massive show of royal power, and she knew the love that a queen consort could expect from her people.

Pageants were held all across the city to underscore this. The first was staged at the Porte of Saint-Denis, which was located on the western side of Paris, and here the coronation of the queen was symbolized by six iconic female figures of the Old Testament—"Sarah, Rachel, Rebecca, Esther, Deborah and Lea, who symbolized the virtues of the queen: faithfulness, kindness, prudence, modesty, the good doctrine and fertility."[20]

While Francis would share his affections with many other women—particularly his chief mistress, the Countess of Châteaubriant—the royal couple took their duty to preserve the dynastic line seriously. The king visited the queen's bed on a regular basis. First this brought them two daughters, and then finally, on Sunday, February 28, 1518, the royal couple were blessed with what they had been praying for, a baby boy.

Both parents beamed with love and adoration for their firstborn son, also named Francis, with Claude cheekily instructing her midwife: "Tell the king that he [their son] is even more beautiful than himself." This was something they would both agree on as Francis rejoiced that his son was "a beautiful Dauphin who is the most beautiful and puissant child one could imagine," adding he "will be the easiest to bring up." Soon, arrangements had been made for the christening of the prince, which would take place at Amboise on April 25, 1518. The castle had been prepared for the event "with tapestries depicting tales from the antiquity."[21]

Many great noblemen and noblewomen of the country and beyond had been invited to witness the ceremony, including the hugely influential figure of Lorenzo II de Medici, Duke of Urbino—nephew of the Pope and future father of Catherine de Medici—who had been named godfather of the dauphin. A few months later, the duke married Madeleine de la Tour d'Auvergne. The ties between the French royal family and the Medicis had just become stronger, creating new dynastic links in the complicated European political world. Anne, as part of Claude's retinue, would have been mindful of these, too.

*

The birth of a son meant that the Anglo-French dynasties could be intertwined once more. A marriage proposal was soon discussed between Princess Mary, daughter of Henry VIII and Catherine of Aragon, and the new dauphin of France. As Stephen de Poncher, Bishop of Paris, said to Cardinal Wolsey, "my master, Francis king of France, is eager to see a closer alliance between the two crowns by promoting the abovementioned marriage."[22]

However, this potential dynastic alliance posed a new problem for England's relations with Spain, since King Charles was apprehensive to see new conciliations between the two kingdoms. With this in mind, he dispatched his own secretary, Jehan de la Sauch, to Henry VIII's court. As he understood it, the marriage between the dauphin and the English princess also involved the restitution of Tournay by the English. Tournay was on the critical border between the Holy Roman Empire—which was a strong ally to Spain as part of the same dynastic family—and France.

The bishop continued: "I do not wish to cause rupture between England and France, as I have always desired only unity between Christian princes so we can send a common expedition against the Turks, my only request is that nothing be concluded to my detriment, or against existing treaties that secure the alliance between England and Spain."

When it came to the Franco-Spanish northern border, Charles was even stricter. "If Tournay is restored, Francis must promise not to send any garrison there, nor harbor the Emperor's rebels or exiles."[23]

Francis would not, however, be told what to do in his own territory. After all, his low opinion of the King of Spain was well known. In other words, the alliance and its possible terms were far from being assured. Francis was, however, determined not to let the opportunity slip away. So, over the summer, he dispatched a commission of four men to negotiate the treaty: Guillaume Gouffier, Lord of Bonnivet, Admiral of France; Stephen de Poncher, Bishop of Paris; Francis de Rochecovard, Seneschal of Toulouse and Governor of Rochelle; and Nicolas of Neufville, Lord of Villeroy and Secretary of Finance. They were all generously received at Henry's English court. Determined to counterbalance Spain's power, they relayed that Francis was willing to pay 400,000 crowns for the restitution of Tournay.

Of course, an alliance with France would itself be a major coup. But as with all such dynastic arrangements, there was a lot of hard bargaining to be done before any such union was finally contracted. For now, Henry would have to be satisfied with the wooing that Francis was ready to offer.

While the details of the dynastic marriage were still being organized, the Treaty of Universal Peace—which, with a certain optimism, was advertised as a means of bringing an end to the proliferation of military conflict between European kingdoms and realms—was signed in October 1518. As with so many peace treaties, it did not last long, but, for the time being, it allowed the negotiations to continue between Henry, Francis and Charles, though it was Charles's voice that began to dominate proceedings.

The French started to grow impatient with the slow progress of the proposed union; the French commissioners were disappointed in their discussions at the English court. They complained that "the Most Catholic King [Charles of Spain] is trying to prevent the marriage and the surrender of Tournay despite our best efforts to come to this conclusion."[24]

Henry knew that he could not linger much longer. As a gesture of good faith on his country's part, therefore, a treaty was drafted in England, with the name "Thomas Boleyn" appearing among the witnesses' signatures.[25]

The French ambassadors were received on October 5, 1518, in Catherine of Aragon's great chamber at Greenwich. She greeted them alongside her husband, Henry VIII, and their two-and-a-half-year-old daughter, Mary.

After an oration *de laudibus matrimonii* (in praise of matrimony) by Cuthbert Tunstall, who served as Master of the Rolls, Lord Bonnivet approached the little princess and offered her a ring; he put it on her fourth finger as a token of her betrothal to the dauphin. Accompanied by the French envoys, Henry then made his way to the chapel in the manor of Greenwich, where he took "the oath to the treaty" between France and England.[26]

Eleven days later, in front of his tribunal, Henry promised to "fulfill the contract of marriage between the Princess Mary and Francis the Dauphin when the Princess was fit of age." In his exuberance, he declared, "Cardinal Wolsey, if I fail my promise, do excommunicate me."[27]

Both parties seemed to be genuine in their willingness to achieve peace, yet the return of Tournay to the French was still very much a thorn in Henry VIII's side. Seemingly convinced that Francis I would keep his oath, he assured Margaret of Savoy—whose territory might be endangered by the return of Tournay to the French—that "the town will be and remain in the condition in which it was before the war and its reduction. Francis is not only sworn to this by an express article in the treaty, under ecclesiastical censure, but is also compelled to give several honorable persons from his court as hostages, who will remain in England for thirteen or fourteen years at least."[28] Henry hoped this act would put Margaret's—and her brother the King of Spain's—mind at ease.

Francis, on the other hand, still needed convincing about some of the treaty's terms. He instructed his ambassadors: "Find the names of the ambassadors who will be sent by my brother, the king of England, and when they are expected to land in my realm."[29]

Soon afterward, he was advised that a special commission—composed notably of Charles Somerset, Earl of Worcester, and Nicholas West, Bishop of Ely—had been sent to France. Although these people were generally reliable and experienced courtiers and diplomats, Cardinal Wolsey felt the need to also send one of his closest informants. He chose one of the rising courtiers who knew how to remain faithful and useful to him: Sir Thomas Boleyn.

It is hard to precisely date when Thomas Boleyn was actually sent to France, but on December 5, 1518, he acknowledged that he had received one of Wolsey's letters, as well as an enclosed letter destined for the French king on November 27, 1518. The cardinal, who sought to ensure repayment for recent losses sustained by English merchants in an affair at La Fontaine, was clearly by this time using Boleyn as his mouthpiece at the French court.[30] The master of England's Hever Castle had now been thrown into the midst of Anglo-French politics, and Wolsey clearly intended to receive more intelligence from him. Meanwhile, Thomas was about to be reunited with his daughter, Anne, whom by now he had not seen in years—at least since early 1515. With her eyes and ears at the heart of the French court, Anne was now the ideal spy for English affairs.

★

The English commissioners were given an enthusiastic welcome at court; the Earl of Worcester and the Bishop of Ely, among others, were even publicly greeted with respect on their way to Paris. The merchants of the city showed how much they were "right joyous of this good peace and alliance": the English diplomats were offered "marmalades and confits" and on Sunday, December 12, 1518, they were finally received by the king, Francis, in his great chamber—"with blue hangings of full fleur de lys, with the floor covered with the same," where seats had been prepared for the gentlemen. The king sat in a chair "raised four steps from the ground under a rich cloth of estate with a pall of cloth of gold."[31]

The secretary to the Venetian ambassador in France, Hironimo Da Canal, recalled that Francis I was wearing no crown and that the ceremony was viewed by "the Queen [Claude] and other ladies from behind a blind."[32]

Anne Boleyn would very likely have been among these women: as hoped by Wolsey and her father, Thomas, she was indeed at the very heart of the French court. For now, she watched carefully, seemingly unobserved by those around her.

King Henry's ambassadors were asked to present their respects to the French king, who then "descended the steps and embraced them with his usual affability." The Venetian secretary noted that around 20 other "superbly dressed" English gentlemen, probably including Thomas Boleyn, were also in attendance.[33] It is likely, then, that he and Anne may have been reunited here, though there is no record of it. There was now no turning back on the marriage proposal and it would be the main subject of discussion. Francis declared what was expected of him: "I strongly desire to maintain the good alliance with my good brother, the king of England, and this marriage is the proof of it."[34]

The next days were packed with more private audiences, including boar and stag hunting and several splendid banquets and tournaments. On December 16, the English ambassadors were received by Queen Claude and her ladies-in-waiting, where she "gave her consent to the marriage."[35] It may well have brought Anne and Thomas into contact again. For Anne, it was more proof of Claude's influence and agency on an international level as a mother to a prince.

Further negotiations between the two crowns was still required on several topics, notably the restitution of Tournay and its payment, as well as the dispatch of hostages to the Tower of London. These were complex arrangements requiring detailed discussion.

Nevertheless, they pressed on, and with success. On December 21, 1518, the Treaty of London—which encompassed and provided some solutions to all the outstanding issues—was finally ratified. To celebrate, yet another banquet was held in La Bastille the next day. Both Thomas and Anne Boleyn were part of the festivities, though they did not attend together.

The main hall was squared and "floored with timber." Torches and chandeliers filled the room, "throwing a marvelous blaze of light on the starry ceiling," and two main tables were placed at the center of the room, where both English and French gentlemen "were seated alternately with ladies." The supper consisted of nine courses and lasted over two hours. Queen Claude and the mother of the king, Louise, oversaw the meal, accompanied by their ladies-in-waiting, "from one of the galleries near the King's dais."[36]

In the midst of all the jubilation, something extraordinary caught Anne's eye. While Francis had kept his wife and mother away from the heart of the celebrations, he ordered his sister, Marguerite of Angoulême, Duchess of Alençon, to be at "his left" side—elevating her above all other royal women and making her the center of attention.[37] This was not the first time that Anne had been in the presence of Marguerite, but it was the first time Francis had elevated his sister in such a fashion. There is no doubt that such privilege would not have escaped the mind of such an ambitious young lady like Anne.

Indeed, Marguerite was one of the most influential figures at her brother's court. Charismatic, determined, resilient and highly educated, she showed an interest in humanist ideas and was even known to have exchanged letters on the subject with great thinkers, including Desiderius Erasmus, Clément Marot and Guillaume Budé. As Anne regarded the scene, the ambitious Thomas Boleyn also close by, she couldn't yet know that she would also play a part in these complex negotiations of power in the years to come.

Meanwhile, those present at the banquet must have surely have thought that the conclusion of the peace treaty through the proposed marriage of Princess Mary and the dauphin, Francis, was a done deal. Yet, nothing could be taken for granted—especially when it came to Henry VIII and Francis I's tumultuous rivalry.

3

Witnessing the Pursuit of Grandeur

No one lives forever. Not even kings or emperors.

In the early hours of the morning on January 12, 1519, Maximilian I, Holy Roman Emperor—who had been fighting a long battle with a disease (probably intestinal cancer or pneumonia)—passed away in Wels, Upper Austria. During his life, he ruled over 1,800 semi-independent territories stretching from central Europe to northern Italy, which were collectively known as the Holy Roman Empire. To become the emperor of such a territory, one first had to be elected by the Imperial Electoral College, comprising the archbishops of Mainz, Trier and Cologne, the King of Bohemia-Hungary, the Margrave of Brandenburg, the Duke of Saxony and the Count of the Palatinate.

The most likely candidate to replace him was Charles of Spain, Maximilian's grandson and Francis's archenemy. Francis, unsurprisingly, utterly abhorred this nomination and felt that he had no choice but to compete for the title. As a result, Pope Leo X was left in a tricky position; he could not support either of the two candidates for fear of retaliation from the one unsupported, so he looked for a third candidate that would help maintain peace in Europe. While Henry VIII had no interest in the role at first, Cardinal Wolsey eventually convinced him to throw his hat in the ring—a decision that would have immense repercussions for

European politics. Such a choice also required a lot of discretion, and several political maneuvers to ensure that Henry would not end up with two powerful enemies at his borders.

A complicated game of political chess ensued.

On February 9, 1518, Francis I wrote directly to Wolsey, informing him that he had been discussing the matter of the emperor's death and its consequences with the papal legate's ambassador, "Boulen."

Thomas Boleyn—like his daughter, Anne—remained at the French court, serving England's interests and, in this case, Wolsey's, too. Indeed at this moment, Anne's role was overshadowed by her father's, but her closeness to Queen Claude and her proximity to court events meant she remained the perfect spy for her father.

At this time, Francis I and Thomas Boleyn were meeting on a regular basis.

"I hope that my good brother, cousin, and ally and yourself will be favorable toward me." Clearly, the French king would not hide his ambition—not to Wolsey nor to Henry VIII. He signed his letter to Wolsey, "Your good friend, François."[1]

On the same day, Thomas Boleyn wrote to Henry VIII. In this letter, he expressed the view that Francis seemed genuine in his desire to maintain peace with England.

Boleyn had been granted a private audience with the French king after attending mass in his chamber—a sign of the heights his reputation had reached. After being taken aside, toward the window, Boleyn listened to Francis as he shared his own hopes of becoming Holy Roman Emperor.

"I have made up my mind," Francis explained. "Many electors expect Maximilian's wish that the King Catholic [Charles] succeed and, if it happens, the political consequences of it will be irreversible."

The animosity between the two kings was already known to all—but now Francis's plans to usurp his rival were revealed to

Thomas Boleyn, who was listening attentively as Francis explained his plans to become emperor himself.

"I have the promise of four electors, under their hands and seals, to support me and I aim to convince the Bishops of Cologne and Trier to do the same," Francis revealed, attempting to appear all mighty. He continued, "I am also rejoiced at the aid promised by your master, the king of England, especially as I have been told by one of your fellowmen that his grace [Henry] doth not pretend to the title himself."

Boleyn, who was unsure if this was a question or not, played the truth card and simply retorted, "I have not received any information on this matter."

The English ambassador's answer did not seem to alarm the French king, who just continued discussing other matters at court. He finished the audience with the fact that his mother, Louise, "expressed her delight at the alliance."[2]

The meeting between Boleyn and Francis thus ended positively—little did they know that the election for Holy Roman Emperor was about to create more tensions than either could have ever predicted.

*

At this time, Anne Boleyn—who is widely believed to have remained in Queen Claude's services—remained at the center of the French court, and in a good position to acquaint herself with most of the scandals, rumors and other tales that circulated. More importantly, she now became acquainted with Marguerite of Angoulême, to whom she would show great fondness later in her life.

Marguerite was known for her interest in the reformed ideas—and it was later assumed, therefore, that she was somehow responsible for Anne's own personal interest in religious reformation. While this may be true, it is also important to remember that, at the time, Marguerite and Anne, particularly Anne, both remained strongly Catholic, and that the line between becoming a Protestant and being Catholic in the period's upheaval could be a thin one—one that perhaps Anne Boleyn never truly crossed. Later in her life, when it would eventually serve her purpose, she undeniably saw the value of promoting Protestant ideas, but during her time in France, Anne remained a pious Catholic.

As for Thomas Boleyn, his diplomatic dispatches now revealed the complex dynamics between, on the one hand, Henry VIII and Wolsey, and on the other, Francis I and his mother, Louise of Savoy.

On February 22, 1519, Francis received Boleyn for an audience; he was eager to know if Henry VIII had made his decision on joining the Imperial Contest.

"Has the King of England revealed his intention?" the French king asked.

Boleyn knew it was a difficult topic and, in all truth, he had been kept in the dark by Wolsey. After all, the cardinal knew that the Pope was growing old and that another important competition might soon take place. He would need the support of the French if he would ever be made pope himself.

"So far, the King of England, my master, declined to advance any claim," Boleyn replied simply.

This discussion continued for an hour. They talked about Charles and his claims to the imperial title—acknowledging the importance of the role for binding together all of Christendom in the struggle against the real enemy: the infidels in the east.

Boleyn now felt comfortable enough with Francis, following his good treatment at his court, that he boldly asked: "If you were made Emperor, would you lead yourself a voyage against the Infidels?"

Grabbing Boleyn's wrist with one hand, Francis put his right hand upon his chest and swore, "If I attain to be Emperor, within three years after I would be in Constantinople or I would die by the way."[3]

Boleyn took this oath seriously, though he also knew that Francis had a tendency toward the theatrical—as, in fact, did Henry VIII and Charles of Spain. What was clear, however, was Francis's determination to do everything in his power to make his imperial dream come true, and he would make whatever promises were required. For it to happen, though, he indisputably needed the support of Henry VIII, who was all too aware of this.

Thomas Spinelli, English ambassador at Charles of Spain's court, had been walking on eggshells since the Treaty of London and the promise of a dynastic marriage between Princess Mary and the dauphin. In his audience with the Spanish king, Spinelli reassured him of a simple but powerful fact that was certainly true at the time (and would remain true for a while).

"Notwithstanding the treaty of amity between France and England, the ancient love of the latter for Burgundy is so rooted it cannot be shaken," Spinelli told Charles before continuing, "since the death of the Emperor, Wolsey has induced the king of England to delay interfering on behalf of Francis." The truth of the matter was "the Pope will probably lean to your [Charles's] side as neither he nor the Venetians, nor any other states of Italy, are in favor of the French king to obtain the empire."[4]

It appeared to be a foregone conclusion that Francis alone did not seem to accept—putting Thomas Boleyn in a tricky diplomatic situation.

More importantly, Boleyn's audiences with the king—which involved disclosing various personal and political ambitions—illustrated how close he was to the royal family. This intimacy had started with his daughter, Anne, who used her position in Queen Claude's service to provide intelligence to her father.

On March 5, 1519, Boleyn reported to Wolsey that Claude, who was heavily pregnant at the time, had been "very sickly," adding that she was "worse than she has been" as he understood it.[5] This detail may seem irrelevant, but it could only have come from the heart of court, showing that father and daughter were communicating with each other about the most sensitive matters in the French kingdom. While the letters between them don't seem to have survived, the detail in Thomas's correspondence with Wolsey clearly demonstrates that the discussions had taken place.

A week later, Boleyn also reported the news that Queen Claude, Louise of Savoy and their respective households had left Paris for Saint-Germain and that, because the queen was unwell during the journey, they had stopped at a village called La Porte de Neuilly. During the night, things appeared to have taken a turn for the worse, as Claude was reported to have been "in great danger."[6] Heavily pregnant with her fourth child—the future Henry II of France—false reports spread that she had died during the night, which would have had great repercussions on the Boleyns' political strategy of having their ears and eyes everywhere at the French court.

A few days later, Thomas Boleyn—probably due to a combination of his daughter's position and his own ambassadorial capacity—was invited to accompany the king and his sister, the Duchess of Angoulême, who had joined the queen and their mother at La Porte de Neuilly. The plan was still to go to Saint-Germain "in close barges with chambers made in them" if Claude could stomach the journey on the water.

In the midst of all this was Anne, following in Claude's footsteps, attending her and ensuring that she was as comfortable as she could be.

Queens were not protected from the hardships of bearing a child. While Anne was usually discreet about her mistress's health, the fact that her father knew so many details of Claude's difficult journey proved, not only that Anne confided in him, but also that she was sensitive to Claude's suffering.

Thomas Boleyn took advantage of his proximity to the royal family in order to pursue Wolsey's political agenda. Francis promised that if support for the imperial title was given to him by the English, he would "not be ungrateful." He also promised: "On the word of a king, if Wolsey aspired to be head of the Church I will secure him on the first opportunity the voices of fourteen cardinals, the whole company of the Ursyns at Rome, and the help of one Mark Antony di Colonnia."[7]

Boleyn was satisfied with this answer and believed Francis's words. Yet, the task was more complicated than it seemed. The English had no true intention of supporting Francis—they just needed him to believe that they would.

Wolsey's ambitions and tactical political maneuvers were one thing; Henry VIII's desires and aspirations were another. When it came to the imperial crown, however, their wishes aligned, as Wolsey revealed to the Bishop of Worcester in March 1519:

> The French king is straining every nerve, by art or cunning, to obtain the election and succeed in his unbridled desires. England thinks it is expedient that every obstacle should be thrown in his way; for if he were successful he would revive many obsolete pretentions. It is not that Henry is inclined to Charles, from whose overgrown power, would he be successful, many dangers might ensure hereafter and perilous dissensions in Christendom, but he admits that this would be the less evil and the Pope should remain neutral.[8]

In late March, a diplomatic incident almost occurred, which—if Boleyn had not been able to convince Louise of Savoy of England's sincerity—could have had irreparable consequences for France and England.

Francis's ambassador in Spain had intercepted a letter from England to Spain, stating that Henry was in fact in "favor of the King Catholic" of Spain.

"I beg you not to believe these lies," Thomas Boleyn pleaded to Louise of Savoy, who, demonstrating her political significance, had asked for an audience regarding the matter. "It is a plot from Spain to sow discord between our two princes," he claimed.

At first, Louise showed skepticism but, at Boleyn's pleading, she appeared to mellow. "I have so much faith in England that I give this no credence," she said. "My son even laughed at it when I told him."[9]

Having been reassured that the French court did not believe the possible treachery, Boleyn and Louise moved on to discuss Princess Mary's and Marguerite of Angoulême's illnesses, as both women had been unwell. Little did the French rulers know that the letter they had intercepted actually told the truth.

The fact that Francis I asked Henry VIII for a loan of 100,000 crowns, which was refused, was a clear indication that England was not fully behind his candidacy for Holy Roman Emperor. Yet the kings' relationship seemed strong when, on June 1, 1519, Francis's second son—born on March 31 of the same year—was christened Henry as a tribute to the English king, who was godfather to the new prince. Thomas and Anne Boleyn also took part in the ceremony, both of them now fully embedded in the French court.

Despite these tokens of a firm and stable friendship, the election of the Holy Roman Emperor was approaching fast, and peace in Europe was at stake.

On June 8, 1519, the seven electors met in Frankfurt to make their decision. With the Pope's reluctant support—but support nonetheless—of Charles V, Francis was forced to withdraw. On June 28, the King of Spain was unanimously elected Holy Roman Emperor.

Without a doubt, this election further complicated European politics.

★

In a world where men dominated any aspect of political, social and cultural life, it is unsurprising that often the records of women's perceptions are harder to come by. Nevertheless, we know that Anne Boleyn would have carefully observed much of what happened at the French court in this tense time. Not only was she one of the confidantes of Queen Claude: now she was also well acquainted with Marguerite of Angoulême—the woman who would rise high at the court of her brother, Francis.

Marguerite was a formidable figure. Though the power and agency she wielded were derived from Francis, she was particularly astute, enough to use her influence over him to promote her own agenda. Since the beginning of Francis I's reign, Marguerite, alongside her mother, Louise, had been promoted above anyone else. Marguerite was given titles, lands and an annual revenue of 20,000 crowns. She was invited to important diplomatic events, including audiences with Venetian and English ambassadors alike, not as an ornament but as a woman keen to participate in the business of state.

As the Duchess of Alençon, Marguerite was Francis's second-in-command—something that did not pass Anne by and that undoubtedly evoked admiration as the two women grew to know each other better.

Born on April 11, 1492, Marguerite spent her early life in Cognac, in her family's stronghold where her father, Charles of Orléans, Count of Angoulême, died in 1496. Raised by her mother, Marguerite soon became aware of their precarious status. Rapidly, due to the complicated French succession to the throne, her brother, Francis, became an heir apparent and, consequently, the family moved to the castles of Blois and Amboise.

Louise of Savoy was a voracious reader, possessing a great library of books written in French, Spanish, Italian, Greek and Latin. Thus, from a young age Marguerite and Francis were exposed to a wealth of classical works, which, for Marguerite in particular, deeply influenced her vision of the world.

At 17, Marguerite married Charles IV of Alençon, a union that had been arranged by Louis XII. By the time her brother came to the throne, however, it was clear that Marguerite's true calling was not the one of an obedient and pious wife, but instead, a political and cultural figure at the French court. Her influence, in fact, went beyond the French court. In 1519 she wrote to the Pope, asking for his authorization to fund and create a monastery for nuns. A year later, her request was accepted.

Marguerite did not hide her interest in humanist and reformed ideas, exchanging letters openly with Desiderius Erasmus, Guillaume Budé and other reformists. Since her brother was her protector, she feared no one; although Francis did not approve of everything she did, he never turned on her for her innovative opinions, and as she grew older these ideas would become deeply rooted in her mind. For Anne, she was another model of political power, and a reminder of the high esteem that respected, forthright women could be held in.

While Anne was in the service of Queen Claude, she and Marguerite met on a number of occasions. Given Anne's own confidence following her departure from France, as well as her own later views on how the Roman Catholic Church should be challenged, one can see the influence Marguerite exerted on her. Some also claimed that Anne might have served as one of Marguerite's ladies-in-waiting. In the Duchess of Alençon's household accounts for the year 1517, there is no mention of Anne, or of any other lady.[10] It is not impossible, however, that Anne served Marguerite after 1517 and before her return to England. What is certain is that, later on, Anne referred to Marguerite as a friend.

Marguerite's rise at Francis's court took a new and important turn after the imperial election. England had clearly played France's ambitions and tightened its relationship with Spain, and now it had done the same with the Holy Roman Empire. Yet the growing power of Charles of Spain could not serve either England's or France's interests in the long run, and Henry VIII and Francis had to find a way to put their differences aside and forge a stronger alliance between their realms.

What became apparent from this competition for the imperial crown was that three powerful kings were at one another's mercy, and that all had at their disposal many men (and women) who were ready to play dirty political games in order to please their respective masters. It could be a long war of attrition. But also evident was the fact that Francis and Henry had to compromise with each other if they wanted to counterbalance Charles's power and, from this, an idea emerged: What if they met in person and made their alliance more tangible? So, a meeting between the two princes was organized—and it would be the meeting of the century. Marguerite and Anne would witness it firsthand. One as the sister of the French king, the other as a lady-in-waiting to the French queen.

*

Two kings together in one place was a rare sight—and, quite frankly, a nightmare to organize.

The architect behind this great royal meeting was Cardinal Wolsey, who had forged his success within the Henrician court and also built a trusting relationship with Francis I. Wolsey's power and influence were substantial, and he was cunning enough to master political games like no other.

The goal behind such a reunion was to ensure England's place as a third power in Europe—one that would offer a balance of power between France and Spain. In 1519, discussions of a meeting commenced, but it wasn't until 1520 that the meeting actually materialized, a sign of the painstaking diplomacy involved.

Evidently, Charles of Spain did not see eye to eye with English ambitions, and needed reassurances that England was not favoring France over Spain. In the spring of 1520, he instructed his ambassador to inform Henry VIII of his intention to visit England shortly.

Henry VIII was ambushed. His meeting with Francis would have to wait a little longer.

*

In April 1520, Francis visited his wife, Claude—who was by now pregnant with their fifth child, the little Madeleine, and was resting in Blois in the company of her ladies-in-waiting. Francis had heard of Charles's trick in visiting Henry VIII before he himself could meet the English king in person. He was not impressed.

"Tell your master that I wish for us to meet first, before his meeting with the Catholic King," Francis told the English ambassador, Sir Richard Wingfield, after boasting about his earlier hunting session and how he had mastered the art of hunting boar.[11]

The next day, Francis, his wife and her court went to Paris. Clearly, Anne's life was cloistered as some historians and contemporaries had presumed; Claude and her ladies-in-waiting, including Anne, would all attend the eagerly awaited encounter between France and England.

Sadly, Francis's plea to meet with Henry first fell on deaf ears.

On May 26, 1520, Charles arrived in Dover, where he was received by Cardinal Wolsey. He made it just in time; Henry was very shortly due to make his way to France for a meeting with Francis.

The next day, Henry and his wife and consort, Catherine of Aragon, met with the newly appointed Holy Roman Emperor in Canterbury. This meeting was not just symbolic; serious diplomatic negotiations took place. The peace treaty between England and the Low Countries was extended for another five years—bringing much joy to Charles, who had feared that France and England's rapprochement would jeopardize it.

Charles's next stop was, in fact, the Low Countries, where he was expected to visit his aunt, Margaret of Savoy—and now a bonus: he was to bring her the good news that England remained a strong ally to Spain and the Holy Roman Empire.

Before making his way to France, Henry VIII agreed to meet with Charles again on the emperor's return to England. Charles's influence over his uncle-in-law was quite clear—especially to the French, who kept complaining about this unwelcome strengthening of relations. Yet the men forged ahead with their plans to meet again.

*

In a world where women may have been overshadowed by men, it is important to remember that they often saw and heard just as much as those men—and were well capable of forming their own opinions. This was certainly the case for Anne Boleyn, whose name is largely absent from French records and chronicles of that particular time, though we know of her close proximity to the court. She was soon to become closer than ever to the action.

Both in their prime—with Henry VIII being 28 and Francis I being 25—the two men were known for their charisma, vitality, athleticism and their love of pleasure, including good food and women.

For months prior to their next meeting, preparations had been made in which no expense had been spared. The idea was clear: impress the respective courts and masters, in order that each demonstrate his own greatness.

The camp—known as the Field of the Cloth of Gold because of the glittering, golden drape that covered it—was to be located in the valley between Guînes and Ardres in the north of France. This location was strategic; it placed the two kings on level ground and was not too far from two other major cities, the English stronghold of Calais and the French city of Boulogne.

Guînes and Ardres had suffered a great deal during the Anglo-French wars, and had lost many of their inns and lodgings. Therefore, tents and pavilions were erected for the guests all over the valley—artisans, tentmakers, smiths, carpenters and other craftsmen worked hard to ensure that the makeshift city was ready for its new arrivals. Female artisans labored to sew and weave the materials that would cover the constructions built by the carpenters. Such an undertaking required everyone's best efforts.

Guillaume de Seigne—a treasurer in service to Galiot de Genouillac, master of artillery for the French king—supervised the construction of the tents and transportation of all materials to the French camp. In his accounts, he listed the workers and people involved in setting up the event. For instance, a trader called Nicolas Allement traveled many times to Florence and Milan to purchase fleurs-de-lys, gold tissue and silk. He was paid 1,500 crowns for his service.[12]

According to reports, Francis I's pavilion was particularly imposing. It was described as being "as high as the tallest tower," "60 paces high" and "120ft high."[13] It was covered in cloth of gold, as expected, with "three lateral stripes of blue velvet powdered with golden fleur-de-lis."[14]

Francis was accompanied by his queen, Claude, his mother, Louise, and his sister, Marguerite. Claude had two tents for herself in addition to small pavilions for her household, which included Anne Boleyn. The tents and pavilions were embellished with gold and silver and violet satin drapes. The entertainment was to include archery and other sporting tournaments, masquerade balls, royal choirs and other musical performances, and of course there was to be luxurious quantities of wine and food for all present.

Among all this preparation, there was another key requirement: enough space for the "feat of arms," a form of entertainment that involved jousts and wrestling, as well as other feats of physicality, a perfect forum for powerful men to showcase their prowess. The two kings were no exception.

On June 7, the feast day of Corpus Christi, Henry and Francis, along with their men, met at the bottom of the Val Doré. They both wore silver cloth garments with precious gems, such as diamonds and rubies, though Francis had opted to distinguish himself further with an additional cloak of gold satin. As they rode down to the valley, their men and their courts held their breath; they "should remain still, on pain of death."[15] After all, not so long ago, France and England had been at war with each other, and distrust remained high on both sides.

All at once, the music transformed so that only the trumpets sounded. Henry was accompanied by the man who had organized everything for the English side—Cardinal Wolsey—along with a few other nobles, including the newly appointed ambassador to France, Wingfield. Francis was flanked by Charles, Duke of Bourbon, Constable of France, and Bonnivet. Footmen—three on each side of the respective monarchs, the French in white velvet and silver, the English in crimson velvet and gold—completed the party.

Once they had approached each other, the two kings halted, rode a little farther, and then, still on their respective horses, they embraced each other. What a relief for all involved! The celebrations could now begin in earnest. It was decreed that, on Sunday, June 10, the King of England would dine with the Queen of France at Ardres while the King of France would dine with the Queen of England at Guînes.

Wearing "a double mantle of cloth of gold made like a cloak (cappe) embroidered in jewels," Henry VIII was received at Claude's lodging. Upon his arrival, he met her ladies, including Anne Boleyn. One of his special envoys recalled the women to be "the most beautiful that could be, dressed in cloth of gold."

Henry was invited to enter the main room, where Queen Claude was waiting. As finely dressed as him—dripping with opulent diamonds and emeralds—she was surrounded by her ladies-in-waiting and, more importantly, flanked by both Francis I's mother, Louise of Savoy, and his sister, Marguerite d'Angoulême. The message was clear: the women of the French court were not to be overlooked by the Englishmen.

They all dined together, with the ladies-in-waiting, including Anne herself, witnessing the event. Whispers of Henry's attractiveness swirled: "He is a very handsome prince."[16]

Now that all the required diplomatic conventions had taken place, and these two powerful kings had been showcased, the demonstrations of power and strength could follow.

*

The feat of arms was desired by both Henry and Francis. It consisted first of jousting at the tilt, then a tournament in the open field, and concluded with combat on foot. Sharp, steel weapons were not allowed, in order to avoid any accidents. Even so, it was quite a sight for the audience, watching these men preparing for combat, one way or another, and hoping to prove their martial worth.

Ladies, including the queens and their households, were part of this audience. Henry's sister, Mary Tudor, the Duchess of Suffolk and former queen of France, was also attending the celebrations. She was accompanying Queen Catherine of England—both borne in remarkably embroidered litters. Catherine's was in crimson satin with gold, with her emblem of the pomegranate of Granada embroidered on it. Mary's was covered with a cloth of gold wrought with lilies.

Queen Claude, wearing a sumptuous necklace, arrived in a litter covered with a cloth of silver and gold. Her ladies-in-waiting, including Anne Boleyn, followed behind her in three luxurious wagons. At the back of these was the queen mother's litter, covered in black velvet. Marguerite, the French king's sister, also followed in her own litter.

The queens, both English and French, met alongside their ladies. While Henry's wife, Catherine, could speak French, it is believed that Anne Boleyn was used as an interpreter between her and the royal French women. Interpreter or not, Anne certainly witnessed the event firsthand.

The women's beauty was commented on by various ambassadors who deemed that the English ladies were well dressed but less beautiful than their French counterparts. At the time, Anne was viewed as one of the French ladies, and she was proud of this.

Her father, Thomas, now with his wife, Elizabeth Boleyn, were also attending the feat of arms, as well as the wider meeting of kings.[17] They sat on the English side, with their daughter on the French side—just as Thomas had planned.

She was a rose among the fleurs-de-lys.

The ladies conversed while the men were attired for the joust, at which Francis's skill was notably impressive; he was said to be "breaking spears mightily" while Henry "broke a lance on nearly every course." At the end of the day of mock battle, the kings joined the ladies and "amused themselves in their company."[18]

A few days later, the kings took each other on again. While they were drinking together, Henry demanded a wrestling match with Francis, who was more than happy to oblige. The French king was known to be a strong and clever wrestler and, during their match, he gave Henry a "tour de Bretagne," throwing him on his back and boldly defeating him. Luckily, Henry had triumphed days before in the archery tournaments—showing his superiority at the sport—and thus saving himself from complete humiliation now at the hands of Francis.

Alongside these masculine activities, music and other entertainments, food was provided. These luxurious meals included the best meat attainable—such as beef, veal and hog—and were accompanied by the finest wines, beers and ales.

The royal kings often ate together without their ladies and nobles, offering a rare moment of shared privacy to the two rulers. Queen Claude—who was heavily pregnant again—was absent from time to time, but when she was in attendance she ensured she was resplendent, adorned in gold and magnificent jewels: diamonds, emeralds and rubies. Her ladies also stood by her side and it is often speculated that Henry VIII first noticed Anne during these royal gatherings. One can easily assume that it would have been impossible for Anne not to notice Henry. After all, beyond his authority and his dashing looks, Henry was a *bon vivant* who sought entertainment and attention in all its possible forms. Boisterous, loud and exuberant, he was not the type of man who could be easily overlooked.

After dinner, the ladies and noblemen were reacquainted with the royals to dance and amuse themselves. Cardinal Wolsey was often seen in the company of Louise of Savoy, the queen mother of France, feasting and dancing. The two seemed to have a lot to discuss—not surprising given that they were the architects of this meeting, and were the representatives of their respective monarchs.

For several days the two parties mingled. By now Anne Boleyn was around 20 years old, and in this meeting of two kingdoms she was finally seeing the English court at close quarters for the first time.

One wonders whether it was at this time that she began to speculate that a woman of ambition and purpose might not reach similar heights in another court—in her home country.

★

On the last day of the festivities, Sunday, June 24, the kings—along with their close advisers and royals—enjoyed one last dinner together before attending the ceremony of "prize-giving," in which the best performers during the feat of arms were acknowledged and celebrated. The French and English queens were tasked with awarding gifts—Queen Catherine to the French men, including Francis I, who had jousted and combatted well, and Queen Claude to Henry VIII, his prize involving precious gems, rings and other jewels.

Before the parties left each other, the queen consorts gave each other gifts as symbols of their amity. Claude presented Catherine with a gold-cloth litter, along with its mules and pages, while Catherine reciprocated with hobbies and beautiful palfreys. Louise, the French queen mother, gave Cardinal Wolsey a jeweled crucifix, which was itself worth a fortune.

Looking on at these embraces and the exchange of such lavish gifts, Anne Boleyn observed the conclusion of the famous encounter of the Field of the Cloth of Gold—with its promise of friendship and alliance between the French and English crowns. Even if this state of harmony was not to endure, she understood the Anglo-French alliance more clearly than ever before. She must have known what an asset this would be for her future.

4

Troubled Waters

All good things must come to an end—even for Anne Boleyn, who saw her fate take a turn when she least expected it.

Though the Field of the Cloth of Gold seemed to have brought France and England's rulers closer together, diplomatic turmoil was never far away, especially when it came to masculine and royal rivalry. For Charles of Spain—now Francis's chief enemy—his desire to make a name for himself was stronger than ever given the union of his two rivals. Ultimately, that meant he needed to be seen, and respected, as the strongest ruler in Europe.

By the autumn of 1520, Charles's power had steadily increased—and his will to control Italy had grown along with it. For decades, the struggle for dominance in Italy had been the principal spur to Franco-Spanish hostility. Geopolitical considerations had virtually forced Charles and Francis into war.

In England, the situation was delicate. Both Henry VIII and Wolsey saw an opportunity to prove their importance on the European political scene; if England could not compete for glory, she had to appear as the rightful mediator of European politics, including the fight for power between Charles and Francis. Whoever prevailed in this tug-of-war would desperately need England's support in order to ensure victory.

In November, Wolsey wrote to Thomas Boleyn and his other

French ambassadors, informing them of recent intelligence reports from Spain and the Holy Roman Empire, as well as England's decision to take a stand against France.

"It is said that Francis of France will not accept a truce and is ready to attack Charles with a great force that he won't be able to resist."

The English had gathered intelligence that Francis was thinking of making a military move on the Low Countries and, as a result, Wolsey informed the ambassadors that England "will declare war on France" in the near future.[1]

This drastic turn of events was potentially disastrous for Anne Boleyn, who was still in the service of Queen Claude. Evidently, she could not remain there. The daughter of a diplomat and courtier, she would soon be among enemies once the war was declared.

Enemies that she personally saw as friends and allies.

Enemies that for her were close to family.

She was soon to be recalled. However, Anne's departure would also be a risky move, and one that would rightfully increase wariness among the French. She had now been at Francis's court for seven years. She knew the entire royal family and had spent a great deal of time in their company, having been particularly inspired by the women in her midst. Repatriating her to England would not be an easy task.

Fortunately for the English, who did not wish to be suspected of breaking the peace with France too early, an explanation for her abrupt departure could easily be given that would not raise further suspicions.

In 1515, Anne's grandfather—Thomas Butler, Earl of Ormonde—had died without a direct heir, with possible inheritors among the Boleyns and the St. Legers. One contender for the title was Piers Butler, another cousin who had fewer rights on the title but who had already been styling himself "the earl of Ormonde" since the death of the patriarch.

As a pretext for Anne's recall from France, and in order to appease tensions between the different branches of the family, a match had been made between Anne and Piers's son, James. Cardinal Wolsey was once again the mastermind behind it all: as close to the Boleyns as ever, he was accelerating their rise at the English court.

He directly wrote to Henry: "On my return, I will talk with you how to bring about the marriage between Piers's son and Sir Thomas Boleyn's daughter."[2]

This was evidently used as a stratagem to fool the French, as no such match was ever actually concluded.

Francis, on the other hand, did not hide his suspicion, or his disapproval of such a decision: "His [Henry VIII's] subjects go and take the Emperor's pay, the English scholars at Paris have returned home, and also the daughter of Mr. Boullan [Boleyn], while ships were being made at Dover, and musters taken in England, the rumor being that it was to make war on France."

The French king, however, was not so easily duped. He knew that the wind had turned and that he had been left in a difficult position.

> I do not know if he [Henry VIII] finds it difficult to maintain the friendship of myself and the Emperor elect, considering the enmity between us, but he must choose between neutrality and a declaration for one or the other. As to neutrality, I should not be dissatisfied, but if he were to declare against me, I should consider it a great wrong, after all the familiarities, oaths, and treaties between us.[3]

And "a great wrong" it was.

Francis, Henry and Charles were soon to be dragged into a bloody war—their egos pitted against one another while their men were slaughtered—and all this in the pursuit of making a name for themselves and for the balance of power in Europe.

In this time of war and defiance, Anne now found herself back in England, once again serving her family's interests the best she could. What would the future hold for her?

In fact, one cannot fully understand Anne's future without understanding Francis's coming years of failures and military setbacks. As the blows rained down upon him, it soon became quite clear that he needed a true ally at the English court.

And so, from 1522 to 1527, without any interaction between them, Anne's and Francis's fates in these years were surprisingly intertwined in a dance of calculation and tenacity—the last of these a quality Anne was about to display as she made her first entrance onto the stage of the English court.

By early 1522, Charles and Henry were strengthening the pact they had made against Francis. Henry was reneging on everything he had promised Francis during all those years of consolidating the Anglo-French alliance. It was a blow Francis certainly had not expected. His friend—or so he had thought—was now pleading allegiance to his archenemy, Charles of Spain. And, to add insult to injury, Henry broke his word of promising his daughter Mary to the French dauphin; instead, he was now conducting marital negotiations between Mary and Charles.

The resulting war was inevitable and would have long-term effects on Francis and his perception of both England and Henry. The French king would never be able fully to trust him again.

By all accounts, Wolsey was also not the friend Francis thought he was, and, in time, the French king's eyes and interests would turn to someone else whom he saw as the perfect agent for his cause: Anne Boleyn herself.

But first, life lessons were to be taught—the hard way.

*

Thomas Boleyn had been reunited with his daughter, Anne, and was now working relentlessly to ensure that her European education would serve him well. Upon her return in early 1522, he offered her up in the service of Catherine of Aragon.

In many respects, Anne was the perfect lady-in-waiting, and it should not have been difficult to secure such a position in the queen's household. Not only was Thomas in Wolsey's good graces, but Anne herself knew the ins and outs of such a role and would be more than an agreeable companion for the queen—and in time, perhaps, a too agreeable one for the king.

On March 4, 1522, Wolsey organized a sumptuous dinner at York Place, his opulent residence on the River Thames, which eventually became the Palace of Whitehall. The dinner was held to celebrate the strengthened alliance between England and Spain. Charles V's ambassadors were at Henry's court, receiving lavish gifts and great ceremony.

Wolsey's dinner needed to be perfect. It was held in the great hall, which was adorned with rich tapestries and canopies of luxurious cloth for the occasion. It had also been decided that here a pageant would take place representing the relentless pursuit of love. It was named the "Château Vert" pageant after the temporary green castle that had been built to house the occasion.

As Wolsey's protégé, it was no surprise that Thomas Boleyn and his wife were two of the guests at this dinner. Thomas had been working closely with Wolsey for years now, and therefore knew how to best serve his master's interests as well as his own. Thomas suggested that his daughters might perform in the pageant to celebrate Anne's return to court, and his pride in her was clear for all to see.

By now an incredibly well-educated woman, Anne had everything going for her. She was of tall stature, elegant and, importantly, charismatic. She was not a typical beauty; Mary, her sister, better suited the beauty standards of the time, which involved fairer, paler skin and blue eyes. Anne was, as portrayed, olive skinned with dark, intense eyes—quite the opposite of what was regarded as "beautiful" in England at the time. Nevertheless, her je ne sais quoi and her poise made her stand out from the crowd, showing that beauty did not always trump charisma.

★

At the pageant, eight beautiful women stood at the center of the event at York Place. All dressed in Milanese gowns of fine white satin, wearing bonnets decorated with precious gemstones, and with their hair tied with strands of Venetian gold, they were a sight to behold.

Each woman represented a feminine virtue of the courtly love tradition: Kindness, Beauty, Honor, Constancy, Perseverance, Bounty, Mercy and Pity. The names of these virtues were embroidered on their gowns in gold for everyone to see, but the masks covering their faces made it impossible to know who was who, making the whole game far more interesting and enticing.

Mary Boleyn; Mary Tudor Brandon, Duchess of Suffolk; Gertrude Courtenay, Countess of Devon; Jane Parker; Anne Boleyn and three other women—Mistress Browne, Mistress Danet and one unknown lady—all took part in this eye-catching show. In the middle of it wall, Anne was standing high in the tower of the green castle, making her debut at the English court with confidence and elegance.

The pageant was not just a showcase of these virtues but a representation of how they were threatened by the "vices" that spread in the Tudor court. The women, therefore, were guarded by men who embodied these vices—Danger, Disdain, Jealousy, Unkindness, Scorn, Malebouche (or inappropriate language) and Strangeness. These "men" were likely played by young boys, and they stood in the lower part of the castle.

Wolsey and his guests took their seats in front of this embellished set and hidden musicians started the show, entertaining the audience. Suddenly, Henry VIII himself entered the room, accompanied by eight other men—dressed in caps of cloth of gold and mantle cloaks of blue satin—who were masked in an effort to conceal their identities. Like the women performing their virtues, the king and these eight men took on their own masculine virtues: Amorousness, Nobleness, Youth, Attendance, Loyalty, Pleasure, Gentleness, Liberty and Honesty. The unequal number of men and women must have been allowed so that Henry's wife, the queen, Catherine of Aragon, could take part after the pageant took place.

Encouraged by William Cornish—master of the royal chapter choristers, who was playing Ardent Desire—the men took the castle by storm and "threw in dates and oranges, and other fruit made for pleasure."[4]

It was certainly an entertaining spectacle, and the mood was light and frivolous.

Henry, handsome as ever, led the chivalric attack on the castle that the vices were trying to protect. After their victory, each were given a "virtue," and the men and women danced together.

Although it was on this night that Anne and Henry first properly met, and though they may have encountered each other earlier when the English and French courts met in more peaceful times, Henry had another woman on his mind. In fact, Mary Boleyn, Anne's sister, had been on his mind for some time. There is no evidence of exactly when (or if) his relationship with Mary started, nor how long it lasted, or when exactly it ended (though it is believed that they had been involved before Anne arrived at the English court), but it is hard to imagine that Henry would have pursued Anne if he had still been involved with her sister. Later, though, Anne and Henry's detractors used his potential previous relationship with Mary to undermine his and Anne's relationship and so the legitimacy of their marriage. Years later—in 1535—John Hale, a devout supporter of Catherine of Aragon, claimed that "Mary Boleyn had borne the King a son."[5] Ultimately, Henry would discard Mary and ardently pursue her sister. But that was all still to come.

The relationship between the two sisters was likely complex. After all, Anne had spent almost a decade far from home, meaning that the Boleyn daughters barely knew each other when Anne was reunited with her family. Some assume that a rivalry of some kind might have occurred between them, but there is no evidence of any long-standing division within the Boleyn family. Later, Elizabeth I—daughter of Anne Boleyn and Henry VIII—treated her relatives from her mother's side favorably, including the descendants of Mary Boleyn, showing that she embraced her Boleyn heritage.

For now, in 1522, the festivities continued long into the night at Wolsey's pageant. That evening, the alliance between the Tudors and the Habsburgs was strong.

Meanwhile, as Henry's court was celebrating its alliance and friendship with Charles, the Holy Roman Emperor, the situation in France—particularly for Francis—took a dramatic turn.

Henry's and Charles's reconciliation continued to be a betrayal for the French king, who now complained that "many French ships were arrested in English ports"—making trade difficult, but also aggravating the situation and good entente between the two countries.[6] Furthermore, several reports confirmed that the English navy was preparing its ships in all ports; a clear sign that Henry was determined to bring Francis to his knees.

To add to France's displeasure, the English navy was only getting stronger. In 1510, Henry VIII had ordered the construction of one of the largest military ships in the navy, which would be a real asset in the wars to come: the *Mary Rose*. Her armament was a mix of old design and new innovations. She contained large iron guns as well as bronze ones, which rested on four-wheel carriages. This warship was an example of English craftsmanship and strength, both past and future, and she soon became Henry Tudor's pride and joy.

The *Mary Rose* first fought the French in 1512, and the rumor that she was being armed again was certainly not good news for them. Now, ten years on, in June—led by her master, John Browne—she was carrying troops that would eventually capture the port of Morlaix in Brittany.

To retaliate against this attack, and against England's favor toward the Habsburgs, Francis sought to bring the Franco-Scottish "Auld Alliance" into play. If Henry was ready to betray him, then he could inflict some damage via Henry's northern border with the aid of the strong leadership of John Stewart, Duke of Albany.

The illegitimate grandson of James II of Scotland, John Stewart was born and raised in France. He was a reliable agent of the French court as well as an avid promoter of his own interests. In Francis's view, as an excellent military commander who had served in the French army, the Duke of Albany was the perfect de facto troublemaker to be sent to the Anglo-Scottish border.

Henry was furious, but Francis shrugged his shoulders. After all, by choosing to turn against France, the English king had made his bed and now he would have to lie in it. However, while this created a useful diversion, the combined forces of the English and the Spanish continued to put incredible pressure on France.

War was now at their doorstep, and from that moment—and into the years that followed—nothing would ever be the same for Henry and Francis. The promises of a perpetual friendship had been broken, and suspicion would always remain between them. Anne would soon find herself caught in the crossfire of the two crowns, both a pawn and a power player in the service of two kings and two kingdoms.

But first, hell would be unleashed on the French king. Francis would face some cruel blows that would scar him forever.

★

With the help of 16,000 Swiss troops, Francis's army descended into Italy with the purpose of once more recapturing the duchy of Milan and ensuring that Charles's power was kept at arm's length.

While the first offensive under the leadership of Francis's commander, the Vicomte de Lautrec, was a success, trouble soon started brewing among the troops. The Swiss mercenaries were not happy, claiming they had not been paid what they were due. On top of that, the forces against the French were better organized, and more prepared for their arrival, than they had expected. While the first battles went in favor of the French, they soon realized that more reinforcements were coming, leaving them in a difficult position.

As the weeks passed, the French army ceased making progress, and it soon became clear that this was an enormous defeat for them—and especially for Francis, who blamed Lautrec for his indecisiveness and inability to follow his orders.

The victory of Marignano in 1515 seemed to be a faraway memory. The glory of Francis was fading.

In an attempt to restore his master's reputation, Lautrec decided to launch a counterattack on Pavia. Once more, however, he underestimated his opponents and faced another dreadful defeat. The situation became even more dire when the Swiss mutinied against the French. Lautrec returned to France, defeated again, and with no good news to offer Francis, who was watching his influence on the European political scene diminish by the day.

While Francis was experiencing his humiliation in Italy, Charles, Duke of Bourbon and Constable of France—one of the French king's closest advisers and a prince of royal blood, which meant he had a claim to the throne—was about to betray him. Bourbon saw an opportunity to ally himself with the Holy Roman Emperor and the English king. In many respects, Bourbon had never truly recognized Francis's right to be on the French throne, and this war was the perfect excuse for him to reveal his true allegiance.

By 1524, the situation had intensified. Most of the Italian territories were lost to Charles, and now Bourbon was threatening to invade the south while Henry sent forces to the north of France. This was the nightmare of all military strategists—enemies on more than one front, and the threat of self-declared "enemies within."

While Francis remained determined to fight on, he knew his options were diminishing by the day. The Scots were not causing enough damage to the English, and Bourbon's betrayal had left a very bitter taste in his mouth. Meanwhile, Charles V of Spain was now asking for Burgundy in return for Milan and for a ceasefire—a proposition unacceptable in the eyes of Francis, who could hardly be expected to cede a huge chunk of territory within the realm of France itself. This, he felt, was just the latest in a long line of insults to be thrown him. Even worse, Bourbon was now promising the French crown to Henry VIII himself.

"If Henry does not fetch the French crown himself, we will bring it to him."[7]

In July 1524, with an army of 20,000 men from the Holy Roman Empire, Bourbon went on the offensive in Var and Provence. By August 7, Aix-en-Provence had fallen. The siege of Marseille began on August 19 but proved to be more complex. Bourbon was hoping that the French, who had been impoverished by Francis's love for both luxury and interminable wars, would turn on their king and country. Instead, the opposite happened. Proud and resilient, the Marseillais fought the imperial army.

Although Bourbon might have been right that they were not huge supporters of Francis, the Marseillais were not prepared to welcome a traitor and foreigner as their ruler, and their tenacity and determination caused Bourbon to suffer a serious defeat. By October, the French army, sent by Francis, had reconquered the territories. Francis promised he would "remember their services for evermore."[8]

In the midst of all this chaos, 1524 was a dreadful year for

Francis in other ways. Before leaving for the south and defending his territory in July, he said his final farewell to his wife, Claude, who possibly died in childbirth but in any case had certainly been ill for quite some time. She passed away on July 20, 1524. The loss hit him so greatly, perhaps more than he expected, admitting to his sister, Marguerite, that "could I buy her life with mine I would do it with all my heart."[9] His misfortunes did not stop there. On September 18 he lost his second daughter, seven-year-old Charlotte, to measles. On top of this tragedy, his mother, Louise, was also taken ill—further troubling the deflated king.

Yet the worst was still to come.

★

In spite of his personal troubles, Francis threw himself into the recovery, as he long hoped for, of his Italian territories. He had regained some of his confidence with the reconquest of Provence, and Bonnivet, his trusted adviser, had recovered from wounds incurred in battle. Now Francis's eyes were on Milan and the pursuit of glory.

Could this be a mistake? Louise of Savoy certainly thought so. In fact, she wrote to her son in September 1524, urging him to reconsider, but it was too late; by early October, the French army, led by the king himself, left Aix for Milan.

Unfortunately for Francis, Milan was riddled with plague, making an invasion impossible. Disappointed, but still determined to humiliate his archenemy, Francis decided to push on and take Pavia.

Pavia was a small town 22 miles away from Milan. Antonio de Leyva, one of the best generals and commanders of Charles V's army, was stationed there along with his 6,000 troops. In November the French started to lay siege to Pavia, but this was a mistake. Francis simply did not have the forces required to conquer it, and de Leyva was an experienced general who knew how to defend a city. The siege would last throughout the winter, and see the French army crumble away—afflicted by sickness and a collapse of morale.

By January 1525, Francis's enemies were conspiring against him, and Bourbon—who personally wanted revenge for what had happened in Provence—was amassing an army of 6,000 troops and a cavalry of 500. Charles V also sent additional forces to Pavia. Francis was now faced with an enemy force of around 17,000 troops and 1,000 cavalry.

For weeks the fighting was intense. Each camp gave it their best. Unfortunately for Francis, and despite some military success, French troops ultimately proved inadequate.

On February 23, Charles's army made a final decisive attack on the French. While the French fought well, maintaining a degree of discipline, they were ambushed and slaughtered. It was a massacre. Bonnivet killed himself, preferring this outcome to suffering at the hands of his enemies. Francis's brother-in-law, Marguerite's first husband, Charles IV, Duke of Alençon, was injured and abandoned the king. He would later die of his injuries, remembered as a coward.

Francis himself fought to the end until Bourbon's lieutenant, Sieur de Pompérant, recognized him and took him prisoner. The glorious French king, who had been the hero of Marignano, the king who had hosted the Field of the Cloth of Gold, was now on his knees, reduced to becoming the prisoner of his archenemy, Charles V. It was the ultimate humiliation.

"I pray you decide in your own heart whatever you may be pleased to do with me," he wrote to Charles.

"I beg you not to lose heart but to employ your usual good sense, for I have confidence that in the end God will not desert me," he disclosed to his mother, Louise.[10]

Francis would eventually regain his glory and dignity but for now, his enemies—including Henry VIII himself—rejoiced at his downfall.

*

In her son's absence, Louise of Savoy was made regent of the realm while his sister, Marguerite—who was now a widow—was about to play the most important role of her life: a negotiator and an ambassador for her mother and brother. These two women, who had so influenced Anne Boleyn in her teenage years, had now been propelled to the forefront of the European political scene. Their first priority was to secure the French king's release from captivity.

There is no doubt that Anne—whose father was still a close informant of Wolsey—had heard the news, and it was likely her admiration for these strong female leaders only increased.

Charles V showed great humility in his victory, and now Henry VIII was the one making things more difficult for the French. He now threatened to invade France and, in so doing, become yet another enemy of Francis.

Tensions between the two realms were at their highest, and the people of France—while being deflated by such a defeat in Pavia and humiliated by having their king imprisoned—were prepared to fight any English invasion. Charles for his part showed no interest in taking advantage of the situation and invading France himself, leaving Henry alone in his quest to capture it—an endeavor that now seemed unattainable if it were to be unsupported by Charles.

In the absence of the French king, the two royal women made a plan. Marguerite turned to negotiation with the emperor while Louise approached the English court.

Using her steely political insight, and probably also her genuine camaraderie with Wolsey, she sought another treaty of peace between England and France, and so the French queen mother had no other choice but to swallow her pride and play the game of thrones. Eventually, her stratagems would pay off.

Louise was a formidable stateswoman. She knew what would appeal to Henry more than a difficult military campaign against France: money. She therefore offered to pay him a total of 2 million gold crowns in exchange for his promise to actively demand Francis's release. Louise also made the promise to no longer ally with Scotland and, on August 30, 1525, the Treaty of the More, re-establishing the Anglo-French alliance, was signed by both parties.

While this was a step toward securing the French king's release, it was not enough.

In secret, Louise also sent envoys to Suleiman the Magnificent—the Ottoman sultan and the only ruler that could now challenge Charles V militarily. She asked him to help her deliver her son out of captivity and urged him to invade Charles's states in the east. At first, Suleiman showed compassion to Louise: in Ottoman culture, the mother of a king was the highest rank after the sultan himself, and he respected her. Yet, despite the fact that Charles's empire was a threat to the Ottomans, he did not want at this point to engage the emperor with force. In proof of his genuine sympathy for Francis, he wrote a few letters to him in support of Louise's position but sent no aid to liberate him.

The news that Francis had fallen ill in captivity aggravated the situation, and Louise was left with no choice but to send her daughter to plead for him. Marguerite, who had been Anne Boleyn's indirect mentor in so many respects, was suddenly at the forefront of these vital negotiations.

She wrote to Francis, informing him of their mother's decision: "I am determined to serve you [. . .] your very humble, Marguerite."[11]

In September 1525, Marguerite was reunited with her brother in Madrid. Though rumors spread that he was so ill he could be dying, to his sister's relief, the king without a throne slowly but surely recovered.

Marguerite still had to ensure that her mission was a success, however, so she journeyed on to Toledo, where Charles resided.

Here, she was received coolly, but nevertheless with respect. Charles's sister Eleanor, one of the more prominent figures at the court, greeted the duchess. As for Charles, his promises bode well: "I am in favor of negotiations and good relations with France, we will further discuss this tomorrow and Saturday."[12]

Marguerite had few real cards to play. She understood that these negotiations were not going to be easy, but she was determined not to have made this journey in vain, and to rescue her brother from Spain. After all, France needed its leader back on the throne. Although her mother, Louise, was now a force to be reckoned with at home, she was facing predictable discontent from the Parlement de Paris and some of her ministers, who would be more than happy to take advantage of the current woes of the Valois-Angoulême dynasty.

Unfortunately, the first round of negotiations turned sour for the French. Charles deemed Marguerite's—or, rather, her mother Louise's—conditions unacceptable and refused to press on with discussions. The duchess in turn refused any *pourparler* that would involve the contentious territory of Burgundy.

There was nothing left to say, and Marguerite was left with no other choice but to leave Toledo for Madrid again.

This trip, however, had not been totally in vain. On her short stay in Toledo, Marguerite had befriended Eleanor, Charles's older sister, and during her time with her brother, she came up with another proposition. She returned to Toledo and, in exchange for Francis's release, she offered Charles 3 million gold crowns and a marriage between Francis and Eleanor.

For Charles, this was still not enough.

Marguerite's diplomatic endeavors proved to be a failure, yet she also showed the extent to which women could be entrusted with delicate and important missions. On her way back to France, she went to see Francis once more, leaving behind a small dog as a companion.

For Francis, these negotiations might have been protracted but they were far from futile; his sister had given him hope. He now hatched a plan that would allow him to rise from the ashes. To Charles he promised Burgundy—as well as some other Italian territories—but insisted that in order to deliver on the deal he would need to be restored as king of France to convince his people of the agreement and avoid their rebellion. He also persuaded Charles to break his promise to Bourbon and agree to an alliance through marriage between Francis and Eleanor, the Holy Roman Emperor's sister.

To everyone's surprise, Charles agreed to these terms. His councillors tried to change his mind, but he believed Francis's word without considering that, at this point, Francis was no longer the Renaissance king he once was. The French king had faced humiliation after humiliation and now had a cunning appetite for revenge—without honor, if need be.

Although Charles had acquiesced to Francis's terms, he needed guarantees—or, in this case, guarantors. He asked for the king's sons—the dauphin, Francis, along with his brother Henry, Duke of Orléans—to be sent as prisoners in exchange for the French king's release. Francis complied.

On January 14, 1526, both rulers signed the Treaty of Madrid.

Now that Francis was free, he started to repair his tattered reputation. Upon his return to France, a marriage was agreed between his sister, Marguerite, and Henry d'Albret, King of Navarre—a strategic territory sitting between Spain and France. At this point, Francis would contemplate any sort of alliance and was prepared to seek agents that would serve his interests at other rulers' courts. He needed to ensure the liberation of his two sons—even though this would take some years to achieve.

Soon, his perfect agent at the English court would rise: Anne Boleyn.

For, while the drama had been unfolding in Europe, Anne had been discovering the thrills of courtly love for herself—before catching the interest of the one who would eventually destroy her.

★

After the success of the Château Vert pageant, Anne was now in the service of Catherine of Aragon, where she could draw upon all the skills she had previously learned in Mechelen and Paris. As a now experienced lady-in-waiting, Anne could converse with and entertain her queen while performing her duties of care toward Henry's wife with great diligence.

Soon, she would draw the interest of courtiers, who were intrigued by her unconventional beauty and elegance. Certainly, Anne was like no one else at court. Her manners and behavior were deemed continental. She showed humility and yet, it was said, "employed the power of her eyes" to charm and seduce.[13] There was no doubt that Anne was magnetic, and it wasn't long before she started to use this to her advantage.

It was also time for Anne to think about marriage. Her sister, Mary—who had not spent her youth at the French court and whose marriage to William Carey had been secured in 1520—was now believed to be Henry VIII's mistress.

Anne, meanwhile, had apparently attracted Thomas Wyatt's attention. Known as the "first great Tudor poet,"[14] Wyatt resided in Allington Castle, which was 20 miles or so from Hever Castle—making him almost a near-neighbor to the Boleyns. The extent to which Wyatt pursued Anne has been disputed, but the contemporary stories linking them have certainly endured. Wyatt's writings were often held up as proof of their affection for one another, Anne described as his muse. Yet, his actual pursuit of her remained timid—especially when compared with that of another courtier who was also mesmerized by Anne.

In the service of Wolsey was a man called Henry Percy, heir to the earldom of Northumberland and therefore, it seemed to the Boleyns, a suitable match for Anne. However, Wolsey—who seemed determined to end any potential discussion of a marriage with Percy—rebuked him: "I marvel not a little of your peevish folly that you would tangle and ensure yourself with a foolish girl yonder in the court. I mean Anne Boleyn."[15]

The courtly love between Percy and Anne, therefore, was short-lived, though she did not know yet the reason for the abrupt ending of his interest. As it turned out, someone else had their eyes on her, someone not accustomed to having his will thwarted or his desire turned down: the King of England himself.

Little did Anne know what exactly was to come: a passion that would change the course of European history. But, buoyed with confidence from her years in France, and what she had learned from the royal women there, she felt ready for whatever might be in store.

Secretly, she prayed for glory.

PART 2

The Pursuit of a Crown

1527–1532

5

Struggle to Power

Could this be love?

One thing was certain: Henry VIII was slowly but surely revealing his feelings for a woman who was not his wife. Also clearly on his mind was the indisputable fact that he currently had no male heir and, as things stood with Catherine of Aragon, was unlikely to secure one.

Soon enough, the name of Anne Boleyn—as well as her influence on the English king—would be on everyone's lips. For some, this new love interest would be a way of ensuring a stronger alliance between France and England. For others, it would make their worst nightmare a reality: destabilizing royal authority and turning the English Church upside down. What would the future hold for this love affair, and the woman at its heart?

Among this romantic turbulence, the tensions between Europe's two ruling powers remained, and though *talks* of peace were on the horizon, peace itself seemed extremely hard to achieve. War, it seemed, was always on the table.

Francis I and Charles V were still at each other's throats, though their courts knew that in spite of their hatred they needed to find a way to make a truce. Pope Clement VII, under Charles's instruction, begged both of them to reach an agreement. Henry VIII was supposed to be the mediator between them, but now he had fallen for Anne, and divorce from Catherine of Aragon was on his mind. This complicated the matter.

Neither Henry nor Francis could look with complete equanimity on Charles's current dominance—not least because of his violent overthrow of papal temporal authority in the recent Sack of Rome, which had led to the imprisonment of the Pope. While they undoubtedly distrusted each other, they were once more left with no other choice than to put their differences aside for the greater good.

Matters between France and England, however, remained far from resolution. In February 1527, Francis sent special envoys to the English court to recommence discussions regarding the marriage between his son, Francis the dauphin, and Henry's daughter, Princess Mary, which had been discussed before the Field of the Cloth of Gold in 1520.

Fears remained that King Francis's old resentments could ruin his chances of obtaining Henry's support against Charles.

Was it a risk worth taking?

Only time would tell.

★

On February 26, 1527, Gabriel de Gramont—the Bishop of Tarbes and an experienced diplomat, who had spent a significant amount of time in Rome—along with Francis, Viscount of Turenne, Antoine Le Viste, president of the council of Paris, and Claude Dodieu, councillor of the Parlement de Paris, arrived at Dover. They were received by another diplomat who had been appointed at the Tudor court: Jean Joachim de Passaut, Sieur de Vaux.

These envoys had two clear missions: to negotiate a new marriage proposal between the dauphin, Francis, and Princess Mary, and to ensure England's support in the release of the French king's son.

The first to receive these envoys and their letters from Francis I was Cardinal Wolsey himself. In many ways Henry's right-hand man, Wolsey ensured that these matters were dealt with swiftly without disturbing the English king, who was preoccupied with other—more personal—matters.

A ruthless negotiator who had years of experience when it came to political and diplomatic matters, Cardinal Wolsey conjured an air of authority and superiority. Always superbly dressed, showcasing his high status and personal wealth, he was a man of power and he knew it. His close relationship with Henry VIII meant that he had the air of an unchallengeable man. When receiving the demands from the French, Wolsey did not even try to hide his disdain:

"You cannot possibly contemplate that we marry the princess to a man with whom we are not sure of perpetual friendship?" he asked, aghast. "While, of course, we have agreed to a peace treaty with Madame [Louise] when your master, King Francis, was captured in Spain, this treaty is only during the lives of the two kings, and while it should be perpetual, there is no evidence of it for now."

The baffled French ambassadors were unsure how to reply. They discussed the promises of perpetual friendship made previously by the two kings, and how this had been enough when, in 1520–1521, a marriage had been agreed between the dauphin and the princess.

Angered, Wolsey retorted: "The treaty was made when they were under age, to preserve the friendship of the kingdoms, but it was never intended to carry it out."[1]

There it was: the stark, unvarnished truth. The English had never intended to marry off Henry's only heir to the French—and especially to a king who had been a prisoner and who now had both his sons at the mercy of Charles V of Spain.

Wolsey also inquired about Francis I's promise to marry Charles's sister, Eleanor, and the consequences of him seeking another marriage when his sons were still in Spain.

Perhaps realizing he'd said too much, Wolsey took the Bishop of Tarbes aside, trying to explain that the French demands were too bold for the Tudor king, who would never consent to such an agreement. As a token of his goodwill, Wolsey promised that he would organize a meeting with the king himself, but asked them to moderate their demands so that Henry would be more receptive to them.

For the French ambassadors, there was still hope for further negotiations.

On Thursday, March 7, the French diplomats were received at Greenwich. The meeting was formal and the special envoys did not seem to be greeted with much enthusiasm. Henry more or less repeated what Wolsey had said two weeks before: he would make an alliance with Francis, but the promise of a marriage between his daughter and the French dauphin was simply not an option. He did, however, reassure them that he was a true friend of their master and that he would support him in his quest to release his sons from captivity.

In many respects, this was merely a ploy to end any further discussions on both matters. Henry had given them nothing concrete to prove his good intentions toward the French king.

The negotiations, therefore, proved to be far more difficult than expected. For days, the ambassadors bargained with both the king and Wolsey. They were sent to Queen Catherine, who inquired about "the universal peace" and how it could be achieved for "all Christendom."[2] The French envoys believed that, through the marriage between her daughter and the dauphin, this could indeed be achieved. While Catherine showed no signs of being against such a match, she noted that it would not be in the best interests of her nephew, Charles of Spain, and in that assessment she was correct.

Many more audiences were granted over the following months and, by May, Henry was showing more patience with—and consideration for—the French ambassadors. No conclusive resolution, however, was to be found. In fact, other matters were now troubling the English king. For Francis, it may have felt like the winds of change were at last upon them—though it would be some time before he derived much benefit from it.

While Henry appeared to be the mediator and the only king who could restore stability to these fractious realms, his own marriage alliance with Catherine and the house of Austria was unraveling, and turmoil was waiting in its wake.

★

From May 17 until May 31, 1527, Wolsey hosted secret and highly confidential meetings with King Henry VIII himself, along with Stephen Gardiner, William Warham, Archbishop of Canterbury, William Claiburgh, John Allen, William Bennet and John Cox, who were doctors of law.

The matter was serious: Henry was seeking a divorce or an annulment from his wife, Catherine of Aragon, and they were there to help him achieve his goal.[3]

While divorces were technically impossible under Church law, annulments could be obtained for noble families under particular circumstances—especially if there was proof that the marriage should not have occurred in the first place. They were not easy to achieve—and, in this case, the dynamics were even trickier. Henry VII had secured a dispensation from Pope Julius II, since Catherine had been married, briefly, to Henry's older brother: Arthur. This dispensation was now questioned, given that Pope Clement VII was now in effect under the control of Charles following the Sack of Rome. In this situation, the granting of such an annulment was impossible—even if he would have wished to do so.

On the last day of these discussions, Warham drafted the reasons for the annulment, making reference to Catherine's first husband and Henry's brother: "It was notorious that Prince Arthur had married Catherine, cohabited with her, and carnally known her."[4] They even explained that Henry himself, "when he came to the age of puberty, made a protest against the marriage," knowing it was wrong to marry his brother's widow. They even quoted Leviticus 20:21: "He that marrieth his brother's wife, doth an unlawful thing, he hath uncovered his brother's nakedness. They shall be without children."

Of course, Henry and Catherine did have children; Princess Mary was the only one who had survived infancy, but they were evidently not childless. However, the quest for a son and his fascination for Anne Boleyn meant that Henry was resolute: this marriage had to be dissolved one way or another.

Henry was a man who did not take "no" for an answer. And there were scholars who were prepared to give him the answer he wanted.

Through these theological—and, he felt, lawful—claims, the Tudor king hoped that Pope Clement VII would have no choice but to grant him the divorce he so desired.

But Catherine was of royal blood and would not be so easily discarded or disrespected. As a rightful Aragon and Castile descendant, she had allies both at the English court and abroad.

On June 22, 1527, a private conversation between Henry and his queen consort, Catherine of Aragon, was leaked to the imperial ambassador, Mendoza (Íñigo López de Mendoza y Zúñiga), by Catherine herself, who told him that Henry had made the following confession to her: "We have been living in mortal sin during all these years. My conscience being so troubled, I was left with no choice but to seek counsel toward canonists and theologians. They all agree that because of your previous marriage to my brother, Arthur, we are in fact sinners." He had paused. "I wish you to choose the place where you should retire."

At those words, Catherine had burst into tears. Inconsolable—and, quite frankly, humiliated—she had no response.

Henry continued, promising "that all should be done for the best. I beg you to keep secrecy upon what I have just told you."[5]

She evidently did not, knowing too well that this was a ploy to keep her away from her supporters and to prevent her from telling her nephew, Charles, the Holy Roman Emperor, of the scandal she was facing. So she confided in Mendoza, who alerted the emperor himself. For this was a humiliation not just of Catherine, but of the Habsburgs and Spain, too.

Yet Mendoza and Catherine had to act with great care. While Wolsey was in France—which in itself was perceived as an alarming sign that a rapprochement between England and France was imminent—they did not wish to aggravate the situation or push Henry further into Francis's arms.

Charles's invasion of the Papal States in May 1527 was certainly not approved of by Henry, who desperately needed Pope Clement VII's support for annulling his marriage to Catherine. Henry could still offer himself as the perfect mediator between Francis and Charles, but his desire for divorce was about to seriously jeopardize the European games of power.

In his reply to Mendoza, his ambassador at Henry's court, Charles gave a subtle yet clear warning: "We are indeed certain that the king of England will act in this case [if he were to serve as a mediator between France and Spain] as a good friend and ally, and zealous promoter of peace, putting aside all partisanship."[6]

This was a scenario that would inevitably include the Howards and Boleyns, who, into the bargain, could scale the heights now that Henry's new feelings for Anne had become public.

*

While the exact dates of the love letters Henry wrote to Anne remain mostly unknown, they were certainly written between 1527 and 1528, when it became apparent to everyone that Henry was pursuing the other Boleyn sister—having ended his alleged tryst with Mary.

The correspondence remaining from his courtship with Anne makes clear his most ardent passion:

"My mistress and friend, I and my heart put ourselves in your hands, begging you to recommend us to your favor and not to let absence lessen your affection to us."

Evidently, Henry wasn't afraid to wear his heart on his sleeve.

"This is from the hand of your servant and friend," he continued, "Henry Rex."[7]

Anne reciprocated his affections, but she must surely have also felt caution. After all, during her years at the French court she had seen Francis pursuing many ladies, and making some his favorites, but others were always waiting in the wings. Of course, Francis's chief mistresses, first, the enigmatic Françoise de Foix, Countess of Châteaubriant, and, from 1526, the blonde-haired, charismatic Anne de Pisseleu-d'Heilly, Duchess of Étampes, did come to wield political influence at court. Yet both their power and reputations remained at Francis's mercy, and he could withdraw affection as quickly as he bestowed it—a thought that was not too appealing to Anne.

Anne had also seen for herself how her lover behaved, and how he treated his other mistresses, potentially including her own sister. Elizabeth Blount, who had been Henry's mistress while Anne was in France between 1518 and 1519, had even given birth to a son, Henry, Duke of Richmond, but she had quickly fallen out of favor. It seemed that Henry's passion never lasted long, and being just another name on his long list of mistresses and lovers was not one of Anne's long-term aspirations. She had seen kings take women to their beds and then forget them, and she had not labored so long at court to be so easily disposed of. Elizabeth Blount had accrued wealth and noble titles for herself and her son but, the truth was, she no longer had the interest or love of the king and she was not a political actor at the Tudor court.

Anne wanted more. It is clear from the tone of Henry's letters that while she entertained his affections, she was not easily conquered, and from this we can deduce that she had made up her mind: if she was going to be anything for Henry, it had to be everything: his lover, his queen, and the mother of his legitimate children.

In total, Henry wrote 18 letters that have survived until today, all of which he signed as Anne Boleyn's "humble servant." She certainly seemed to hold his heart in her hands.

In one of these love letters, Henry revealed his profound, carnal desire for her. He wrote that he was looking forward to being "in my sweetheart's arms, whose pretty dukkys [breasts] I trust shortly to kiss."[8]

This declaration proved that, for the moment, Anne was still refusing to succumb to his advances. Henry, however, continued in his relentless pursuit, trying to find a way finally to be united with his new love interest.

In another letter, Henry made his own goal clear: if Anne would not be his mistress, he would want her as his wife. In response, Anne had sent him a gift (*une étrenne*): a trinket representing "a ship with a woman on board and with a (presumably) pendant diamond."[9] Her own message was also clear: she would consent to marriage and nothing else.

Henry was delighted with this response:

> For a present so valuable that nothing could be more (considering the whole of it) I return you my most hearty thanks, not only on account of the costly diamond, and the ship in which the solitary damsel is tossed about, but chiefly for the fine interpretation and too humble submission which your goodness has made to me. [...] The demonstration of your affection is such, the fine thoughts of your letter to cordially express that they oblige me forever to honor, love, and serve you sincerely. [...] That hereafter my heart shall be dedicated to you alone.[10]

Mendoza, the imperial ambassador, revealed what was now known to all: "It is generally believed that if the king can obtain a divorce, he will end by marrying the daughter of Master Boleyn."[11]

Mendoza, seeing the storm ahead, warned: "Henry is so blinded by passion."

Indeed, Henry was utterly obsessed with Anne. It was a tumultuous passion. Despite her promise in the form of a gift, Henry was never satisfied, questioning her feelings at times and doubting her affection for him. Anne had him enraptured as no other woman ever had before or, arguably, would again. Assessing Anne's own feelings, and the strength of her love for Henry, is a difficult task, given the lack of Anne's own writings. We can deduce much, though, from Henry's letters. At the beginning of their relationship, she seemed almost to play games with his affections—at least from his perspective.

Henry wrote:

> To my mistress, because the time seems to me very long, since I have heard from you, or concerning your health, the great affection I have for you has obliged me to send this bearer to be better informed both of your health and pleasure, particularly because since my last parting with you, I have been told that you have entirely changed the opinion in which I left you, and that you would neither come to court with your mother, nor any other way; which report if true, I cannot enough wonder at, being persuaded in my own mind that I have never committed any offense against you; and it seems a very small return for the great love I bear to you, to be kept at a distance from the person and presence of the woman in the world that I value the most.[12]

Anne did reply to Henry, but the letters are believed to be lost. It would be fair to assume, however, that in these letters, she did not surrender herself too easily, but delicately played hard to get, without discouraging his interest. She would need to carefully consider her position, but she must surely have also known that her unique access to both the English king and the French court could make her a political asset, particularly having observed the games of rival kingdoms from her position as lady-in-waiting. Although it is hard fully to determine where her loyalty ultimately lay—with the French or with Henry—what is certain is that Anne was her own woman, moving carefully toward her own destiny. Henry's infatuation offered her the opportunity to carve out a role for herself at the heart of European politics. The French, however, did not yet know that, one day, Anne could provide them with access to the heart of the English court.

*

In November 1527, Francis I sent a more permanent ambassador, instead of the usual special envoys, to Henry's court. This new arrival was someone who was well acquainted with his goals and family: Jean du Bellay.

Born around 1492 at Souday in Glatigny, Jean was the second son of Louis du Bellay, Sieur de Langley, and Marguerite de la Tour-Landry. Along with his brothers, Guillaume, René and Martin, he had received a thorough humanist education and was well connected to several courtiers by the time Francis I ascended the throne. After Francis's release from prison, the du Bellay brothers saw their loyalty to the French royal family rewarded. Guillaume was sent to Italy as an ambassador. René was given the position of councillor at the Parlement de Paris, and Jean was given the abbey of Breteuil and made bishop of Bayonne.

These titles mattered—especially as Jean was then dispatched to the English court as a representative of the French crown. He had previously been sent as a special envoy in September of the same year, but this time it was an attempt to tighten the diplomatic relations between the two crowns. As a close adviser to Anne de Montmorency, who had been made constable of France after Bourbon's treachery, du Bellay also benefited from the patronage of another key political figure in France: Marguerite, Queen of Navarre, sister of the king, and indirect mentor of Anne herself.

Du Bellay was not exactly an imposing figure, though he could be recognized by his striking physical features: closed, narrowed eyes, a bushy beard, and the long Greek nose that all du Bellay men seemed to have inherited from their ancestors. He also had what could be considered as a long beard for the time and, as bishop of Bayonne, he was usually seen in his religious attire.

Du Bellay's first few months at the English court were tense. He was mostly received by Cardinal Wolsey; Henry, who evidently did not regard him as entirely trustworthy, tended to ignore du Bellay's requests for a direct audience.

Du Bellay was certainly himself cautious when sending intelligence back to France, as he revealed to Montmorency himself: "I have not written to the king, nor to Madame [Louise], to ensure that they would not be suspicious of my letters being too big."[13]

His packages were always checked by the English before they were sent, making his role difficult. In other words, he was not among friends at the Henrician court, and he knew it.

Around January 1528, the French ambassador and the special envoy, Jean de Brosse—who had been dispatched a month after du Bellay to assist him—were both finally received by Henry VIII. The French hoped this was a sign of conciliation.

Henry VIII met the Frenchmen at his court after mass. Du Bellay later revealed that he and de Brosse were invited to the king's private chamber where they were entertained by courtiers—notably Sir Thomas Boleyn, Viscount of Rochford. They were then introduced to "the ladies" of the queen, including Anne herself, who was still in the service of Catherine.[14] There is no record of what the relationship between the two women was like at this time, but one can imagine that it was fraught with tension and rivalry. After all, they were vying for the same man's attention. However, in 1527, Catherine and Anne were offered two Books of Hours from France that were highly similar, indicating that perhaps they spent time reading them in each other's presence.[15]

Perhaps, despite the challenges, they may have shared some peaceable moments.

In the months to come, du Bellay would become a close acquaintance of, perhaps even a friend to, the Boleyns.

All throughout this time, discussions regarding the king's "great matter"—his divorce—continued. Eventually, Wolsey decided to take the matter into his own hands, and it was du Bellay's job to try to discover what the king's, and Wolsey's, intentions really were. In late 1527 and early 1528, there were rumors that Uberto Gambara, who had been named nuncio (an important ecclesiastical diplomat) at the French court, had agreed secretly to carry a letter from Wolsey to the Pope. The cardinal's demand was simple enough: Wolsey asked to be granted special powers that would enable him to annul the marriage between his master, Henry, and his wife, Catherine.

In February 1528, du Bellay reported that Gambara's departure was imminent. He also revealed that his brother, Guillaume, who was in Rome, had informed him that yet more discussions were taking place regarding Henry's divorce. Every diplomat at court now dwelled on the same questions.

Du Bellay wrote: "Even if the marriage was declared null, their daughter [Mary], who was born of a father and mother in good faith, still needs to be esteemed as legitimate and not bastard."[16] This was an important point for the French, who were still trying to obtain a dynastic match between the two royal houses.

The political situation deteriorated rapidly. While Pope Clement VII was technically no longer a prisoner of Charles V, who had freed him later on in 1527, he was still restricted in his actions. Furthermore, the fight for dominance in Italy continued to rage between France and Spain and, while Charles had officially recognized Henry VIII as a mediator between the French king and himself, the reality was more complex, not least with Francis launching new military offensives in both the Low Countries and northern Italy. His sons were still hostages in Spain, but his pursuit of glory always prevailed over sentiment. Besides, he had a third son, named Charles, who was safe in France. His legacy seemed protected.

In mid-February 1528, as the war continued, du Bellay informed Henry that several French and English ambassadors had been arrested on Charles of Spain's orders. It was a reminder that diplomats weren't immune from arrest.

Henry VIII did not react well to the news. "This is an outrage!" he exclaimed in front of du Bellay.[17]

The truth was, Charles was determined to find any intelligence regarding Henry's "great matter." The reputation and dignity of his aunt, Catherine, were at stake. He would not let her suffer the humiliation of a divorce.

Once more, the reconciliation of France and England was needed and, in March 1528, Francis dispatched another special envoy to assist Jean du Bellay in his endeavors: Charles de Solier, Count of Morette.

An experienced soldier and diplomat, Morette was a long-serving gentleman in the chamber of the French king. He was around 12 years older than du Bellay and had been sent to England once before, in October 1526. He was tall of stature and had an imposing, authoritative presence. His arrival at court put more pressure on the English and ensured that they would eventually stand against the Spaniards, just as they had before. During this period, Margaret of Austria acted as another agent of peace; she feared that any military action from the French in the Low Countries would further jeopardize trade and stability in the region.

Meanwhile, du Bellay and Morette discussed with Henry and Wolsey a potential truce between Margaret of Austria—who had been dragged into war by her nephew, Charles—and Francis. The French ambassadors were sharing intelligence with the English, striving to convince Henry to support France's actions.

In an audience at Richmond Palace, Henry professed his genuine intentions toward Francis: "My good brother, Francis, and I are made of the same thing," he said before swearing that he bore a "great love" for his French counterpart.[18]

Yet negotiations were soon suspended. Not only were Francis's sons still prisoners of Charles, but Henry's demands regarding annual payments and the surrender of French cities also continued to complicate the already complex and thorny situation. All the while, the other burning question, that of the divorce, continued to linger.

By now, Jean du Bellay was also in a tricky position; the payment for his services kept being delayed, and his personal struggles were affecting his ability to negotiate. He wrote with despair to Montmorency: "My god, I am indebted to the tune of two thousand five hundred crowns. You would be amazed at the expenses I am forced to spend and how expensive the goods are here."[19]

Francis and his constable, Anne de Montmorency, would have to reassess their budget if they wanted to keep a resident ambassador at the English court.

In the months to come, Jean du Bellay's role would become more significant; his personal connection to Marguerite of Navarre would make him the perfect ally for the Boleyns, particularly Anne. And in the midst of these crises, only one thing seemed certain: Henry continued to adore her.

*

The French forces in Naples—led by Odet de Foix, Vicomte de Lautrec—were making progress, further forcing the emperor to reassess his situation. The French armies pressing in Italy and the Spanish Netherlands remained problematic.

In June 1528, a truce was agreed for eight months between the Spanish Netherlands and France. This was a relief for everyone—especially Henry, who could now focus his efforts on getting a divorce, as well as perhaps acquiring more support from the French.

By this time, Henry's love seemed to have been more or less secured, and what remains of Anne's confident correspondence suggested that, as the relationship had blossomed, her political sense had also grown. A letter to Wolsey demonstrated her careful but powerful way with words:

"I desire you pardon me that I am so bold to trouble you with my simple and rude writing," she shrewdly claimed, "proceeding from one who is much desirous to know that your Grace does well." She even promised that all she was doing was "in loving you, next unto the King's grace, above all creatures living."

Her letter was not, however, just an expression of pure allegiance or devotion to the second most powerful person in the realm. It was a political tactic to show Wolsey that she was in control, for now, of the king's will.

"I long to hear from you news of the Legate, and hope they will be very good."

Anne was of course aware of the king's efforts to secure an annulment.

The king signed Anne's letter, another demonstration of their intimacy, and simply wrote: "The not hearing of the Legate's arrival in France causeth us somewhat to muse; but we trust by your diligence shortly to be eased of that trouble."[20]

For Wolsey, the pressure to succeed—to give Henry what he most desired—had increased considerably. This Boleyn girl was becoming more and more of a thorn in his side.

★

The Tudor king's great matter was now pushed to the forefront of diplomatic discussions.

On a warm afternoon in June 1528, du Bellay and Wolsey were walking in the gardens of Hampton Court, miles away from the city of London.

"It is an outrage that the Pope has still not agreed to grant the king his wishes," Wolsey claimed.

Du Bellay pondered his reply. "In my humble opinion," he said eventually, "sending Cardinal Campeggio to follow through on that matter was the right thing to do. There is so much that the emperor [Charles] can do."[21]

All was clear. The French also had a stake in this resolution, as it would damage Anglo-Spanish relations and would therefore undoubtedly reinforce trust between France and England.

Yet these discussions were in their early days, and du Bellay did not want to give too much information to Wolsey. Instead, he preferred to appear as some sort of confidant, listening to Wolsey's frustrations regarding Henry's patience, which was not known to be the king's strength.

"This matter needs to be resolved soon, as this realm would be in great danger if the king was to die without this marriage to be declared null first."[22]

While the two spoke informally in the gardens, discussing these potential dangers, another very real threat was spreading in the city of London: a case of the potentially lethal sweating sickness had been detected.

In his report to Montmorency, du Bellay conveyed his alarm:

> My lord, the sweat is a disease that seems to have appeared in the last four days and is the deadliest disease known to us yet. At first, people suffer from a headache and heartache, suddenly they start sweating. There is no need for a doctor as it spreads so fast that the fever is untameable. [...] The last time such a disease occurred, people say it was twelve years ago and it killed ten thousands of people in ten days.

He also revealed that the illness was now close to one of the most important people in England.

One of the ladies of Mademoiselle Boleyn has been affected with the sweat. The king left in haste toward the countryside, twelve miles away or so from the city, and the lady [Boleyn] was dispatched to Kent, with her father, the viscount. Their love for each other, however, seems unaffected.[23]

If anything, in fact, their correspondence suggests that their love for each other seemed to grow during this time, even more so when reports reached the king that that Anne herself was now suffering from the sweat.

A distraught Henry wrote directly to Anne:

There came to me in the night the most afflicting news possible. I have to grieve for three causes: first, to hear of my mistress's sickness, whose health I desire as my own, and would willingly bear the half of yours to cure you. Secondly, because I fear to suffer yet longer that absence which has already given me so much pain—God deliver me from such an importunate rebel! Thirdly, because the physician I trust most is at present absent when he could do me the greatest pleasure. However, in his absence, I send you the second, praying God he may soon make you well and I shall love him the better. I beseech you to be governed by his advice, and then I hope to see you again soon.[24]

Fortunately, Anne and her father, Thomas—who also contracted the disease—both "escaped it" and would recover fully.[25] In many ways, though, this frightening episode strengthened the king's feelings for Anne, who in her absence only played more on Henry's mind.

By the end of July 1528, du Bellay was reporting that Anne had returned and "had been seen at court," but of course the matter of the divorce was still unresolved. He confessed that Wolsey "was unsure of what to do next."[26] Wolsey had confided in du Bellay, predicting that "if the marriage [between Henry and Anne] ever happened, this would cause great despair" as the emperor would never let such an insult to his aunt go unpunished.[27] The drama now threatened to come between Henry and his closest adviser.

Meanwhile, Cardinal Lorenzo Campeggio, who had been sent earlier in the year to convince the Pope to grant Henry an annulment, came back to England in October 1528 with clear instructions.

First, he had to try to dissuade Henry from his purpose. This, of course, was quite impossible; Henry insisted that the best available interpretation of scripture and canon law demonstrated beyond reasonable doubt that he'd been living in sin because he had married his brother's wife. There was no changing his mind on this: he was a man used to getting his way. Another of Campeggio's lines of attack was to convince Catherine herself to retire to a convent. This was not received well either. Catherine was not the type of woman who would go from queen to nun. Campeggio's final tactic was to delay things as much as possible—buying time and hoping that Henry's infatuation with Anne would burn itself out.

It did not.

Anne knew how to play the game of courtly love. She teased the king by being briefly present at court and then removing herself for weeks to Hever Castle with her family. Was it a ploy to make herself seem more appealing? It is hard to know for sure. But if so, it seems to have had the desired effect.

Henry's best hope now was for Rome to issue a decretal—a papal decree on a specific canon law, which would give power to another member of the clergy, instead of the Pope, to annul the marriage. But whether this would be granted was far from certain.

By December 1528, Anne had become the center of attention at court, with du Bellay reporting: "Madame de Boulan has joined the king at Richmond and is well received, in a great and luxurious house that King Henry himself ensured was close enough to his own royal apartments. They both spend time at court where everything is made to be magnificent, even more so than when it was made for the queen herself."[28]

Their relationship was truly out in the open, and as Anne became more established in her role as Henry's new love, so, too, did her own political sensibilities grow. She was becoming a woman to be reckoned with.

6

Ainsi Sera, Groigne Qui Groigne

The long and the short of it was that a courtier and ambassador's daughter was now the center of political attention.

She was not the kind of woman expected to be so close to the crown, and as her status grew, so, too, did her list of enemies. Her influence on the king, they feared, had become too powerful.

In February 1529, Mendoza stated how alarmed he was by this influence: "The lady who is the cause of this king's misconduct, perceiving that her marriage, which she considered as certain, is being put off, begins to suspect that the Cardinal of England is preventing it as much as he can, from fear of losing his power the moment she becomes queen," he disclosed to Charles, Holy Roman Emperor. "This suspicion has been the cause of her forming an alliance with her father, and with the two Dukes of Norfolk and Suffolk, to try and see whether they can conjointly ruin the cardinal."[1] While the Boleyn clan was still influential, they were now led by Anne herself.

A few days earlier, Jean du Bellay had also noticed the growing tension between Anne and Cardinal Wolsey. Sir Thomas Cheney, an experienced diplomat and politician at Henry's court, initially became a fervent supporter of Anne (a support he would, however, later withdraw). Wolsey tried to banish Cheney from court in early 1528, but "the lady [Anne] rehabilitated him"—showing that she was now in charge of whom should or should not be at court. Du Bellay recalled how "the duke of Norfolk and his partisans [and therefore Anne's] have started showing off their power at court. However, they should be wiser as their opponents outsmart them."[2]

Wolsey and Anne were now locked in psychological and political arm wrestling. Who would be the victor? Only time would tell.

What was certain was that Henry could not have two close advisers, and Anne, in the French fashion, was determined to be his one and only.

*

The pressure to have the king's marriage to Catherine of Aragon dissolved continued to intensify by the day. Henry was determined to marry Anne as soon as he possibly could, especially as his pursuit of a male heir depended on it. This problem haunted him, and he had lost all patience.

Du Bellay was adamant that "the cardinal of York [Wolsey] is in the greatest pain he ever was. The dukes of Suffolk and Norfolk, and others, are convincing the king that he has not done as much as he could have done to promote the marriage [with Anne]."

The French—Francis I and his mother, Louise—were more than willing to have this new marriage arranged. The divorce from Catherine of Aragon meant the end of a strong and stable Anglo-Habsburg alliance. But, even better, having a lady who had been raised and educated in France as the new queen consort of England implicitly meant more French influence at the English court. Suddenly, Anne's close connection to the French was starting to bear fruit. Could they be the answer to her and Henry's prayers?

The Pope, meanwhile, was still refusing "to declare the enlarged brief null and void," though du Bellay asserted that everyone "expected that the matter once commenced will only last two months." "But," du Bellay wrote to Anne of Montmorency, primary adviser to Francis I, "I promise you, it will last more than four."³

As it turned out, it lasted far longer than four months. It would last for years.

Francis sent another special envoy to England to assist du Bellay in promoting the Anglo-French alliance: Jean de la Sauche. He also dispatched other legates and ambassadors to Rome, including Gabriel de Gramont, Bishop of Tarbes, who had been in England before—he had assisted Henry's own diplomats in putting more pressure on the Pope to grant the English king his annulment and dispensation to remarry.

When it came to choosing a queen and a dynastic alliance, the French clearly indicated that they were on Anne Boleyn's side. In due course, the new English royal couple would surely seek more reassurance and protection—especially Anne, given her vulnerabilities and her enemies. For now, though, other matters preoccupied the French, who had to remain moderate in their show of support.

After all, Francis's sons were still imprisoned in Spain, and fears of another conflict were never far away from people's minds.

*

By June 1529, the situation had become yet more complex. The Duke of Suffolk, Charles Brandon—Henry's brother-in-law, who was residing in Paris as a special envoy—reported that "the Turk [Suleiman the Magnificent, Ottoman Sultan] will invade Hungary with 200,000 horsemen."⁴ The pressure on Charles to make peace with Francis I and Henry VIII was now quite intense. The future of the whole Christendom could depend upon it.

For Henry, this was in one respect some good news. The threat of the Ottomans at the borders of the Christendom meant that his divorce and remarriage might seem to be less of a worry for others than the peril of Ottoman hordes overrunning Christian

Europe. In the context of European overthrow, surely a divorce would seem like a minor affair.

He did not wait; once again, things were set in motion.

The facts of the matter remained the same: one of the cardinals, either Wolsey or Campeggio, would have to declare Henry's current marriage to Catherine of Aragon null and void before he could marry Anne Boleyn. Du Bellay continued to monitor matters and had his eyes and ears wide open. On June 15, he reported to Anne de Montmorency and Francis that:

> the king, coming by water, landed, in passing at my lord of Rocheford's, with a small company of ladies and gentlemen, where he waited for the tide and then went to Greenwich. The queen had already passed by land, and had seen Campeggio. I have no doubt that for some time the king has become closer to Anne Boleyn, therefore do not be surprised if they want to hasten the wedding.[5]

Campeggio was unwell, and when Catherine visited him, "being very anxious and perplexed about her affairs," she showed great concern. "My advocates, who ought to have come from Flanders, have not come because it seems that the Emperor has given them to understand that he did not wish them to do so as the place is not safe. I have no one to plead for me that I trust. I beg you for your aid and counsel," she said, distraught.

Catherine was left with no other option than to beg, now without any true allies within her husband's court, all of whom knew now that divorce was a likely outcome.

"Keep a good heart and rely upon the king's justice and upon the conscience and learning of those prelates who have been assigned to you for counselors. I assure that nothing inconsistent with justice and reason would be done by us Legates," Campeggio promised. "What is the state of the case? How can any proceedings be taken during the trial of the cause at Rome before the Pope? Do you know anything about the matter?"

Catherine was lost in the face of all these questions. She only had her own. How could this love affair have gone so far? How could she risk losing everything she had built in her adoptive country over the past few decades? How could she, daughter of Ferdinand of Aragon and Isabella of Castile, be so badly treated?

"The cause has not been brought into court yet and the Pope, having delegated two Legates for this process, will not revoke it without great forethought and consideration. My mistress, you need to pray God to enlighten yourself, to take some good course in this great difficulty," said Campeggio, who also felt that his hands were tied.

"I regard this fact as the great solace of my mind and as the firm foundation of my righteousness, that from the embraces of my first husband I entered this marriage [with Henry] as a virgin and immaculate woman. I solemnly swear of it," Catherine stated.[6]

Campeggio never doubted her sincerity; there just wasn't much more he could do for her and her cause. As she left, even she knew that the divorce proceedings must surely be imminent.

Never before had she faced such humiliation.

Yet, as a true, strong, Spanish royal woman, she retained her pride, and she would certainly not go down without a fight. So, Catherine wrote to the Pope, pleading her case. She had allies and supporters beyond the court, she said, and she would seek their assistance. Henry might be king, but she was his only queen and she would not let Anne Boleyn take her crown so easily.

Mendoza, who was about to leave England due to an illness, tried once more to reason with the king: "The only reason the Emperor is intervening between your majesty and your wife is not to set you at discord but to labor that you might live in the same concord and harmony in which you have always lived. In acting thus, he belies he is acting in accordance with his conscience and honor, and with the authority of his person and that of the queen, to whom he was so greatly bound." Mendoza paused. "Anything he has done for the said defense has been done with so much moderation as to be evidently done out of love for your majesty."

Henry, absolutely furious, spat, "The more he defends the queen, the more he injures her cause!"

Henry loathed Charles V's mediation in his marriage difficulties.

Standing his ground, the imperial ambassador retorted: "Even if the queen insisted, the Emperor would not abandon her defense as she does not deserve any greater ill-treatment."[7]

Henry, who by now had had enough, adjourned the conversation. The legal proceedings, he repeated, would take place. Charles could grumble all he wanted; Catherine's fate was nigh.

*

The first sitting of the legatine court took place on June 18 at Blackfriars in London. One of the judges explained the rules that would govern proceedings for the two rival parties: "They must receive the original letters of citation. If the King and Queen have not appeared they must be publicly summoned. The proctors of the King and Queen must exhibit their proxies [...] If one party does not appear, the judges must perform the first three articles."[8]

The second court sitting, in which the case got underway in earnest, took place three days later and, according to du Bellay, who attended the session, it was open to some of the public. He reported what he had seen and heard to Francis I, who was to follow the proceedings with intense interest. Both king and queen were present.

With dignity and courage, Catherine of Aragon had declared that she refused the authority of the judges.

Henry cut her off: "I desire you [the judges] to determine the validity or nullity of my marriage about which I have from the beginning felt a perpetual scruple."

"After so long a silence," Catherine snidely replied.

"It is because of the great love I had and have for you," Henry said, "for which I'm sorry."

Henry continued his plea that her request to have this case tried in Rome was unnecessary, "considering the Emperor's power there, and this country is perfectly secure for her as she has had the choice of prelates and lawyers."

At these words, Catherine fell to her knees, now begging her husband, "Please consider my honor, our daughter's, and yours. You should not be displeased with me for defending it and you should consider the reputation of my nation and my relatives who will be seriously offended. Rome has concluded that this matter is over."[9]

She was sincere in her troubles, and her suffering was clear to all.

The proceedings were adjourned and Henry departed without another word to anyone, neither his wife, nor any other in the room.

He would not change his mind.

By now she knew it, and she was crushed with despair.

Outside, some of the women who had attended the proceedings showed their loyal support to the queen. "Hold on, good Catherine, and do not worry," said one as she passed by.[10] Despite the still-significant public support for the king's wife, however, the proceedings were to go on.

The next day, Campeggio—now under pressure from Henry and Wolsey—declared that he could not accept the queen's protest. Yet he was still not ready to betray his own conscience and, before a verdict could be found, he adjourned and delayed the proceedings on the pretext of awaiting important information from Rome.

Anne was furious but not surprised; she had distrusted Campeggio and his motivations for some time, and she felt sure that his procrastination was the main reason for these constant delays. Her only hope, she felt, lay in the hands of Stephen

Gardiner, Wolsey's former secretary, who had been sent to Rome in January 1529 and who was now on his way back to England.

During Gardiner's time in Rome, Anne had written directly to him and had thanked him for his letter, "for that is but a rejoicing hope which puts me into more pain," as she was still waiting for the matter to be resolved. She also prayed for a "better ending."[11] Ideally, it would be one with the Pope's blessing.

For his loyalty to the king and to his cause, Gardiner was made chief secretary to Henry. The Pope, in the meantime, revoked all powers given to the commissioners in England and asked for the case to be tried in Rome. This order probably came from Charles himself.

Henry, however, was not the type of person you could push around. Neither, it seemed, was Anne. Both still hoped for both a legal and papal resolution. But there was a worry that they had already gone too far, exposing themselves to the full gamut of rumor and gossip, and of course the hostility from those who thought that Catherine was being grievously wronged.

That damage, of course, could not be undone. And so there was no going back.

Du Bellay watched the situation develop with great interest. The longer and more complex Henry's affair became, the safer Francis's interests in Italy were, and the more the pendulum of power swung toward the French. Henry realized this. The English king had no other choice, therefore, but to now agree to Francis's terms and assist him in his quest to release his sons from Spain, in order to secure his support in the question of the divorce and new marriage.

Predictably, if cynically, the French ambassador could see how the stuttering process could turn to the King of France's benefit. The ambassador wrote to Montmorency:

> Cardinal Wolsey begs his majesty, the king [Francis] to support the English king's affair and to write to Campeggio himself,

asking him to expedite the affair. If he [Francis] did, Wolsey would see it as a personal favor to him and show eternal gratitude. To tell the truth, I do not see how this will help their cause, but if it was to end it would be to our advantage as beyond the great friendship that unites our kings, it will be a means to bring this king [Henry] on his knees to you in the future.[12]

Cardinal Wolsey, formerly the second most powerful man in England, now felt absolutely powerless. He knew that this annulment threatened to extinguish him politically. Anne Boleyn would eclipse him at court and his enemies on the council would oust him. He also knew that if he failed to satisfy the king's wish, that could very well be the end of him. It was a thankless task. The lesser, it seemed, of the two evils, he was left with no option but to try to secure the king's wishes.

Henry's disappointment in Wolsey, however, was clear, and Anne—and her supporters, including her father, her uncle, the Duke of Norfolk, the Duke of Suffolk and Gardiner—saw the cardinal as an enemy to their cause. Ultimately, Wolsey had failed in delivering an annulment.

Years had already passed, and yet more would pass, it seemed, before a desirable outcome could be achieved. This was utterly unacceptable to them all.

★

Henry now spent most of his time with Anne and her supporters, hunting and feasting as well as discussing these ongoing political matters. Wolsey, however, was no longer invited to any of these events. Anne had supplanted him, although, as a mistress, she could perhaps never truly wield as much power as he could. Her strength was, of course, her proximity to the king. But their relationship was not just a physical one. Henry clearly enjoyed Anne's company in other ways, and he was known for soliciting her opinions and listening to her responses, which might have surprised those who knew Henry for his impatience. Of course, it helped that on many issues their opinions were aligned.

Beyond the domestic turmoil that England was facing, on the continent Francis and Charles were about to make an indirect peace: Francis through his mother, Louise of Savoy, and Charles through his aunt, Margaret of Austria. Both women had agreed to meet in Cambray in the summer of 1529 to discuss peace between the two Christian kings and the possibility of, together, confronting the Ottomans.

The peace talks began on July 5 and lasted a month. They were successful and, on August 3, 1529, the Treaty of Cambray—known as "the Treaty of the Ladies" or the "Ladies' Peace"—was signed. They had finally found common ground to put an end to the war in the Italian territories. Louise and Francis consented to surrender Arras, Lille and Tournai, but Burgundy would remain French on account of 2 million *écus* being given to Charles. Upon receipt of the payment, the two French princes would be released from Spain and allowed to return to France. The marriage agreement between Francis I and Charles V's sister, Eleanor, would also be ratified. It is striking that Louise and Margaret's more intimate negotiations had succeeded where others had failed, and back in England Anne Boleyn must have heard of such developments with interest.

Despite the substantial dent in the French king's finances that this treaty caused, it could be seen as a success for Francis—though the military advantage had still rested for the most part with Charles. Diplomatically, however, Francis was now in the stronger position, as Henry's affair and desire for a divorce had undermined his relations with Charles.

Now, overall, the balance of power in Europe seemed more equal.

With peace having been made between France and Spain, Henry was more determined than ever to seek a French alliance again, reminding Francis of how he had supported him during his trouble with Charles.

With the divorce still not proclaimed, however, Henry's patience, already notoriously limited, was beginning to wear very thin.

In October 1529, Campeggio began his journey back to Rome. On his way to Dover, he was stopped by English officers working on Henry's orders. His luggage was searched, and his passport and permit of safe conduct were revoked. He complained to the king, who showed to what extent his patience was diminishing when he said: "A rumor has prevailed that you and the cardinal of York [Wolsey] had been guilty of collusion in our cause; and that you would not leave England until this calumny has been cleared up, and satisfaction for so atrocious claim be wrong."[13]

As for Wolsey, his time had finally come. He had failed in his duty to the king and all his powers, privileges, lands, goods and offices were revoked.

He was distraught and pleaded directly to Henry himself: "Though I daily cry to you for mercy, I beseech that you will not think it proceeds from any mistrust I have in your goodness, nor that I would molest you by my importunate suit. The same comes of my ardent desire, that, next unto God, I covet nothing so much in this world as your favor and forgiveness."[14]

The reality, though, was that he failed to secure the king's wishes.

★

Wolsey's downfall meant the further rise of the Boleyns and their associates. George Boleyn, Anne's brother, and the Bishop of London, John Stokesley, were sent to the French court as ambassadors, strengthening the family's much-wanted Boleyn–French alliance.

Sir Thomas Boleyn approached Jean du Bellay and, in a ciphered letter to Montmorency, the French ambassador explained that the Boleyns had become prominent figures at court through Anne, and were responsible for taking down Wolsey. He also revealed that Thomas Boleyn expected "his little prince," George, to be well received once in France, taking up Anne's former mantle as the family's eyes and ears.[15]

While it is hard to differentiate Anne's own political agenda from her family's, their goals of securing the family's increased influence seemed to have been aligned, and this would surely have been a consideration of Anne's when lobbying for her marriage.

However, du Bellay now seemed to have been discarded by Henry. Eustace Chapuys, the imperial ambassador who replaced Mendoza, noted that the French ambassador "had only been received at court once."[16] Indeed, in late October 1529, Wolsey and du Bellay met privately a few times, during which the deposed cardinal begged the ambassador to plead on his behalf to Francis and his mother, Louise, for their support.

Du Bellay reported to the French court the extent of the cardinal's downfall: "Wolsey had just been put out of his house, and all his goods taken into the king's hands. [...] The duke of Norfolk is made chief of the Council, Suffolk acting in his absence, and, at the head of all, Mademoiselle Anne. We don't know yet who will be in charge of the seal." The seal had been in the possession of Wolsey as long as anyone could remember. Later, it would be given to another of Henry VIII's close councillors: Thomas More.

Wolsey now feared for his life. Du Bellay was sympathetic to his impossible position, sharing with the French royals that the cardinal "begs the king [Francis] for the mercy of God, thus to protect him from the fury of his enemies, who would bring his old age to the most shameful and miserable end." Du Bellay may have felt sorry for him, but he maneuvered carefully in order not to take sides: "As for me, I have no business to meddle further, or to give my advice."[17]

The articles against Wolsey, sealing his fall, were drafted and presented to him on December 1, 1529. In them, he was accused of over 40 breaches of English law and of contravening his duty to the king himself, including

> for having in divers letters and instructions to foreign parts used the expression "King and I," and "I would ye should do thus," and "the King and I give unto you our hearty thanks," using himself more like a fellow to your Highness than a subject. For having caused his servants to be sworn only to himself, when it has been the custom for noblemen to swear their households first to be true to the King.[18]

The enemies at Wolsey's throat—including Thomas More, the Duke of Norfolk, the Duke of Suffolk and of course, Thomas Boleyn himself—all signed these articles. With that, the game was over.

The Venetian ambassador reported that Wolsey "was taken bare-footed in his shirt into the king's presence [...] at the close of the proceedings, he was condemned to death, the people exclaiming 'Stone him'; but the King rose, saying that for the honor of the Cardinalship; he did not choose him to be put to death, and has confined him in a small village belonging to him [Wolsey]."[19]

The cardinal had no friends left, even where they might have been expected. No letters from Francis defending the cardinal can be found; given the political situation in Europe, with the Turks at the door of Christendom, as well as other complications between the French king and the Holy Roman Emperor, it is unlikely that the French king tried to protect him, particularly given the fact that Anne Boleyn had been a familiar and trusted face at his own court once.

And, after all, there are no real friends in politics.

Wolsey was banished from court, though permitted to live in

his lands in the north. Stripped of his power and influence, he would never forget the humiliations he had suffered.

In December 1529, Eustace Chapuys lamented what he was witnessing: "Certain relatives of the Lady [Anne] were lately created earls, for it was considered essential that before her being raised to the rank of Queen her own family should be somewhat exalted." He reported to Charles that Anne's father was given "two earldoms, one in Ireland, and the other in this kingdom."

If Chapuys was shocked by this, what happened next was unfathomable to him. A feast was organized to celebrate the new earldoms and, therefore, essentially to celebrate the ascent of Anne herself. All of the most important ambassadors, courtiers, and noblemen and women were invited. Ladies such as Mary, Duchess of Suffolk and dowager queen of France, were all led in to the feast by Anne, who had never looked more regal.

Chapuys gasped in shock when Anne was "being made to sit by the King's side, occupying the very place allotted to a crowned queen, which by the by is a thing that was never before done."[20]

Anne had never been closer to the crown, and seated beside Henry, her position looked unassailable.

*

Anne and Henry had been showcasing their affections at court for years now, yet marriage still eluded them.

Rumors were spreading that if the king could not get his union to Catherine annulled—or receive a divorce and a dispensation for a new marriage from Rome—that "he will take the license for himself, on the ground that many [legal authorities] are of the opinion he may do so, and that he will do worse to remain in sin, rather than ascertan whether his marriage with the Queen is legitimate."[21] Such a course of action might previously have been considered unthinkable, but desperate times were cause for desperate measures. Henry's relationship with Rome had stretched to a breaking point.

When asked by Rome to contribute financially to the war against the Ottomans, Henry answered that he "will send money, but first requires the sentence of divorce to be passed."[22] He was using all the political tools at his disposal to obtain what he desired the most.

The power struggle between Charles of Spain and Henry continued as the question of the annulment rumbled on. Therefore the English king was once again left with no choice but to seek Francis I's staunch support—and this time it would come at a high price.

Frankly, Francis was delighted with the rift between Charles and Henry; he could not have hoped for a better situation while he recovered from his own years of hardship and the Pavia humiliation. This shift in power certainly did not escape Charles, who could see how this was likely to unfold when he wrote to his brother, Ferdinand:

> I cannot tell you yet how this affair will end, but of this I am quite certain, namely, that the King will commit this folly and with or without the Pope's consent marry Lady Anne, which I need not point out to you will be a great evil and a sufficient cause for new wars. I really believe that the French king will help and do his utmost to set us both at war on that score.[23]

Henry and Anne's main goal now was to obtain enough solidly supportive opinions from scholars and universities all around Europe—people who would agree that Henry's first marriage could not continue. This, they thought, would help them circumvent Rome in their pursuit of divorce.

In this new world, Francis I's influence on the couple was soon to reach new heights.

Jean du Bellay and his brother Guillaume were welcomed warmly at the English court. Chapuys noticed their closeness to Anne, in particular, and how this reflected her own confidence in her new power. "There was much dancing, and the Lady [Anne] entertained them splendidly here; nothing could have given the king greater satisfaction than to see the French ambassadors thus take leave of the Lady and pay their respects to her."[24]

The French elite already believed that Anne was the future of England.

Later, in mid-1530, the du Bellay brothers were recalled from England. Jean Joachim de Passaut, Sieur de Vaux, replaced them, gladly reporting to the French king, "Your brother, the king of England, is at your mercy and seeks your assistance in his great matter."[25]

Unfortunately for Henry, French universities and their theologians still sided with Catherine of Aragon. The grounds for an annulment were, in their eyes, too weak.

Henry pressured Francis to use his influence to overturn their judgments—especially when it came to the Faculty of Theology at the University of Paris—as he truly believed "to have the most just cause, for the satisfaction of his conscience he will peradventure take expedients which will seem more appropriate to you [Francis] and your good counsel."[26]

Francis's new role in English affairs changed the balance of power between the two kings. It would have been inconceivable for Henry to pursue such an alliance with Francis if it had not been for his love—or infatuation—for Anne. In order to marry her and obtain his long-awaited male heir, he was ready to damage his own reputation on the European political scene.

While Francis knew he would be able to extract his own demands in exchange for such favors, he also knew how difficult it would be to convince the theologians of such radical departures from religious convention. The English needed more than just the support of French theologians, however: they also needed the French to side with them in Rome itself. Soon, two clear factions appeared in Rome: the imperials and the French, each supporting their own interests when it came to the Italian territories but also now divided according to their view on English affairs, too. Some Italian cardinals sided with the French, and therefore with Henry's demands, but the overall thrust of papal policy here remained in the hands of Charles. However, this clear alliance between the English and French kings was not something Charles took lightly.

Anne never stopped hoping for a good resolution, but the anxiety must have been crippling. Although she and her supporters had been given so much, granted status, lands and titles, she was still not queen of England.

*

During the summer of 1530, George Boleyn was struggling to perform his duties as ambassador of France as Francis, who wanted to support Henry, was reluctant to offer formal support at this time. As for Thomas Boleyn, he had been instructed to stop in Paris to continue his son's work before going on his way to Bologna and plead Henry's cause once more to the Cardinals in the city. George was, therefore, replaced by his father, Sir Thomas Boleyn, Earl of Wiltshire, who had just failed in obtaining a resolution in Rome in March of that year—partly because of Charles's political maneuvers.

In June 1530, du Bellay was sent back to England to strengthen the alliance between France and England. The Boleyns, who trusted du Bellay and viewed him as an ally, rejoiced at the idea of having him back at court. It was a sign that Francis was mindful of their rise, and was in favor of it.

While traveling from Bordeaux—where he had been sojourning with Louise of Savoy—to London, du Bellay stopped in Paris for a few days. He noted that the scholars of "the Theology

Faculty of Paris were still in process to discuss the matter of the king of England."[27] Evidently, Francis was still in conversation with his theologians, too, encouraging them to approve a divorce or an annulment. It was an encouraging state of affairs for the English.

Finally, on June 15, 1530, du Bellay reported the good news. At one of the recent sessions of the Faculty of Theology, it had been agreed that the union of Henry and Catherine was unlawful, and they would declare it as such.[28] With this breakthrough, clearly secured through the tenacity of the French king, du Bellay felt more confident in approaching Henry again.

After this victory at Paris, in front of the court of European public opinion, other universities followed suit and soon there was a new wave of support in favor of the divorce. With the tide seemingly flowing in the Boleyns' favor, Thomas Boleyn returned to England in August, confident that the marriage would soon be secured.

So, too, was du Bellay, who stated: "I am of the opinion that Henry should not wait any longer and marry Lady Anne, and with the support of the French king himself, Pope Clement will be brought to ratify the marriage."[29]

To du Bellay, and indeed others, it must have appeared that the French court was on the verge of doing what was supposed to be impossible—that is, breaking an existing dynastic marriage alliance. And given Anne's own history at the French court, one could even argue that she was remaking those dynastic alliances in favor of the French, almost a French princess herself.

On Sunday, June 12, 1530, a summons was issued to the noblemen of the English realm. They were ordered to come to court "to write conjointly to the Pope, explaining the necessity there was for the King to divorce the Queen and make another marriage [...] in conformity with the opinion of the most famous universities and most learned men in Christendom, to declare the marriage between the King and Queen illegal, and authorize the King to take another wife."

Chapuys was outraged. Fortunately for Charles and Catherine, the English council opposed du Bellay's plan and voiced their own concerns on the matter of the marriage. Led by the Duke of Suffolk, who viewed the Boleyns as too ambitious, these dissident voices were about to become highly problematic.

This turn of events made Chapuys hopeful that Henry would change his mind: "If the lady Anne could only be kept away from court for a little while, the queen might still regain her influence over the king, for he does not seem to bear any ill-will toward her."[30]

But Anne had no intention of going anywhere. If anything, she only became more of a presence. Despite the opposition at court, the fact that Henry and Anne had persuaded French universities to declare the marriage to Catherine illegal actually strengthened their position. It also reflected a tendency among some European Christians to play down the authority of the papacy. Inevitably, there was a public association between these tendencies and the rise of a reformed mode of religion, which was by now much-discussed among scholars and therefore threatened the stability of the Holy Roman Empire as well as the position of the papacy at the center of western European Christendom.

Anne was starting to align herself openly with these positions. She was reported by Chapuys to have said that "the Emperor has it not in his power to do you [Henry] any harm, and my family alone will provide for one year 10,000 men for your service at our own expenses. Let's not forget that the Emperor has not suffered any qualms of conscience in marrying his own cousin [Isabella of Portugal], he could not decently ask others to be more scrupulous in this matter." This was a bold position to take.

In another conversation between the couple, which Chapuys also seemed to have overheard, Henry reminded Anne: "You are under great obligation to me as I am offending everyone and making enemies everywhere for your sake."

Anne dramatically retorted, "That matters not, for it is foretold in ancient prophecies that at this time a queen shall be burnt: but even if I were to suffer a thousand deaths, my love for you will not abate, not one bit."[31]

Anne's love, and her ambition, were both clear, and her confidence was unshakable.

*

With growing tension at court between factions with different political interests, Wolsey believed it was the right time for him to capitalize on these differences and plan his revenge on Anne and her father—and, more importantly, to attempt to regain his power and influence.

With the aid of secret agents, he was hoping to get himself reinstated in his former pomp. This treachery, however, was uncovered by the Duke of Norfolk, who had discovered the nature of this correspondence and was adamant that although "the Cardinal might use all the artifices he could conjure up, he would never again either see or speak with the king."[32]

Norfolk—like any astute courtier or political player—knew that access to the ruler was everything in a monarchical court in which the political was personal, and the personal political.

Nevertheless, while aggrieved that his attempts at regaining his former status and power had failed, Wolsey continued to plot. After all, he felt he had nothing left to lose.

In November 1530, the pursuit of a papal dispensation and annulment was still on the cards. Once more, papal legates were sent to England and, once again, the negotiations and discussions dragged on. Meanwhile, Wolsey made a bold move that would cost him even more than his titles, lands and wealth.

The cardinal was accused of contacting the Pope to ask "to

excommunicate the king and lay an interdict on his kingdom, unless he immediately dismissed the Lady Anne from court." Wolsey's aim was to inspire an uprising throughout the country, and "in the midst of confusion seize again the reins of government."

De Vaux, the French ambassador whom Wolsey believed to be an ally, was in fact some sort of double agent, and reported the news, blaming the cardinal for "his malignity and bad conduct."[33] With this evidence, and the gravity of the accusations made against Wolsey, his arrest was imminent. There was nothing he could say or do to save his life.

Norfolk, now at the helm of the government, saw his opportunity to capitalize on this to consolidate his own power. He would show no mercy. Nor would the king.

Wolsey was arrested at Cawood and was sent down to London, where, in the Tower, he would await his fate. During the journey, however, he fell gravely ill and, at Leicester Abbey on November 29, 1530, the former second most powerful man in England breathed his last breath. With Wolsey dead, the path to the crown now seemed clearer for Anne Boleyn, but it was certainly not yet quite within arm's reach.

What was certain, however, was that Anne's pursuit of the crown was making her a target, meaning that, more than ever, she needed to call upon her allies. This meant she needed the support of her friends in France.

But though the circumstances were grave, Anne's attitude was one of fortitude. At Christmas of 1530, she had "the livery coats of her servants embroidered" with a motto she would temporarily adopt. It was a phrase she had learned during her time in Mechelen, at Margaret of Austria's court: *Ainsi sera, groigne qui groigne* (Let them grumble, that is how it is going to be).[34]

She would not be cowed.

7

Every Rose Has Its Thorn

One enemy was down, but there would be more to rise.

These tensions, and the protracted negotiations, brought other problems. Anne's patience was wearing thin, as was Henry's, which surely created friction in their relationship—one in which both parties, the king in particular, were used to achieving their desires with few obstacles. But they had come so far: there was no way back for them now. Anne was in pursuit of her glory, confident that French support could propel her to her destination.

*

In late December 1530, the experienced diplomat Gilles de la Pommeraie arrived in England to assist Jean Joachim de Passaut, Sieur de Vaux. Anne gladly received him, and it was said that King Henry offered him "apartments in his own palace at Bridewell."[1]

The French were now undeniably in the ascendant at the English court.

De la Pommeraie's mission was clear: he was here on behalf of Francis I to discuss how the French king could support the English king's dynastic project. This was music to Anne's ears, who was said to have claimed that her grandfather, Sir William

Boleyn, was in fact a "descendant of a Norman knight." The Duchess of Norfolk—her aunt-in-law, Lady Elizabeth Stafford—mocked her niece for making such a claim.[2]

French lineage or not, Anne was certainly trying to play the role of a kind of French substitute princess—she must have reckoned that this would confer on her an additional layer of protection, if dynastic push came to factional shove. But would the French play the game? No one could be sure, though Anne certainly hoped so.

Meanwhile, the animosity between Catherine of Aragon and Anne Boleyn had inevitably grown worse as they continued to be in close proximity to each other at court. Pitted against each other—fighting for the hand of the same man, and of course, fighting for a crown that was already in Catherine's possession—made an already fraught situation even more challenging for Anne. After all, Catherine was of royal blood, the daughter of two great monarchs. Anne needed equal prestige on her side to compete against her ultimate rival.

Behind her confident exterior, which suggested she could handle all the insults hurled at her, Anne was not made of wood and must surely have felt them, even if she could absorb their anger. She had a fire in her belly and she was certainly not going to let her enemies win.

*

In January 1531, Anne was in Greenwich with Henry. Rumors were circulating feverishly at court that plans were afoot to dissolve Henry's marriage to Catherine at the next parliamentary session. Even more insulting to her enemies, Anne was now displaying overt disdain for Catherine and was said to be "fiercer than a lioness." It was a fitting analogy for someone who intended to marry a Tudor.

"I wish all the Spaniards were at the bottom of the sea!" Anne was believed to have shouted at one of her ladies-in-waiting, who retorted: "You should not for the sake of the Queen's honor express such sentiments."

"I do not care for the queen or any of her family and I would rather see her hanged than have to confess that she was the mistress or wife of the king," Anne allegedly replied.[3]

According to her detractors, Anne was becoming increasingly arrogant—but under this apparent self-importance must surely have been a sense of self-protection: she must show her good side, and hide her fear of losing it all.

On January 5, 1531, Pope Clement VII wrote to Henry:

> At the request of the Queen, we forbid you to remarry until the decision of the case, and we declare that if you do all issue will be illegitimate. We forbid any one in England, of ecclesiastical or secular dignity, universities, parliaments, courts of law, to make any decision in an affair the judgment of which is reserved for the Holy See. The whole under pain of excommunication.[4]

Henry was furious. So was Anne.

As someone who had always been seen to be a strong and devout Catholic—and who, in 1521, had earned the prestigious title of the "Defender of the Faith" for guarding the Roman Catholic Church against the attacks made by Luther—Henry was (or at least feigned to be) devastated.

On the one hand, he had locked himself into the rhetoric of the need to break the status quo in order to guarantee the succession in the direct line, but in favor of a male heir—without one, he firmly believed (and it was so often proven the case with other rulers) that his legacy was in mortal danger. And, of course, his love for Anne remained.

In any case, he must have raged—how could a foreign power have so much control over a king and his realm? Here, in the courtly display exhibited by Henry and Anne, was a manifesto for a vastly more authoritative version of royal power. Anne, as much as Henry, must have known what was at stake here. Beyond their own feelings, the English couple were fighting for self-determination.

*

The English court often took up residence at Greenwich and, at this time, the Duke of Norfolk and Thomas Boleyn were there with the king, underlining their ascendency. The French ambassadors, de Vaux and de la Pommeraie, were also visibly on the up. They were often invited to join Anne, her uncle and her father for dinner, and they always stayed for the *de rigueur* postprandial entertainment, too.

Reports sent to Rome warned the Pope of the seriousness of the situation in England: "The king of England is so passionately in love with the woman [Anne] whom he wishes to marry, that, having some difference with her, he summoned certain of her relations, and implored them with tears to make peace. By this he has shown himself so forgetful of what is right, and of his dignity and authority."[5]

For so many, Henry and Anne's relationship was an absurdity, an anomaly that they hoped would end before the status quo was fractured beyond repair.

It was true that they sometimes quarreled at court—no surprise given the circumstances, but despite this they maintained their affections. In fact, and more problematically for the men who wanted the king's utmost favor, including her uncle and father, Anne seemed to have become a primary adviser to Henry. It was said that Anne was "becoming more and more proud and brave with every day that passes, using words and authority toward the king."[6] Although Anne was still not queen by 1531, she was certainly making it clear that she would not be a pious, quiet consort. Full of passion, fire and life, she had found her own taste for decision-making.

After Wolsey's death, another man was rising up at court: Thomas Cromwell, who for years had been working for the cardinal, hiding in his shadow. A well-educated man who had risen despite humble origins, Cromwell had also learned how to navigate factions at court. In 1530, he had been made secretary to the king, and now he showed favor to the Boleyns, and particularly Anne.

In his opinion, the only way to resolve the king's "great matter" was to change policy when it came to the deadlock with Rome: the key, he felt, was to force the English clergy to accept royal authority in place of that of the papacy. A revolutionary idea was forming: the king and those around him were evidently starting to imagine an independent national Church, with Henry at its head, free from the confines of Rome.

Cromwell would use all his cunning, all his considerable powers of persuasion, to bring the clergy under the sway of the English monarchy—until eventually there passed into law a range of fundamental changes to the Church's legal and ecclesial identity.[7] It was evident that the clergy, or much of it, would balk at such laws.

In the meantime, the French still publicly supported Henry's and Anne's version of the future. Henry sent books and other pamphlets to Francis concerning his annulment "to obtain the approval of the university of France."[8]

By June 1531, Henry was receiving legates from Rome, and the discussion soon became a heated one: "The Pope is evidently doing his utmost to retain the cognizance of this affair but he must not be deceived and lose his time in addressing to me persuasions and remonstrance, for I shall never consent to his being the judge in that affair. Even if his Holiness should do his worst by excommunicating me, and so forth, I shall not mind it, for I care not a fig for all his excommunications. Let him follow his own at Rome, I will do here what I think best!" Henry shouted after receiving one such legate.[9]

The papal nuncio was appalled by such words: defying the authority of the Pope, the only representative of God on Earth, was an outrage.

These tensions were felt elsewhere. Anne's temper was now reported to be at its worst. Chapuys claimed that after Anne heard Lord Guildford, the comptroller, insisting that he would not support the marriage, she furiously threatened him: "Once I am queen of England, I will have you punished and deprived of your office."

The comptroller was said to retort, "I will be the first to resign my post."

Guildford went to the king to complain of Anne's outspoken behavior. Henry tried to convince him to retain his position, but it was said that he "was really indisposed, insisted on giving up his office, and went home."[10]

The list of Anne's enemies was certainly growing. But Henry's support for her was, for now, unfaltering.

★

In the summer of 1531, the court resided at Hampton Court Palace, where the king hunted on a daily basis, with Anne by his side; Catherine was not allowed to join them and had firm orders to remain at Windsor. Further isolated, Henry's wife had surely lost faith that she would ever be able to rescue her marriage. The more time her husband spent with Anne, the more humiliation she had to endure.

After a month of hunting in the parks near Hampton Court, and spending most of the season in each other's company, Henry and Anne decided to make their way to Windsor Castle. They sent orders ahead to Catherine to vacate the premises and go to the More, a house the Abbot of St. Albans had been forced to concede to the king. Anne was becoming queen in all but name.

To overcome her detractors, she sought to reward those who favored the divorce and her marriage to Henry. John Stokesley had been made bishop of London, Stephen Gardiner was awarded bishop of Winchester, and the archbishopric of York was offered to Dr. Edward Lee. Anne's cousin, Sir Francis Bryan, became ambassador to France to ensure stable relations between the two realms. Unfortunately for Anne, some of these men's loyalties would later be swayed.

De Vaux, the French ambassador at Henry's court, was also favored by the king and often invited to dinner, at which he usually found a seat not too far from Anne; they would discuss her education in France and how it had influenced her. Evidently, Anne was enjoying her association with the French and sought to take advantage of it as much as she could. They were her most obvious allies as she took on the role of queen in other ways, such as asking for the royal jewels, including those that were in Catherine's possession—a request Henry did not deny. The Duke of Norfolk happily obliged to make the request to Catherine, who staunchly refused it.

> I will not dare send my rings and jewelry to the king, my husband, knowing that he has forbidden it on a previous occasion, and moreover it would cause much distress on my conscience to deliver up my jewels for so bad a purpose as that of decorating a woman who is a scandal to the whole of Christendom, and a cause of infamy to the king himself [...] if the king wants them, he can come and ask for them himself.[11]

Jewels or not, Anne would eventually take everything from her rival, Catherine: her husband, her title and her crown.

★

The fact that the French court had reasons for supporting Henry did not necessarily make their motives and calculations entirely straightforward.

Gilles de la Pommeraie, who had spent time in Venice before being dispatched to England in late 1530, showed considerable shrewdness during his encounters with Eustace Chapuys, the imperial ambassador.

"Your master, the emperor, is one of the greatest rulers in Europe and I sincerely hope that there will be a greater friendship than ever between him and my master, Francis," he stated.[12]

Could there have been any sincerity in his words? Unlikely.

The French had not forgiven Charles of Spain for the humiliations he'd caused them over the past decade. These emollient sentiments were just another move in the diplomatic game to position France as the strongest power in Europe—one that could now play the role of mediator between the English king and the Holy Roman Emperor.

But the fact was that there were now real plans for Henry and Anne to formally meet with Francis I. Fears that the couple would marry in France, however, were quashed by Anne herself: "I will never consent to the marriage taking place out of England, but only on the very spot and with the same ceremonies used by the English queens at their marriage and coronations."[13]

Anne might have French connections, but it was clear that England had her heart.

As Anne got closer to the consort's crown, the discontent around the relationship continued to grow, and her enemies were not afraid to express their hatred. According to French reports that were sent to Venice, in November 1531, a mob of around 8,000 people—women, and men allegedly dressed as women, with the clear intention to kill Anne—"went out of the town to seize Boleyn's daughter, the sweetheart of the King of England, who was supping at a villa on a river." Henry was not with her, and she had to escape this attempted murder by "crossing the river in a boat."[14]

There are no reports of Anne expressing her upset at these

plots against her: she would not lose face. The threats, however, must have unsettled her.

Besides, Henry did not fear this opposition and continued to favor her extravagantly. For the New Year, he showered her with gifts and offered nothing to his wife, Catherine. Among the treasures Anne received was "a bed covered with gold and silver cloth, crimson satin, and embroidery richer than all the rest." More controversially, Anne now had the same number of ladies-in-waiting as Catherine, "as if she were already a queen."[15]

Maybe Anne thought that she could, in time, win over her domestic enemies and detractors, once the union had been made official. Perhaps even the papacy's stick-in-the-mud attitude over the legalities of the divorce could be sidestepped.

However, a serious obstacle remained: Charles of Spain and his imperial forces, who were threatening to take military action if his aunt, Catherine, was further humiliated. And this was no small threat. Charles's power and military prowess were known by everyone, including Henry and Anne. A stronger alliance, and a pact of mutual assistance with the French, was now essential for the English couple.

French diplomats all over Europe were certainly fascinated by how things were playing out. Jean du Bellay—who was now in France at the service of the constable, Anne de Montmorency, and who was in the midst of the speculation running rife at the French court—corresponded with Francis de Dinteville, cousin to Jean de Dinteville, who would later be sent to England himself, and who was ambassador in Rome, serving both Francis's and Henry's interests.

Du Bellay bluntly revealed that, although la Pommeraie was inclined to sarcasm about the English king, he had told him that "once it is all done" they would have "a king [Henry] on the right path." Du Bellay warned Francis de Dinteville not to share this with anyone, as the risk of "being excommunicated" for their support of Henry's divorce and remarriage remained high.[16]

Du Bellay, who was known for his own reformed ideas, had a particular interest in the outcome. Nevertheless, such discussions around what the "right path" meant were dangerous territory for bishops and other representatives of the Roman Catholic Church.

In January 1532, Cardinal Antoine Duprat—who had been ordered by Francis I to support Henry's demands—wrote to Pope Clement VII and insisted "that the king of England frequently complains that justice is denied him in a cause too important to be proceeded by proxy, while he cannot go to Rome without great danger."

The Pope continued to insist that this affair should be settled in Rome—which meant that Charles, the Holy Roman Emperor, would participate in the proceedings. Duprat countered that "the English and the French, especially the Kings, have always been accustomed to have their cases settled in their own country. [...] This course will be pleasing to the kings of England and France, and worthy of your Holiness, and calculated to avoid many evils."[17]

Francis himself wrote to the Pope with the same intent: "There is no reason to hope that the affair will come to a speedy issue. [...] Moreover, the king of England has been given to understand that you, Holy Highness, insisted on causing him to be cited to go to Rome for the decision of his cause. This is contrary to the privileges of his realm as most learned persons of my realm assured me."[18]

Alongside Francis's representatives in Rome, Henry sent other legates to insist on having his case resolved in England. Clement sent a sharp reply to Henry. "Since the beginning of your suit with Catherine touching the validity of your marriage, you have treated her as your queen, but recently you have removed her from your court, and cohabited openly with a certain Anne," Clement wrote. He continued, "Remember how Catholics will grieve and heretics rejoice to hear that you have repudiated your queen, who is the daughter of kings and the aunt of the emperor and the king of the Romans." He ordered him to "take Catherine back again, and put away Anne."[19]

The Pope was not changing his mind, however, and Francis, like Henry, took exception to having his own authority challenged. There was also the irritating question of Charles's influence over the Pope. Neither Francis nor Henry could let this affair set a precedent where their authority would be diminished and Charles's expanded.

*

In early January 1532, Francis took another step toward a stronger Anglo-French alliance; he instructed la Pommeraie to conclude a better treaty between France and England. Francis promised to provide "five hundred lances and a fleet mounted by 1,500 men" in case England was attacked by the emperor and his forces. In exchange, Henry had to promise to reciprocate by offering "five thousand archers and a similar fleet."[20]

The nightmare scenario for the French was that, in some way, the Tudor regime would fail, and that Charles would intervene and set up his aunt, Catherine, and his cousin, Princess Mary, as de facto sovereigns—and the English would become a client state of the imperialists.

On April 30, 1532, Henry signed and ratified the treaty. Between January and April, as the negotiations took place to do so, parallel discussions about the marriage between Henry and Anne were now at the center of all privy council meetings.

The Duke of Norfolk, Anne's uncle, was in charge of convincing the peers and members of the lower house that "matrimonial causes ought not to be judged by ecclesiasticals but by lay tribunals."[21] They did not agree with him, which further postponed the wedding date.

Henry was furious at this failure and claimed that he would marry Anne at once. La Pommeraie agreed with this plan: "If this king [Henry VIII] wishes to be married again he should not listen to those who advise him to waste time and money in that pursuit, but marry at once the woman he likes most as King Louis XII did in similar circumstances."[22]

This was, however, a course of action that the Duke of Norfolk and Thomas Boleyn themselves opposed; they believed that a marriage with Anne, before the divorce from Catherine was proclaimed, would only reinforce the hatred against Anne and her family, including them. They were still of the opinion that the clergy of England should agree to the divorce first.

With Cromwell's help, therefore, Norfolk and Boleyn once more made a plan to put further pressure on the clergy. They decided to convene royal ministers to insist that "the clergy had no right to make ordinances in provincial councils without the royal assent."[23] William Warham, Archbishop of Canterbury, opposed and denounced such measures. He would not support the couple nor their attempted ecclesiastical reforms.

Worse than that, Warham had no fear of making his opposition to Anne public.

He drafted a speech that he intended to read in the House of Lords, expressing his discontent regarding a potential marriage between Henry and Anne. He claimed that he "would be sorry to do anything prejudicial to the king's authority, especially as it was myself who anointed the king and put the crown upon his head," but he feared that he had to remind the king—and the woman Warham saw as his concubine—that "the liberties of the Church are guaranteed by Magna Carta, and several kings who violated them, as Henry II, Edward III, Richard II, and Henry IV, came to an ill end."[24]

This was a big blow to Henry's authority, and it would have caused far greater problems if this speech had been delivered in parliament. Fortunately for the English couple, the archbishop's health was deteriorating and, on August 23, 1532, William Warham passed away—another enemy down. But the path to victory remained full of obstacles.

Despite the Archbishop of Canterbury's death, the situation remained dire. Anne and Henry needed further support—they needed more than a better treaty with France. They needed to acquire Francis's public support to further pressure the Pope into reconsidering his past declarations. Evidently, Francis I was becoming their only hope.

They needed to see him again.

*

In the summer of 1532, Guillaume du Bellay, brother of Jean du Bellay—the latter known as a staunch supporter of the Boleyns and a quite radical evangelical under Marguerite of Navarre's protection—was sent to the English court to assist la Pommeraie in organizing another meeting between Henry VIII and Francis, this time with Anne. Her presence at such a meeting was a sign of just how far she had come.

It was agreed that the encounter should take place first in Calais and then Boulogne.

In late August 1532, Jean du Bellay—who had been staying in Nantes for some time—was told the news by his brother. Delighted by this decision, he in turn communicated the details to Francis de Dinteville, Bishop of Auxerre, who was residing in Rome: "It will be in a town called Marquise and it will happen at the beginning or the end of October, I will invite you if you wished to attend it."[25]

Such information had to be shared sensitively, as the whole situation was still problematic. After all, the meeting would mean Francis declaring strong public support for Anne, which could be perceived as an insult to the Pope.

Meanwhile, Chapuys tried to gather as much intelligence as he could to report to Charles of Spain: "La Pommeraie asserted that no ladies would be present. However, I think Lady Anne will be there, considering the preparations of ladies and servants to accompany her."

What an outrage if this information was true! It would leave the Pope with two undesirable choices: either "an injustice to the queen and all her adherents" or having "the two kings for enemies."[26]

Anne must have felt confident in her strategy. She spent her time hunting and feasting with the French ambassadors, enjoying their company. In a letter that is wrongly attributed to Jean du Bellay in *Letters and Papers, Foreign and Domestic, Henry VIII*, Gilles de la Pommeraie—its actual author—disclosed his agreement with Anne to write on her behalf to the King of France, asking him to bring his sister, Marguerite, "the queen of Navarre to Boulogne, to feast with them."[27]

Marguerite declined to meet the couple. Despite likely having been a former mentor to Anne and sharing reformed ideas with her during the Boleyn girl's time at the French court, Marguerite may have wanted to avoid the controversy. In 1532, Marguerite was queen of Navarre, and although she was a religious evangelical and an enemy of the Habsburgs, she did not seem to approve of Henry's new love.[28] Anne was not of royal blood, which was something Marguerite held in high regard—as had her mother, Louise of Savoy, who'd passed away on September 22 of the previous year.

This first betrayal, from someone she respected and had learned so much from, must have been a bitter pill for Anne to swallow.

Marguerite's position could also be explained by her own political situation at a time when she needed to tame her religious beliefs. She was queen of Navarre, but her brother did not approve of her evangelical beliefs, making it impossible for her to approve a union that could potentially anger the Pope. She needed to remain discreet, but she did maintain good relations with the du Bellay brothers—especially Jean, who did not hide his support for Anne, which suggested that Marguerite was not entirely unsympathetic to her.

Francis also declined to bring his wife, Eleanor, niece of Catherine of Aragon, to the meeting, likely out of respect for the English queen. His own presence, he thought, would suffice. Even without the ladies, the meeting was already a powerful symbol of support.

Anne, however, had her own supporters, such as la Pommeraie, who was now favored by Henry on account of Anne: "The king of England treats me familiarly and I am alone with him all day, hunting and talking about all his private affairs." Guillaume du Bellay was equally well treated: "Whenever they come to any house of the king's, the king shows his favor to Du Bellay and tells him what he has done and what he is going to do."

Anne appreciated the support. She gifted a "hunting frock and hat, horn, and grayhound" to Guillaume du Bellay, promising him: "This is to show you how the affection of the king of England for Francis, your master, increases, for all I do is by the king's order."[29]

With Anne at the helm of the realm, the Anglo-French alliance seemed to be strengthening.

*

Before Anne could accompany Henry to the second most important royal encounter of the first half of the sixteenth century, this meeting among kings, her status needed further enhancement. She was made marchioness of Pembroke, a title created especially for her, and was granted land accordingly. On Sunday, September 1, 1532, at Windsor Castle, a grand ceremony was organized to celebrate the occasion. Dressed in "a surcoat of crimson velvet, furred with ermines, with strait sleeves," Anne was led by Elizabeth, Countess of Rutland, and Dorothy, Countess of

Sussex, and kneeled before the king.[30] The dukes of Norfolk and Suffolk, and her father, Thomas Boleyn, were naturally also in attendance. Anne's power seemed to be at its peak.

Chapuys could not help but remark on the intimacy between Anne and the French: "I have no doubt that Francis wishes to see her, to thank her for daily good offices, which la Pommeraie says he can hardly be sufficiently grateful. Francis has lost nothing by the death of the cardinal of York [Wolsey]; for, besides that, the lady is more mischievous and has more credit than he had."[31]

The meeting between Henry, Francis and Anne would finally take place—and it could change the course of history.

8

"The Most Happy"

Once the momentous occasion had passed, Anne would surely reflect that the meeting in France had gone as well as she could have expected.

She would never forget that moment when Francis I ordered the Provost of Paris to gift her an impressive diamond worth about 15 crowns—a symbol of their friendship and a symbol of her own Frenchness for so many. The diamond could only be perceived as a token of loyalty and support from Francis I to the royal couple. Anne's reunion with Francis had been successful, and the support she so desperately needed had been secured.

Besides, Henry and Francis had made other important agreements during their meeting between Calais and Boulogne—"to preserve and defend our Holy Faith and Christian religion" and to fight against the Turks together if needed.[1] Their alliance had been reinforced once more, and with Anne at Henry's side, nothing seemed to be able to alter the Anglo-French friendship.

As for Anne, this was the needed hope and relief she had been waiting for. She had met Francis I in person again and he had publicly shown his support. There was more to do, but she must surely have felt protected by this seeming endorsement. Her desires seemed more attainable than ever.

She was determined to honor the alliance, but she had been disappointed by so-called allies before, and she also knew nothing could be taken for granted. Was Francis's endorsement more complex than it appeared? Was she being duped? Was Francis a true ally?

In truth, while Francis was broadly in favor of Anne, he also had his own political agenda that was quite separate from English affairs. So, he agreed to continue putting pressure on the Pope to change his mind, and to counterbalance Charles's growing power in Europe, but as for openly supporting a marriage that went against the Pope's wishes—that was perhaps a step too far. For now, Anne had to be content with what had been achieved to date.

★

The journey back to England was laborious. A terrible storm had been raging in western and northern Europe for over a week—hitting Normandy in the north of France, as well as the south of England.

On Sunday, November 10, 1532, the English king and Anne hoped to sail back home, but a Channel fog prevented their return. Two days later, they finally managed to start their journey back and, on the fourteenth, "after a painfully slow crossing of twenty-nine hours," they arrived in Dover.[2] It has been rumored that the couple consummated their carnal relationship on this particular journey back to England, although no contemporary evidence exists to support this theory. It is certainly likely that Anne would have waited this long to consummate their relationship, because becoming queen was her goal, and she could not have afforded to give him an illegitimate child.

On November 13, while Anne and Henry were crossing the Channel back to England, the French king instructed his ambassador in Rome to remind the Pope of where he stood: "The king of England and myself are so united that our interests are the same and if his Holy Highness provokes us by undertaking anything against the king of England, great damage may ensue." The damage that Francis was referring to was the kings' "demand of a General Council" to discuss the matter of Henry's proposed annulment. If it was refused, they would "hold the Council" themselves. He offered to meet the Pope in "Nice or Avignon" to discuss the matter (an encounter that would eventually take place in the summer of 1533), and also reminded his ambassadors in Rome that they had to "do what they can in the matter of the king of England, as if it was my own affair."[3]

Francis was bold in his demands, but his support of Henry did not necessarily mean he would approve of a clandestine union—even with a woman whom he knew and trusted.

*

Throughout December 1532, in Rome, Francis de Dinteville, Bishop of Auxerre—alongside other French legates in the holy city, such as the Cardinal Francis of Tournon—had been receiving strict orders from Francis I to continue insisting on a resolution for Henry's divorce. Rumors spread in Rome that Dinteville, a fervent Catholic, had displeased Henry VIII, but the ambassador assured his friend, Jean du Bellay, that "I have followed our master's orders and continue to support the king of England's affair."[4]

Tournon—who also received instructions to put further pressure on the Pope to agree to grant a divorce and a dispensation for another marriage—clearly stated his disapproval to the French king: "For the love of God and for yourself, and as his Holiness begs you, try to discreetly convince your good brother, the king of England, that he is making a mistake."[5]

Francis ignored this advice and continued to instruct his ambassadors to support Henry's great matter. In fact, his orders were the same as before the meetings that had taken place in Calais and Boulogne: Francis would continue his foreign policy as long as the rules set by the Pope were respected.

However, without Francis's consent, Henry and Anne—probably empowered by their meeting with him—made the decision to play a dangerous game, one that could cost them allies and friends. It was a game that Anne could really not afford to lose.

For now, there was still hope that glory could be achieved. In early 1533, a protégé and ally of the Boleyns—who had been Sir Thomas Boleyn's chaplain—came back to the English court. This was Thomas Cranmer, and he was about to be consecrated archbishop of Canterbury. With this act, a clear message was sent to everyone in England and abroad: Henry would marry Anne regardless of the Pope's threats and papal bulls. The English king had evidently decided to assert his freedom in this matter.

More importantly, this nomination surprised the imperial ambassador. In late January 1533, Chapuys pondered it: "Formerly it was not the custom of the king to fill up the vacancies before the expiration of the year within the vacancy actually occurred, whereas the archiepiscopal see of Canterbury has not been vacant four months." Chapuys was unsure of the reasons behind such a rushed nomination. He knew "there is a rumor afloat that Dr. Cranmer, who is considered to be a Lutheran, has renounced the whole of his temporalities in favor of this king."[6] This would have been a source of anxiety.

Cranmer was known for being a pious man who had joined the orders after his wife died in the late 1510s. Well-educated, witty and patient, he was an excellent orator who showed grace and talent in his storytelling. He was a flexible man, and his religious and political views seemed to have been influenced by his benefactors, which included the Boleyns.

Cranmer's nomination as archbishop of Canterbury was then confirmed by both the Pope and the Holy Roman Emperor—who

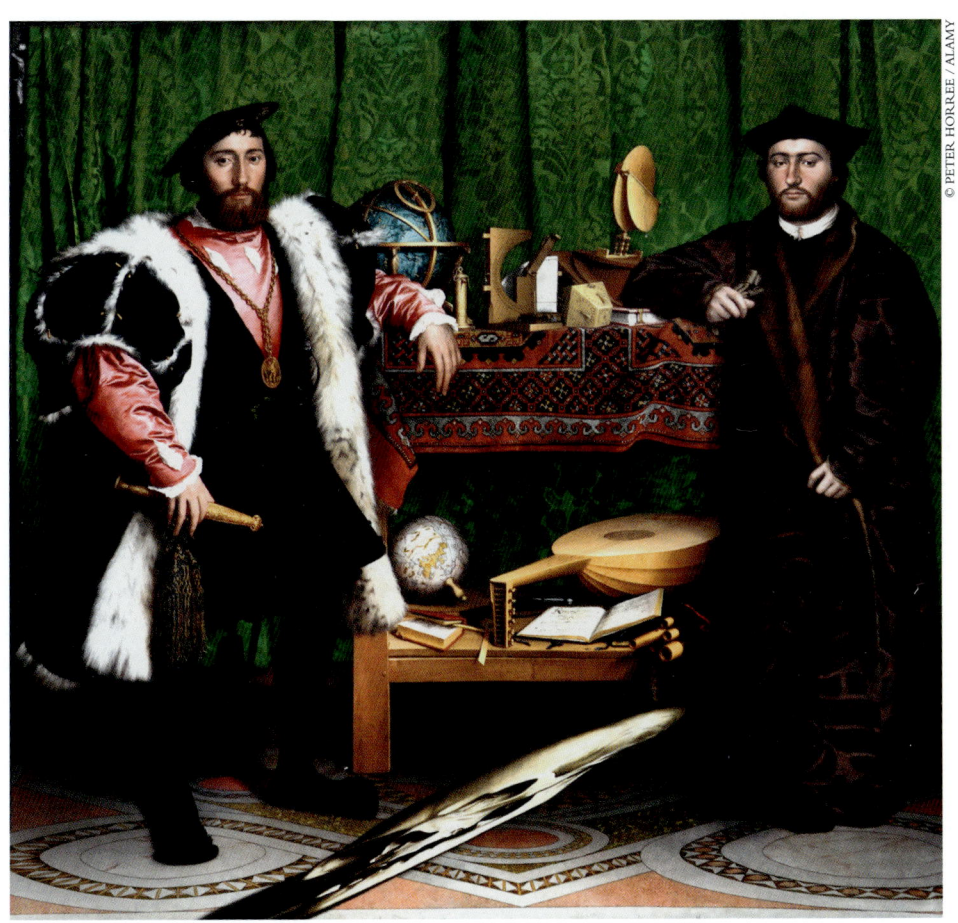

The Ambassadors by Hans Holbein the Younger, 1533. The painting depicts Jean de Dinteville, left, on his second diplomatic mission to England on behalf of Francis I of France, and Georges de Selve, Bishop of Lavaur, to the right. This portrait was completed during the religious tensions as Henry VIII sought to annul his marriage to Catherine of Aragon against the pope's wishes.

BOLEYN·REGINA·ANGLIÆ·153

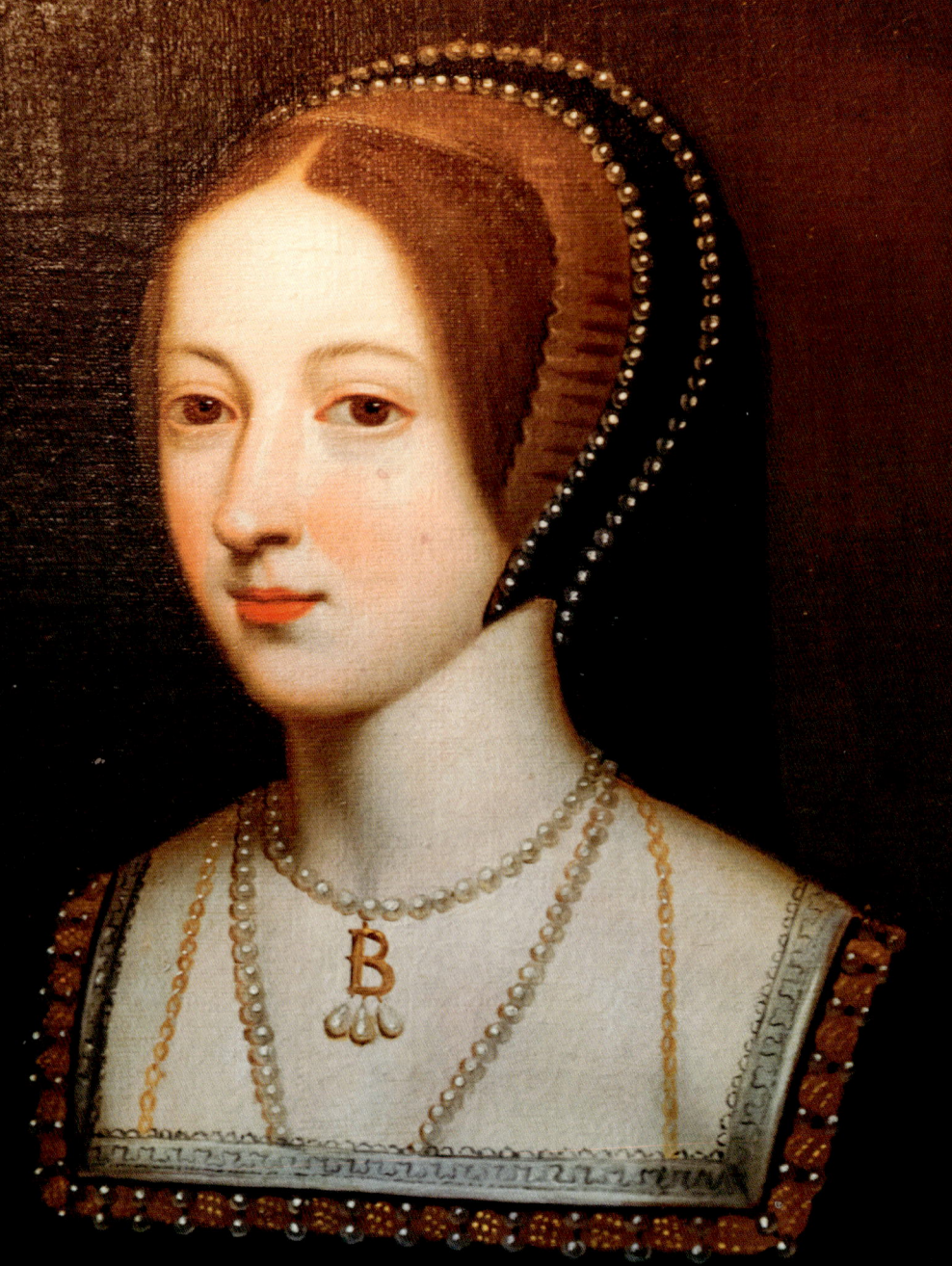

Opposite: A portrait of Anne Boleyn by an unknown artist, held in the collection at the Boleyn family home, Hever Castle. Known as the "Zouche" portrait, it is likely an eighteenth-century copy of a Clouet portrait, made for Alexandre Lambert's Chateau de Thorigny. By 1897 it was in the collection of Robert Curzon, Fifteenth Baron Zouche of Perham Park, hence the name. © STEVE VIDLER / ALAMY

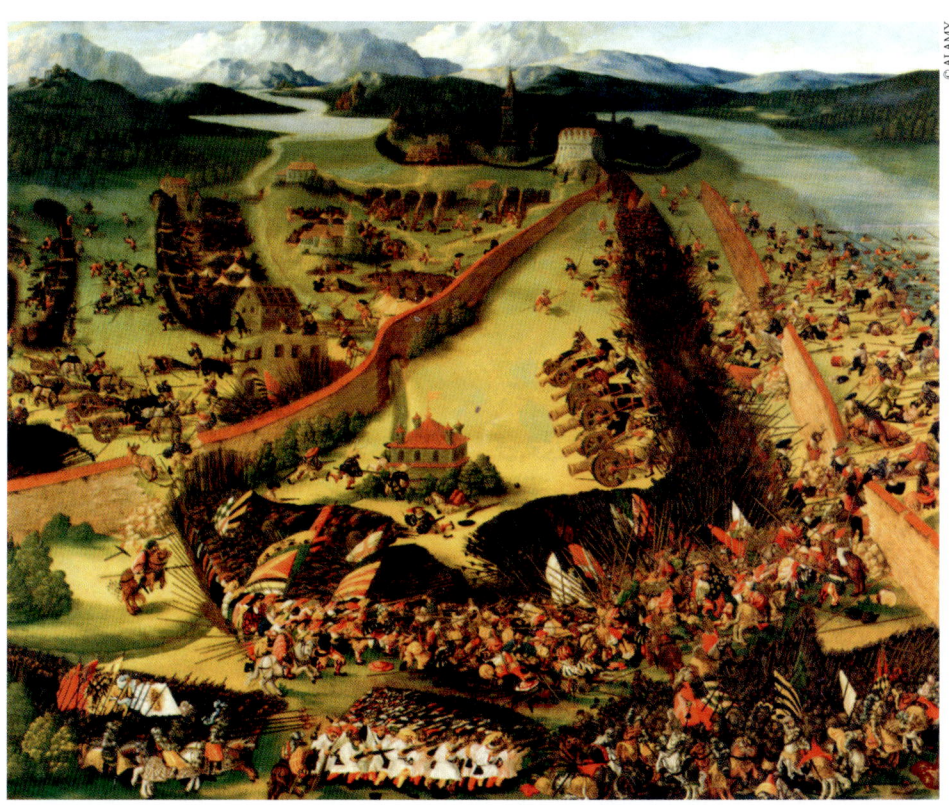

A painting of the Battle of Pavia by an unknown artist. The battle, on February 24, 1525, was a decisive part of the Italian War of 1521–1526, which pitted Francis I of France and the Republic of Venice against the Holy Roman Emperor Charles V, Henry VIII of England, and the Papal States. The conflict arose from animosity over the election of Charles as Emperor in 1519–1520 and Pope Leo X's need to ally with Charles against Martin Luther.

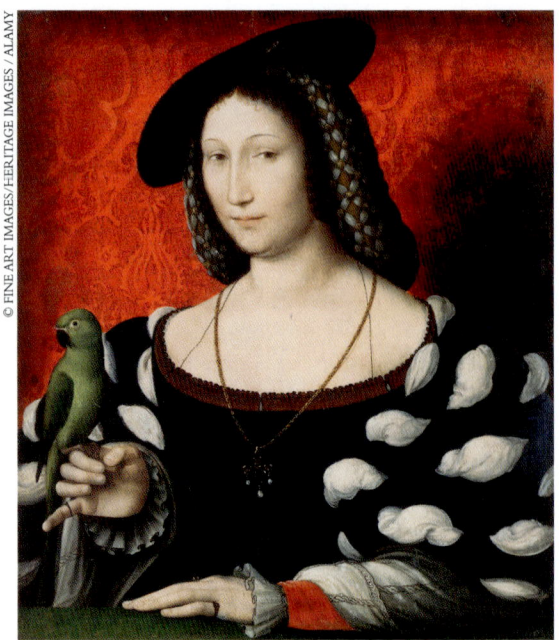

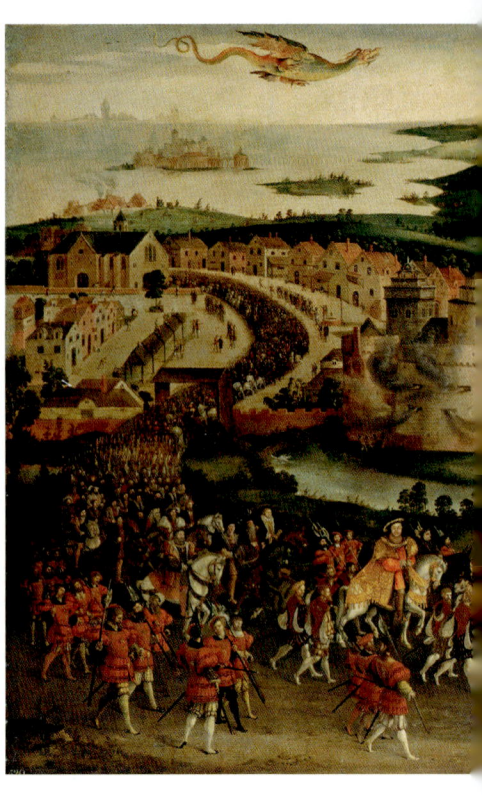

Portrait of Marguerite of Navarre (1492–1549) by Jean Clouet, circa 1527. Sister of Francis I of France, Marguerite was an author, humanist and religious reformer, and was a key figure in the French Renaissance. She was described by Samuel Putnam as "the first modern woman."

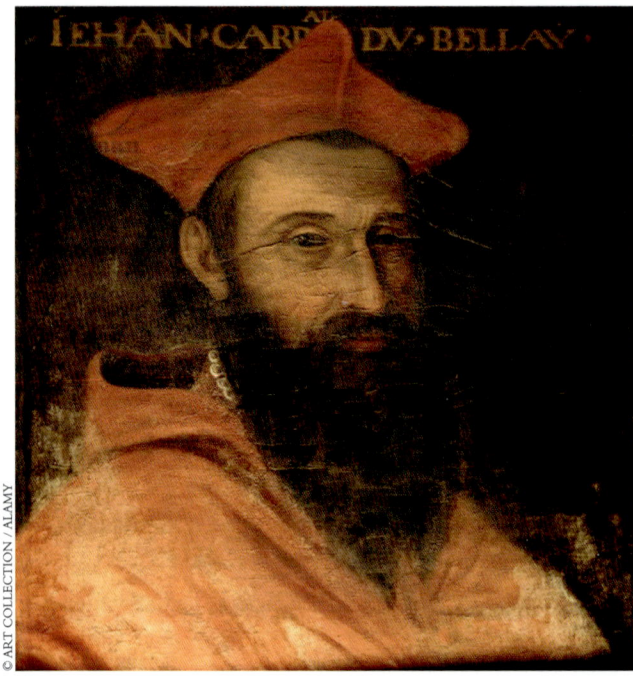

A portrait of Cardinal Jean du Bellay (1492–1560), by an unknown artist. A leading French diplomat, he undertook several diplomatic missions in England as an ambassador during the reign of Henry VIII.

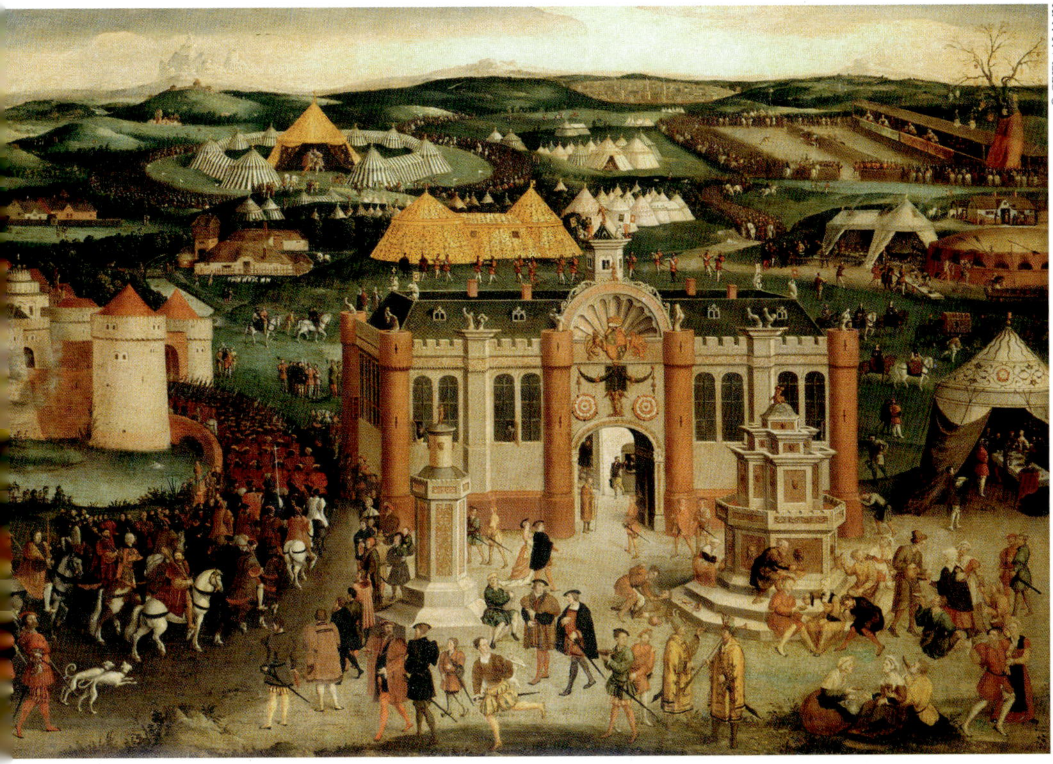

A painting depicting the Field of the Cloth of Gold, a famed meeting between King Francis I and Henry VIII held at Guisnes, south of Calais, by an unknown artist. This scene shows the arrival of the British party for the grand festival held in June 1520.

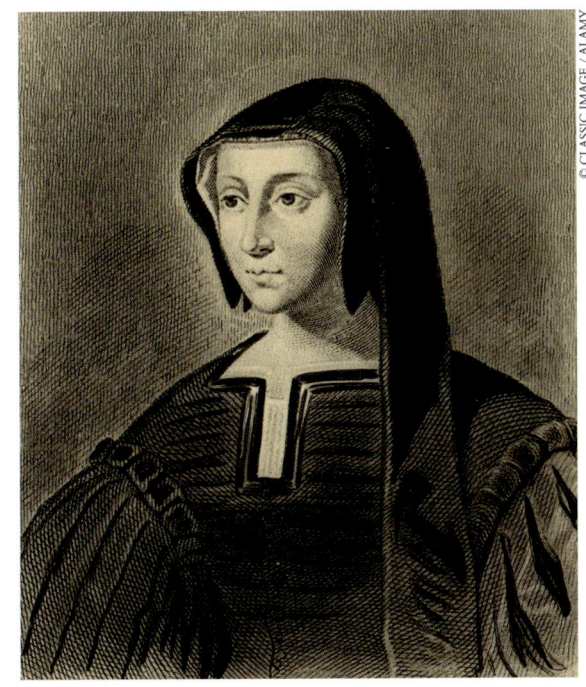

Louise of Savoy (1476–1531), by an unknown artist. A French noble and regent, Duchess of Auvergne and Bourbon, Duchess of Nemours, she was the mother of King Francis I.

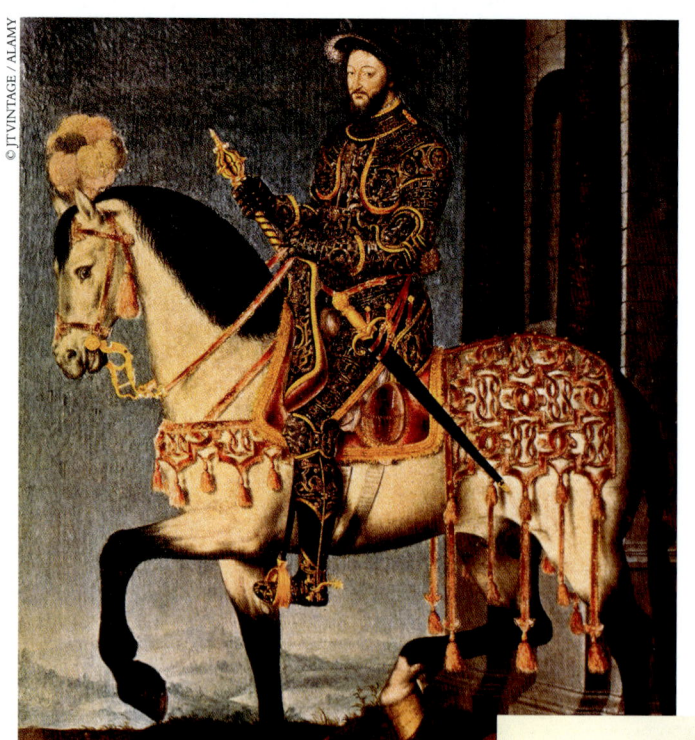

Portrait of Francis I (1494–1547), King of France (1515–1547), by Jean Clouet, circa 1540.

Claude of France (1499–1524), the Queen of France and the first wife of Francis I, by an unknown artist.

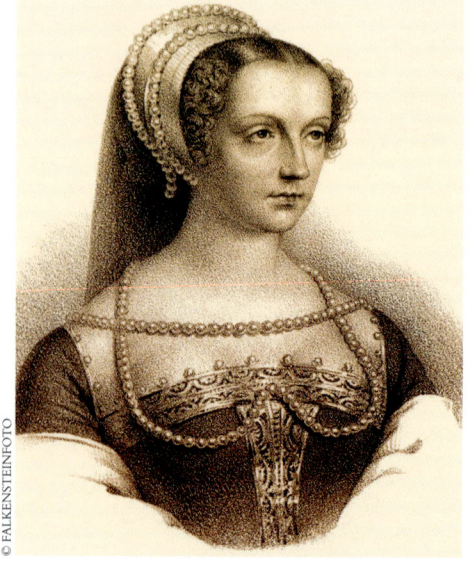

Thomas Boleyn (1477–1539), father of Anne Boleyn, 1st Earl of Wiltshire, First Earl of Ormond, First Viscount Rochford, English diplomat and politician. Hand-colored copperplate engraving by Francis Bartolozzi after Hans Holbein from Facsimiles of Original Drawings by Hans Holbein, London, 1884.

A striking portrait of King Henry VIII by the workshop of Hans Holbein the Younger, circa 1537.

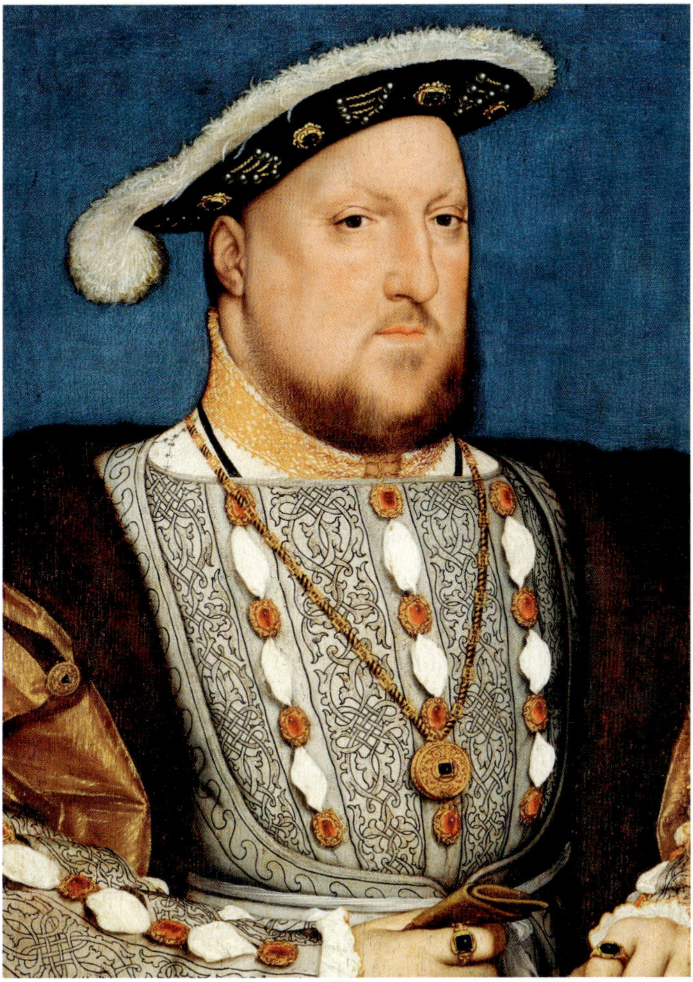

A Victorian reproduction of Henry VIII with Anne Boleyn in the Gallery at Hever Castle, circa 1530. The Victorians were fascinated by Anne and Henry's marriage.

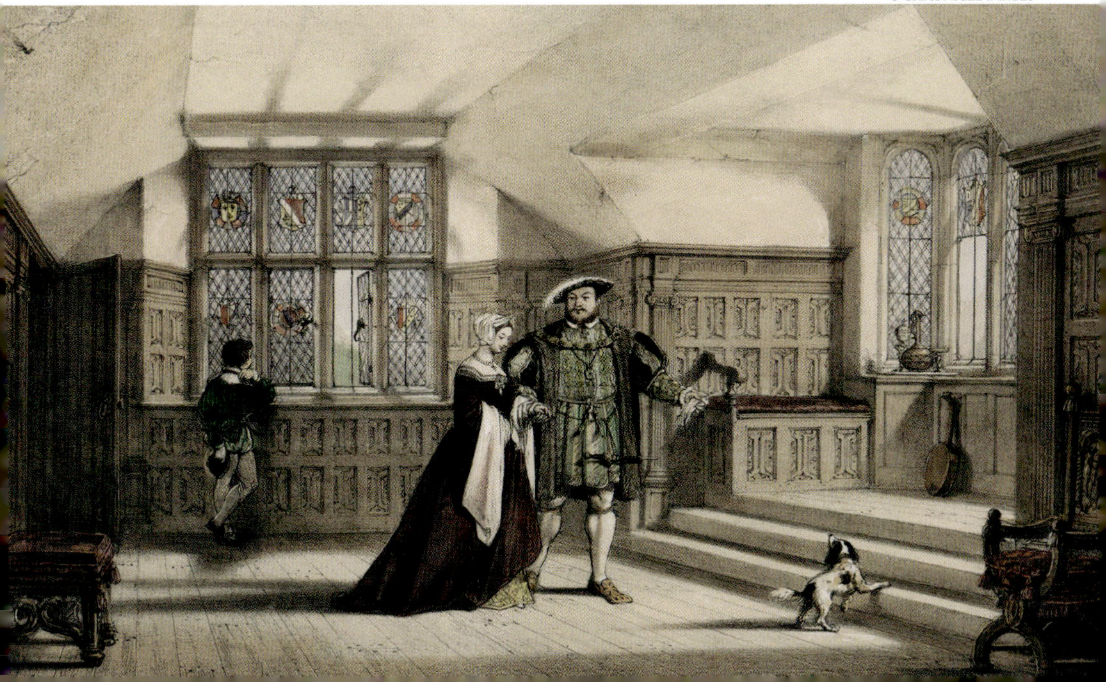

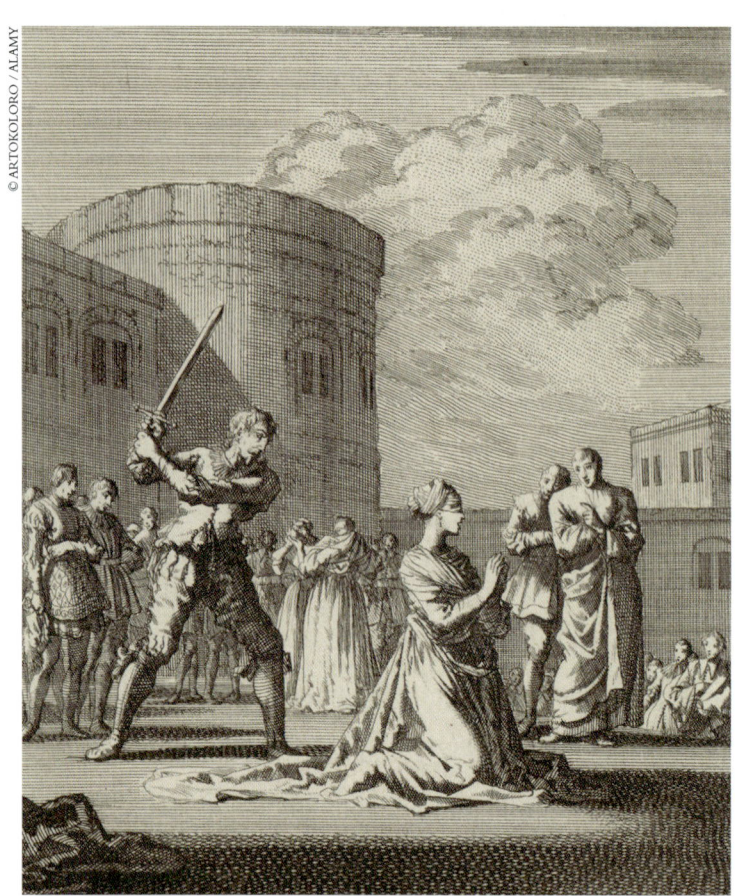

Beheading of Anne Boleyn (1536) by Jan Luyken, circa 1699. The powerful image shows that Anne's legend had continued to grow in the centuries after her death.

Part of a tapestry depicting Anne Boleyn held in the collection of Hever Castle.

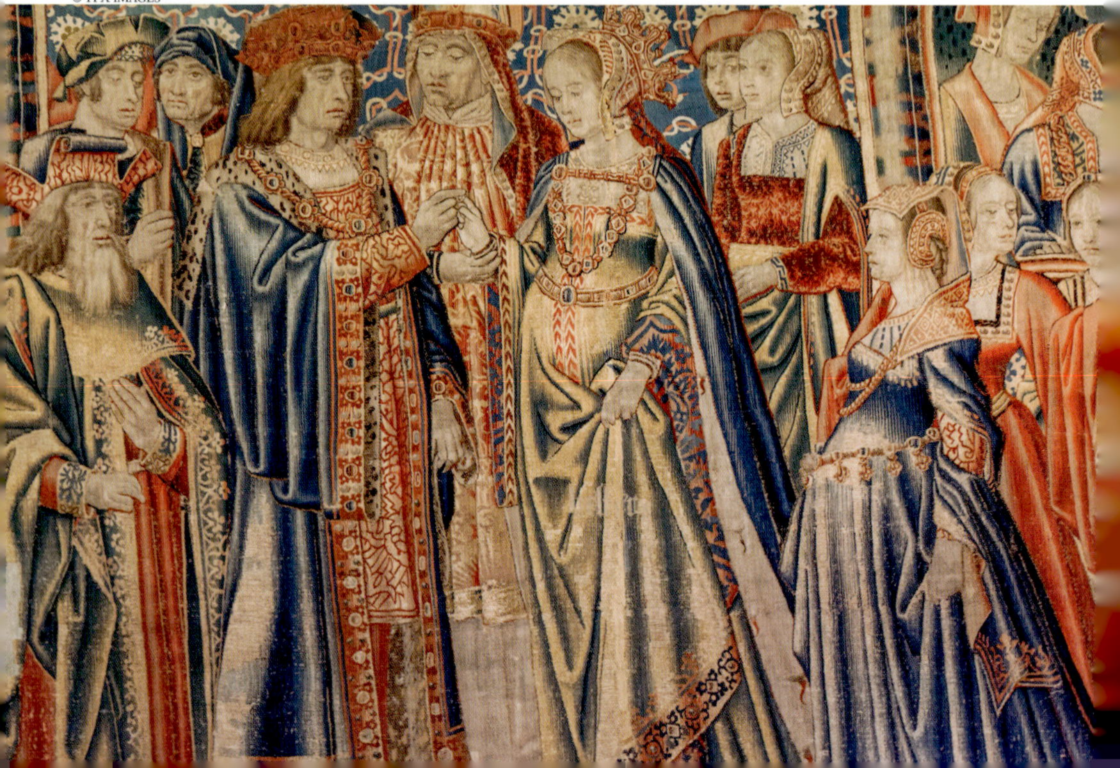

were themselves unaware of Cranmer's political views. During his time at Charles of Spain's court in the early 1530s, Cranmer had shrewdly hidden his true opinion of Henry's great matter and had instead spoken in favor of Queen Catherine of Aragon and her daughter, Princess Mary. By fooling both the emperor and the Pope, Cranmer—who opposed their authority as much as Henry did—used his dissimulations to grasp power.

Sometime in January 1533—probably on the twenty-fifth at the Palace of Whitehall, and officiated by Cranmer himself—Henry and Anne had a secret wedding ceremony.[7] This news was kept under wraps for some months, but in time it percolated through to the rest of Europe. The real reason behind this hasty wedding was the belief that Anne was pregnant.

In March 1533, George Boleyn, Lord Rochford, was sent to Paris to tell Francis I about the union. He was in charge of giving the French king two letters written by Henry himself. Henry showed trust in his letters, but also vulnerability. He informed Francis that,

> according to your advice given at the last interview, and given my anxiety to have male issue for the establishment of my kingdom, I have proceeded effectually to the accomplishment of my marriage, trusting to find that your deeds will correspond with your promises, and that you will assist and maintain myself as king of England in the event of any excommunication from the Pope.

Henry also expressed his hope that Francis "will, as a true friend and brother, devise whatever you can for the establishment of the said marriage, preventing any impediment to it."[8]

While the news must have been a surprise, Francis did not outwardly show any emotion and did not comment publicly on the secret union. He may have shared his true feelings privately, but there are no records of any correspondence. Luckily for the couple, Francis instructed his ambassadors—in Rome and in England—to continue supporting Henry's cause.

*

In January 1533, Francis sent a new ambassador and experienced diplomat—Jean de Dinteville, Bailiff of Troyes—to the English court. Troyes was, like his cousin Francis de Dinteville in Rome, a devout Catholic, who came from a family of diplomats. During his time in England, Troyes commissioned the talented portraitist Holbein to paint a portrait of himself and the special envoy, George of Selve, who would be sent to England for Anne's coronation.[9] Tall and athletic, Troyes was painted as a handsome, wealthy, powerful man. The white fur of his coat conveyed an air of royalty, and at Henry's court, now also Anne's court, he was treated as such. Francis I instructed Troyes to continue to support and to maintain good relations with his "brother" the King of England, as well as ensuring that he would refuse to "listen to the proposals of meeting with Charles and the Pope." Despite Henry's and Anne's clandestine wedding, Francis still supported the English couple.[10]

Indeed, the French king must have felt compassion for Henry when it came to the question of male heirs to secure his dynasty; he, too, understood the importance of establishing a strong dynasty, as he was the first of the Valois-Angoulême branch. Luckily for Francis, he had three sons to succeed him, an heir and two spares: Francis, Henry and Charles.

In fact, Henry's marital woes were serving Francis's political interests and ambitions. While he was advocating for the English king, he was also negotiating for a union between Pope Clement VII's niece, Catherine de Medici, and his second son, Henry, Duke of Orléans. This match would further strengthen Francis's authority on the European political scene, emphasizing the power of his mediation. Indeed, his position as a mediator between

England and Rome continued. Francis instructed his ambassadors in Rome—the cardinals of Gramont and Tournon—to continue in their efforts to convince the Pope to grant Henry a divorce.[11]

While Francis was still hoping for a papal resolution, Gilles de la Pommeraie—who had remained at the English court with Troyes—wrote to the ambassador in Rome, Francis de Dinteville, informing him that "the parliament of this country [England] will be held until after Easter." De la Pommeraie expected that the authority of the Pope "will be greatly diminished."[12] He did not provide any further information, but the fear was that Henry would follow the laws of his country in lieu of the papal ones, which might imperil the negotiations taking place in Rome.

By now, the ties between France and England were at their strongest. Montmorency—the Constable of France and de facto the second most powerful man in France after its king—sent to Troyes "letters in Francis's own hand for Madame the Marchioness," Anne.[13] Francis I was likely aware of Anne's pregnancy. The letters themselves appear to have been lost, though there is no doubt, given the circumstances and the letters that Francis continued to send to Rome, he was prepared for the time being to side with Anne.

On the other hand, and unlike the French ambassadors, Chapuys continued to be kept in the dark when it came to the wedding. On March 31, 1533, he reported that "it is expected that the new marriage will be solemnized before Easter or immediately after"—not realizing it had already taken place.[14]

There was another man who had been kept in the dark—and who disliked it very much. When the news of the wedding reached Jean du Bellay, who had repeatedly demonstrated his goodwill to the Boleyns, his reaction was unexpected. Instead of expressing relief at the couple's decision to marry (particularly given that he himself had suggested the couple proceed without papal dispensation a year or so before), he disclosed his disapproval of Henry to Jean de Dinteville, Bailiff of Troyes, who was at the English court: "I have never seen until this day a man so unreasonable."[15]

The truth was, given the work that the French and English legates and ambassadors were doing to try to achieve a divorce and new marriage, this secret union made their endeavors obsolete. Frustration was naturally expected to be found in their diplomatic dispatches as a result. However, perhaps du Bellay simply felt hurt that he had not been let in on the secret; his disapproval seemed to pass, and he continued later to support Anne.

For those who were still desperately trying to prevent the king's plans, the door was now slammed firmly shut. On April 5, as had been anticipated by la Pommeraie and Chapuys, the Convocation of Canterbury officially proclaimed the divorce between Henry and Catherine, stating that "the Pope has no power of dispensing in case of marriage where the brother's widow has been *cognita*."[16] The meeting consisted of 66 theologians, and only 5 or 6 of them voted against the proclamation. After years of humiliation and fighting for her rights, Catherine was repudiated.

The news was a victory for Anne—but at what cost?

As the news broke, England's position in Europe was now threatened. Chapuys did not hide his contempt, nor his desire for revenge, when he bluntly disclosed his personal feelings to Charles: "It can hardly displease you to make an enterprise against this kingdom, considering the enormous injury done to your aunt; for when this cursed Anne has her foot in the stirrup, you may be sure she will do the Queen all the injury she can, and the Princess likewise."

The insult to the Habsburgs felt irreparable. Furthermore, Charles of Spain, Holy Roman Emperor, also realized that Francis and Henry were now in a stronger alliance than he had previously anticipated, with fears that France "might do something new against your coasts."[17]

Without a doubt, Charles was furious but, for the time being, his focus remained on the Turks at the door of eastern Europe.

He could not afford another war and therefore relied on the Pope to intervene. Yet there were rumors that "the Pope has secretly sent or may send absolution" to Henry[18]—a repulsive thought for the Habsburgs and their agents all over Europe. Fortunately for them, this was not in Clement VII's mind. The Pope must have believed Henry would understand that his course of action could not be sustained. After all, no one had ever truly believed that Henry would actually divorce Catherine for Anne. The situation was unprecedented.

Later in April, Chapuys was further scandalized. On his arrival, he expected to be received by Henry, but instead the Duke of Norfolk informed him that the audience would take place with him instead of the king.

"What I have to say is of very great importance. I have never been denied an audience before and I could not think that the King would wish to break a custom without any occasion, seeing that my master, the emperor, always willingly hears his ambassadors," Chapuys replied.

In response, the duke made excuses and the audience was postponed.

When the audience finally did take place, Chapuys hastened to inform the king that a peace treaty was about to be concluded with the Turks, noting: "at which he remained half stupefied, and entirely mute, without uttering a single word."

Given the circumstances, it is not difficult to speculate on Henry's thoughts on the matter. With a peace treaty between Charles V and Suleiman—the Ottoman sultan—his position in England was in far greater danger than he had previously thought. In all, Henry had relied on the war continuing in order to secure his decision to divorce Catherine.

Chapuys inquired about the situation. "It was many days since I have heard some rumor of what was going on in Convocation, as also in Parliament, in prejudice of the queen, her right and justice. Yet, I had not been willing to take notice of it, because I could not believe that so virtuous, wise, and Catholic a prince would consent to such things."

Henry let Chapuys finish his polite remonstrance before informing him that "God and my conscience are on very good terms."

The imperial ambassador could not believe his ears and asked to speak to him privately, without witnesses. The king replied, "I have spoken without dissimulation," and dismissed his request.

This was another shock for Chapuys. "I cannot believe you wish to give such an example, seeing how Christendom is already troubled by so many heresies," he said before pausing briefly. "I have never heard of so strange a case of one leaving his wife after twenty-five years."

Henry seemed amused. "It is not so long a time, and if the world thinks this divorce was extraordinary, still more the world would find it strange that the Pope has dispensed it without having the power to do so."

Chapuys felt challenged. "I know the cases of five Popes who dispensed in similar situations and though I do not wish to dispute the matter with you, I have to say that there is not a doctor in your kingdom, if it comes to the point, that will not confess the truth. Though you have the seal of the university of Paris, I wish to show you the letters and names of those who have held the queen's side."

"I do not want to see them," Henry tartly replied.

"No one in Spain, Naples, nor elsewhere, has a different opinion," Chapuys continued, feeling empowered by Henry's discomfort.

"I simply wish to have a successor to my kingdom," Henry muttered.

"You have a daughter endowed with all imaginable goodness and virtue, and of an age to bear children, and that as you have received the principal title to your realm by the female line, nature seems to oblige you to restore it to the Princess," Chapuys said. Clearly, he did not fear speaking his mind to the king.

"I know better than my daughter and wish to have children," Henry responded.

"But there is no guarantee you will have them," Chapuys said boldly.

"Am I not a man like other men?"[19]

Chapuys was puzzled, fearing that this question meant Anne was with child.

The dispute between the two continued, now moving onto Catherine's virginity after her marriage to Henry's brother, Arthur. In reality, Chapuys knew he had little chance of changing Henry's mind, but he felt that the right thing to do was to continue showing his unwavering support to Catherine and Princess Mary.

On Easter Eve, Anne made her way to mass "in Royal state, loaded with jewels, clothed in a robe of gold frieze." She was followed by 60 young ladies, and she asked to no longer be referred to as "marchioness" but instead as "queen."

Chapuys reported that Francis had sent a letter to Anne through her brother, Lord Rochford, referring to her as "queen" alongside the gift of 2,000 crowns. Catherine was believed to be using a new title: "the old widow princess." As for Princess Mary, for now, her title was unchanged, "till the lady has had a child."[20]

Anne seemed to be reaching the zenith of her courtly powers just as Catherine's humiliation was complete.

★

Anne's critics were predictably enraged. On April 27, Chapuys reported that on "this feast of Easter, the prior of St. Augustines, in his sermon, recommended the people expressly to pray for Queen Anne; at which they were astonished and scandalized, and almost everyone took his departure with great murmuring and ill looks."

Henry was outraged by the reaction, and—according to

Chapuys—as a result, he forbade Catherine to use the title of "queen." He also forbade Princess Mary to write to her mother. The more Anne endured at the hands of her detractors, the more Henry avenged her by hurting Catherine and Mary.

After years of longing for the ultimate title, Anne was finally to be crowned queen of England.

"Preparations are being made for the coronation of the Lady," Chapuys reported, "which will exceed in sumptuousness all previous ones. It is said it will take place on Ascension Day. The said Lady will be bravely crowned, seeing she has all the queen's jewels, with which she adorns herself every day."[21]

Anne Braye, Baroness Cobham—wife of Sir George Brooke, Baron Cobham, and distant cousin of Anne Boleyn—received a letter from Henry VIII himself, appointing her as the attendant horsewoman for Anne Boleyn's coronation: "You will need to arrive at Greenwich on the previous Friday to accompany the queen to the Tower of London; on the next day to ride through London to Westminster; and on Whitsunday to attend at the coronation in the monastery."[22]

It was important for Anne Boleyn to be supported by the nobility and to display her own pedigree and lineage. After all, she was not of royal blood—like Catherine—and therefore her status could be easily mocked and undermined. This is something Thomas Cromwell might have been sympathetic to.

Further instructions were sent by Henry to all nobles, knights, lords and ladies of the kingdom: "The mayor, aldermen, commoners, and crafts of London are to meet the queen before she comes to the Tower. The king will meet her at the Tower. [...] Two bishops to go every side of the queen. The verge of ivory to be borne. The scepter. A rich crown of gold."[23]

Francis I had continued his support of the English couple, instructing Gramont (who was in Rome) to ensure that the Pope understood "that he must not consider it strange that I support the king of England as our love is such that no man can separate us, and that I consider his affairs as my own."[24] The love Francis was referring to was a pure and strong brotherly love; never before had either of the kings expressed themselves with quite so much affection.

Francis even served as a mediator between Henry and the rest of Europe—including Henry's nephew, King James V of Scotland, who had been threatening the northern borders of England for some time. Francis ensured that a peaceful resolution could be found, despite the mutual hostility displayed by the kings of England and Scotland. Of course, this would be somewhat complicated by the fact that Henry disregarded his advice to continue negotiating with the Pope for a divorce.

Meanwhile, rumors of Anne's pregnancy continued to spread. Troyes reported this rumor to Francis in his letter dated May 23, 1533, which explained (in his eyes) the reason that the coronation was taking place on Ascension Day. Troyes also disclosed that Cranmer had pronounced the divorce, which in his view was a great mistake and would complicate the negotiations conducted in Rome by the French and English emissaries there.

"I begged the archbishop to either postpone it or keep it as a secret. He refused, as did the king of England, your good brother," Troyes wrote to Francis.[25] The reason given was that the legitimacy of the child she was bearing could not be contested. Anne was also determined to not risk the future of her child.

★

Chapuys continued to report his ill treatment, complaining that he had to wait six days for an audience and that he refused the proffered dinner invitation "under these circumstances." Once received at court, he was told by the Duke of Norfolk, Sir Thomas Boleyn, and other privy councillors that he "ought not to interfere with the jurisdiction of the archbishop of Canterbury."

Chapuys was left feeling powerless, though he continued to

express his unwavering support to Catherine of Aragon at any opportunity. Furthermore, he grumbled at the favored treatment of the French ambassador, the Bailiff of Troyes, who was always summoned to court and who could often be found by Anne's side or discussing matters with Henry himself. It seemed that no man could have come between the two kings, as Francis had previously said himself.

On Whitsunday, June 1, 1533—after arriving at the Tower of London two days before to prepare for the greatest event of her life—Anne got ready to make her way to Westminster Abbey to be crowned queen of England.

At around 9:30 a.m., Anne entered the abbey, wearing magnificent "coronation robes of purple velvet, furred with ermine, with the gold coronet on her head which she had worn the day before." She was flanked by the Bishop of London and the Bishop of Winchester.

Then, in front of all the assembled nobles, lords and ladies of the realm, Thomas Cranmer, Archbishop of Canterbury, presented Anne with St. Edward's Crown. The heavy crown only rested on her head briefly before being replaced by a more appropriate, lighter crown for the rest of the coronation. She was officially anointed. In being crowned, she had accomplished the virtually impossible: the daughter of a courtier had eclipsed a foreign royal princess and replaced her as queen consort.

After the ceremony, an exquisite banquet was organized in Westminster Hall, in which a long marble table was set up for the feast. Henry sat on a marble chair "mounted on the dais twelve steps up, under a cloth of estate," overseeing the dinner without being seen, and in the company of the French and Venetian ambassadors. Cranmer accompanied Anne while the other tables were occupied by the nobles according to their rank. The next day, in the usual tradition, a tournament took place to celebrate the new queen.

Some accounts of the coronation were unfavorable to Anne,

claiming that no one in London kneeled, nor did they cry, "God save the King, God save the Queen!" Even worse, some reported that "the crown became her very ill, and a wart disfigured her very much. [...] The French ambassador and his suite were insulted by the people."[26] It was clear, then, that the dissent had not been entirely dispelled.

Despite these adverse reactions, Anne—who was by now six months pregnant—maintained her composure.

For the coronation, Francis I ensured that Anne received a wedding gift from him: "a most beautiful and costly litter" with three mules.[27] It was clear that, whatever he might have felt about the tensions with Rome, he continued to support the new royal couple's cause. And Anne was also buoyed by her supporters, of whom there were many. Indeed, despite the dissent in some quarters, the coronation was happily received in others:

> The great lords of the country who were appointed to be there gave, by their very presence, honor and reverence to the princess, and they couldn't do more for her if she had been of royal parentage. [...] For English hearts never ceased to honor the new princess: not that it pleased them to do so, I think; but in order to conform to the will of the king. [...] He would distract her from any troubling thought, or would appease her if she were offended, and he endeavored solely to satisfy her in all things.[28]

With Anne having finally obtained her greatest desire, it was now time for Henry to obtain his: a male heir.

★

Anne's pregnancy now entered its third trimester, and reports claimed that Anne had some difficulties during these last months. Henry made the decision to retire with her to Windsor, where she could rest awaiting their heir's arrival. She was then expected to "take to her chamber," which meant that she would be isolated with female practitioners and helpers for a month or longer before giving birth.[29] It was a tense time for the couple, and elsewhere there were other tensions.

The Duke of Norfolk had been dispatched to France to convince Francis I to further defend the English couple's decision to the Pope, whom he was either to meet in mid-July 1533—or to refuse the meeting altogether. Francis knew that this was something he could no longer afford to do, as he was negotiating a union between his second son, Henry, and the Pope's niece, Catherine de Medici. This meeting was now paramount to secure his own relations with Clement VII and he would not risk it for Henry.

While the duke was in France, he seemed to keep missing Francis, who had made his way to Nice. He was at first received by the king's sister, Marguerite, the Queen of Navarre, in Paris. She now showed much interest in securing an alliance between France and England against the Habsburgs, and even the Pope, whom she distrusted. The truth was, by now Marguerite was promoting the evangelical reformed thoughts and religious ideas in France and abroad—despite her brother's objection. In June 1533, she wrote a letter to Troyes, the ambassador in England, which enclosed a friendly message to Anne. Perhaps her former disciple could help Marguerite achieve the great anti-Catholic alliance she was now seeking?

The Duke of Norfolk was also entertained by former French ambassadors, including Jean du Bellay and Charles de Solier, Count of Morette, and in Lyon, he was received with splendor. It was then that he heard the news everyone in England had been dreading: on July 11, 1533, Pope Clement VII annulled Henry and Anne's union and declared their children illegitimate. Jean du Bellay recalled Norfolk almost "fainting" at the news.[30]

Pope Clement VII felt duped, betrayed by the usurpation of his authority, which had instead been bestowed on Cranmer. The

French cardinals of Tournon and Gramont no longer wished to advance Henry's interests and instead now sided with the Pope. Francis, despite his promises, was now left with very little leverage. He had claimed that no man could come between him and Henry: he perhaps could not have predicted that it would be a woman who would create such great upheaval all around Europe.

That August, Anne may have been confined to her chamber to prepare for the birth of her child, but it felt as if the world still had its eyes on her. Henry had done the seemingly impossible in order to have her as his wife and queen—he had wronged the most powerful man in Europe, the Holy Roman Emperor. He had wronged his former wife and his eldest daughter. And now he had fatally undermined his relationship with Pope Clement VII.

All of this could be worth it, for a son. Anne's future depended on it.

She may have been "the most happy" woman at Henry's court, a motto that she seemed to have recently adopted, but there was always a chance she could lose it all.

PART 3

The Pitfalls of Glory

1533–1536

9

A Tudor Rose Cannot Replace a Lion Cub

By the end of summer 1533, Henry was in good spirits; he had consulted "physicians and astrologers" and all their reports suggested that Anne "would bear a son."[1]

Jean de Dinteville, Bailiff of Troyes, also reported that Henry had even made a decision regarding the name of the future prince—it would be "Edward or Henry."[2] The English king's excitement was obvious to all who saw him. And then the day he had waited for finally arrived.

On September 7, 1533, at around three or four in the afternoon, Anne Boleyn gave birth to a child. Midwives and doctors rushed to be in attendance of what they believed to be the arrival of the new prince of Wales, and everyone at court celebrated the news of a healthy heir. However, when it became clear that the child was in fact a princess, the disappointment was palpable. This is perhaps more true for Henry than for Anne, who was devoted to her daughter, Elizabeth, right from the moment of birth. As there is no evidence to the contrary, it is believed that this was Anne's first pregnancy as well as her first child, and she doted on her baby as any new mother would. Elizabeth seemed to have a strong constitution, and Anne was adamant that a healthy baby girl meant that healthy sons would follow.

Henry, on the other hand, could not hide his sorrow. After all, this was not just a personal disappointment but also a real political blow; he had burned bridges with the Pope for this child and had therefore been left with very little support from Continental Europe, which mostly now saw England as a land of heretics. If they'd had a boy, perhaps those who hadn't supported the couple might have changed their minds, and seen the expediency of the marriage finally realized, but now that they had another princess, this scenario was unlikely.

For Henry, it was a humiliation, especially with his enemies rejoicing at the news. All of these efforts, and still no male heir.

Francis I was also frustrated at the news, knowing it did not do much to ease the tensions. Nevertheless, the French king was touched by "the good words and tokens of friendship the queen my good sister has shared" with Jean of Dinteville, Bailiff of Troyes.[3] He continuously and respectfully called "the queen, my good sister," and spoke of his contentment at her safe and good delivery—albeit of a girl.[4] Prior to the delivery, Francis had also sent her a ring to celebrate the birth of her first child.

But it had not been the joyful moment Anne had hoped for.

★

Three days after her birth, on Wednesday, September 10, 1533, baby Elizabeth was christened at the Church of Observant Friars, which had also been the setting of her father's christening. On the large octagonal stage inside the church was a great silver font. It had hanging over it "a crimson satin canopy fringed with gold, and around it was a rail covered with red say." The citizens of London were invited to witness the ceremony, as well as the usual "gentlemen, squires, chaplains, the aldermen, the mayor alone, the King's council, his chapel, in copes; barons, bishops, earls."[5] Elizabeth was christened by the Bishop of London, and Thomas Cranmer, Archbishop of Canterbury, was named her godfather. Plunged into the waters of the font three times, Elizabeth was made a "Princess of the Realm." She was named after her grandmothers on both sides—Elizabeth of York and Elizabeth Boleyn—as a reminder of her bloodline.

Chapuys reported that Anne's critics were glad to hear of the birth of a princess rather than a prince. As he stated, they "mock those who put faith in such divinations, and to see them so full of shame." He also, however, wrongly reported that Anne's daughter was to be called "Mary" after Henry's first daughter. Sometimes his informants made mistakes, which was partly due to the fact that Chapuys himself was far from being favored at the English court—particularly by the king and the newly crowned queen.

At this time, the imperial ambassador was desperately seeking new alliances at court—and he would find one in an unexpected place. Earlier in the summer of 1533, Chapuys had sought the company and advice of Thomas Cromwell, whose power had been steadily increasing over the last few years. Cromwell offered Chapuys a horse, which he promised to be "one of the finest in England," so that he could hunt with him. Quite troubled by this sign of favor, Chapuys refused the horse but accepted the invitation to go hunting. There, they discussed the imperial ambassador's worries about Henry's behavior toward Catherine and Charles of Spain. Cromwell listened patiently.

"I would like you to remember, Master Cromwell, that the late Cardinal [Wolsey] was incredibly successful when he was taking the side of the emperor, but after he turned away, all went wrong with him," Chapuys pointed out.

"Thank you for the advice," Cromwell replied, cautious with his words. "All to be true, it should not be my fault if everything did not go right," he said.

Prudence was Cromwell's motto for the year 1533; Chapuys reported to Charles that, in all, he thought that the English secretary was "a clever man who understands affairs and is reasonable."[6] He played his cards close to his chest.

Around six weeks later—in late September 1533, after the birth of Princess Elizabeth—Cromwell asked for another private audience with Chapuys in order to discuss Henry's situation. The imperial ambassador suggested that Henry recognize his error in marrying Anne, annul the union, and return to his lawful wife, Catherine, "who has shown great patience" in the midst of this frustrating situation. He continued by assuring Cromwell that it would not be seen as "inconstancy," as there were several princes before Henry who had "by force of justice" been "compelled to return to their lawful wives and give up others as adulterers."

Cromwell himself was seeking a rapprochement with the house of Austria, mostly to minimize the dangers of a potential invasion, and this may have guided his response.

"Thank you for the affection and good words you have toward my master [Henry VIII] and I praise your suggestions and motives," he humbly replied before alluding to the Pope's declaration of the marriage as illegitimate—including any descendants from Henry and Anne. "It is not regarded as of great importance, for as the king found by the opinion of several doctors of this realm and of the University of Orléans, it was unjust and invalid, and the king and every one of them expect it to be revoked."

Cromwell ended the conversation by revealing that his judgment on the matter had much to do with the strength of Henry's feelings for Anne: "The king's love is too vehement."[7] Perhaps if his feelings changed, things would be different.

The rapprochement between the emperor and the English king would, then, have to wait a little longer—but the discussion itself was an interesting sign that she was not infallible, and that Anne's enemies were once more colluding against her. Among these men, which would soon include Cromwell himself, were John Fisher, Bishop of Rochester, and Reginald Pole—who had a claim to the throne through his mother, Margaret Pole, Countess of Salisbury, a descendant of the Plantagenet line through her father. Chapuys and Reginald Pole discussed the possibility of

Pole marrying Princess Mary and claiming the throne for themselves—restoring the authority of the Pope over England. She may have thought that a child would bring her security, but now, Anne was vulnerable. She would need her allies.

*

For Francis I, the situation had worsened. His steadfast support of Henry VIII and Anne had created tensions between him and Clement VII. But now his mind turned to other things, chiefly the importance of a marriage between Catherine de Medici, the Pope's niece, and his second son, Henry; the papal visit and the wedding were to take place in Marseille later in the year. Henry VIII talked Francis into demanding that the papal bull of the summer be revoked—which Francis did, several times, with the help of his ambassadors at Rome.

Francis was conflicted. On the one hand, he needed Henry's alliance in order to achieve his designs on the Low Countries. On the other, however, he could not afford to be on bad terms with the Pope, whose friendship he would need if he ever pursued his claims on some of the Italian territories, particularly with the marriage to Catherine in sight. Having felt compassion for Henry's desire for a male heir, however, Francis shared his disappointment in the birth of Elizabeth. He had also staked his support on the birth of a son.

Francis no longer had any interest in defending Henry's schism, which was naturally problematic for Anne, who depended on it. For now, however, Anne still had the love of Henry, and—to some extent—a little remaining goodwill from Francis. Anne continued to show favor to the French ambassador, Jean of Dinteville, Bailiff of Troyes, inviting him for dinner and ensuring that he was better treated than any other ambassadors at Henry's court. This displeased others, who felt snubbed.

In early October 1533, Francis promised again that he would

vouch for the couple to the Pope, asking for the sentence against them to be revoked.

"I will do all that I see necessary for the resolution of my good brother's affair," Francis promised.[8]

On October 11, Clement VII landed in the south of France, not far from Marseilles. The next day, he made his solemn entry into the city and was received by Francis, along with the rest of the government and much of the royal family.

The Pope's niece—the young orphan of Florence, Catherine de Medici—was accompanying him so that she could be betrothed to Francis's son, Henry, Duke of Orléans, and the reception for Francis's guests was phenomenal. Musicians and other performing artists were out in force for the occasion, and the Marseille crowd was cheering, delighted to receive His Holiness and his niece.

While the focus was on the union of Henry and Catherine, Francis and Clement had to undertake some difficult discussions—not only regarding the prosperity and protection of the Christendom against the infidels, but also Henry's marriage to Anne Boleyn. The diplomatic talks began on October 16, and—as promised to Henry and Anne—Francis asked for the revocation of the papal bull declaring their union and children illegitimate.

"This cannot be done as the acts of the cause are in Rome and, without them, my hands are tied," the Pope amicably replied. "Furthermore, I have no intention of changing my mind on their union and my good son's [Henry's] behavior regarding his desire for a divorce from his lawful wife, Catherine of Aragon, and his foolishness when he moved in with his concubine and declared his relationship with her legitimate and lawful."[9]

Francis remained quiet; he was unwilling to upset his guest or compromise his own rapport with the Pope, which he desperately needed in order to counterbalance any threat from Charles's power in Italy.

Stephen Gardiner, Bishop of Winchester—who had been sent by Henry to attend the meeting between the French king and the

Pope—was greatly displeased to hear of this conversation. He informed Viscount Lisle, Henry's uncle and Lord Deputy of Calais, that Henry would be disappointed in "his good brother's lack of support."[10]

Three days later, the conversation continued in the lodging of Cardinal Antoine Duprat, as the Chancellor of France, Clement VII, Gardiner and the *papal* ambassador Giacomo Simonetta sought a solution.

"Your Holiness, you have annulled the marriage between the king of England and Anne, but Anne has never been cited to answer the charge against her; and whatever might be the faults of Henry, she should not be punished for them," the cardinal said.

"She was aware that the pope threatened to excommunicate any woman who should contract marriage *lite pendent* with Henry," interrupted Simonetta. "Her marriage has been annulled because it was contrary to the papal inhibition, and she has no cause of complaint."[11]

Duprat's point was a valid one; imperial cardinals and ambassadors had discussed at length the fact that Anne was never cited. It was indeed against the lawful proceedings.

However, this was not enough to make Clement change his opinion.

Ultimately, a compromise was found. It was proposed that Henry's cause would be heard in Avignon by legates who had never before been involved in the matter. The condition for such a hearing was that Henry would have to fully recognize the Pope's authority, and promise to agree to the final judgment made by the new council of legates. Gardiner was asked to accept on behalf of the king, who had declared he had the power to do so.

Feeling uncomfortable at this turn of events, he muttered: "I have not spoken the truth and I cannot bind my master, the king of England, to such conditions."

Francis was enraged after such painstaking work had been done to find the compromise. "I have been fooled by all the promises made by my good brother. If you, bishop of Winchester, representative of the king of England, cannot negotiate on his behalf, what are the reasons for your appointment and presence?"[12]

Feeling insulted, Gardiner left, also indignant, while Francis went to the Pope to deliver the bad news that they remained in a deadlock.

At the end of October, Francis made one last attempt to resolve the issue. This time, he sent Guillaume du Bellay to talk to Gardiner about sending a special envoy to England in order to obtain Henry's blessing to proceed with the new council.

Unfortunately, Henry had read Gardiner's previous letter declaring that the negotiations had not been conclusive, and he felt betrayed. In fact, Chapuys reported that, at the news, the king's face "changed color, and he crushed up one of the letters in his hand for spite, saying that he was betrayed and that neither the French king nor he was such as he thought; and of the Pope he said a thousand ill things."[13]

In an audience he eventually gave to Troyes, the French ambassador, Henry did not hide his anger and disappointment: "I am very disappointed in the king, my good brother, your master [Francis]. The marriage between his son, the duke of Orléans and the Pope's niece, should not have taken place, as he promised to use it as leverage to fight for my cause, which he did not in the end," Henry said.

"I am sure that whatever my master did with the Pope does not diminish his affection toward you," the French ambassador replied, politely but firmly. "He had long promised the Pope the resolution of this marriage and surely you would not want him to break his word. You are also aware of the importance of having an alliance in Italy." Henry was annoyed, and Troyes promised him that his concerns "are taken seriously and that I take the matter very much to heart and I am confident that Francis's closer alliance with the Pope would eventually be beneficial for England."[14]

This rift between the two kings was the perfect opportunity for Cromwell to assert himself; he convinced Henry VIII to turn down Francis's offer. Now, the Anglo-French alliance was in jeopardy once more. Anne—who naturally had little interest in having the case of the divorce reopened—this time supported Cromwell's tactic and went against the desires of the French. It was a very risky strategy.

Henry was avoiding the situation, refusing an audience with the French ambassador. More alarmingly for the French, however, Anne was also dismissive and now seemed less pleased to receive Troyes. They had taken her support for granted, and she would not always follow them blindly. This time, her views did not align with the French agenda—something the French would not forget.

As Troyes was desperately trying to obtain his audience with the king, he ambushed Anne's uncle, the Duke of Norfolk, after mass, sharing his discontent: "If the king, your master [Henry] is a true ally to the king, my master [Francis], he would want him to be a good friend of the Pope, as the greater the alliance with the Pope, the better it is for England's affairs."[15]

His appeal, however, did not resolve a thing. Instead, Henry sent another representative of England to Marseille: Edmund Bonner.

The English envoy was not well received by Francis, who claimed that "your king thinks of himself a wise man but he is simply a fool." He certainly made his opinions clear. "Let him know that if, in consequence of his behavior, he is excommunicated, I have declared and declare that I shall not assist him against the pope."[16]

The outrage did not stop there. The Pope was furious with Henry and his ambassadors' disrespect toward him. He kept being ambushed by the English, who did not observe proper protocol, which was utterly unacceptable to him.

Clement warned Francis: "Being your guest, I allow people to enter without insisting on all the formalities conducted when in

Rome. These men are taking advantage of this and come in without asking the permission of anybody and have just done what, in Rome, would entail capital punishment." The Pope paused. "I have done all I could for the sake of the alliance with the king of England, but he has acted in a very poor manner. You have to forsake this alliance with him and unite with the Holy See against him."[17]

Francis had never yet been put in such a difficult situation. An alliance with England was still desirable for his land in Flanders and for good commerce in northern Europe, yet it was true that Henry's behavior was a step too far—even for Francis with his goodwill toward Anne.

Francis, who was endeavoring to find another compromise, promised: "I will no longer support his cause, as I am displeased as you are with him. However, if the king of England becomes desperate, he might throw himself into the arms of people whose alliance would be hurtful, not only to you and myself, but to the whole of Christendom."

The Pope did not seem impressed, responding: "He told me that if things came to the worst, he might take back his wife and keep the other as a mistress, and make an alliance with the emperor to jointly make a war upon the French."[18]

Francis took this threat seriously.

Clement, on the other hand, did not. He insisted that Francis's support of Henry had to stop. However, although Francis had been annoyed with the English special envoy's arrogance and with Henry VIII's own insolence, he was not ready to turn his back on an Anglo-French alliance entirely. He suggested that, in order for him to make the decision, he would need the return of Calais.

The loss of Francis's support would have considerable repercussions for Anne, who was about to learn the hard way that the French king's friendship was always flimsy and unpredictable.

The interests of his country would always come first—regardless of his promises and the seeming affection that he had displayed to her in the past.

While the Pope was receptive to such a proposition, Duprat and Montmorency disclosed their own impatience with Henry's erratic behavior. Little support for the English could be found at the French court. However, the Count of Cifuentes—the imperial ambassador sent to Rome, who was accompanying the Pope to Marseille—was adamant. Calais was in safer hands with the English than it was with the French.

Edmund Bonner, a clergyman, was sent by Henry VIII to Marseille in another attempt to reverse the decision made by the Pope. Bonner remembered being well received by Clement VII as he was called "to a window, where, after reverence, I showed him I was commanded to intimate your appeal." The Pope blamed the current situation entirely on Henry, claiming that the English king's decisions had left him with no other choice but to make papal bulls against his new union.

"I cannot ignore the queen's [Catherine's] appeals," the Pope insisted.

Bonner felt powerless and could not help but notice the new alliance between Clement and Francis I—an entente that he made sure to report back to Henry. The friendship between the two seemed stronger than ever: "Laughing merrily, they talked for three-quarters of an hour," and spent a great deal of their time in each other's company.[19]

This was not considered a good thing for English affairs.

Bonner persisted nevertheless and asked for another audience with the Pope, explaining that another council was required to discuss Henry's great matter. This drew the retort that "Henry has no authority to call a General Council."[20]

For the French, the situation was also far from ideal. Jean du Bellay insisted that, despite the fact "it is very hard to bear, to do all one can for a friend, and get neither liking nor thanks, but, on the contrary, disgust and suspicion," he was of the opinion that Francis "must try to reconcile the king [Henry] with the Pope and the Apostolic See, offering to make a defensive league between the three."[21]

After all, all parties needed to be reminded that their true enemy was Charles V and his empire, not Anne Boleyn and her faction at the English court.

Nevertheless, Henry—who was left with no clear possible reconciliation with the Pope—couldn't help but feel betrayed by his good brother, the King of France.

★

In England, the situation had worsened. Henry was furious at what he perceived as Francis I's disloyalty. He had forbidden all printers to report on the Pope's entry to Marseille "and the obedience shown him by the king of France," as this was against all the treaties and agreements settled between the two realms.

Furthermore, Henry had several other worrying matters to deal with. Whether or not he was superstitious (he had, after all, consulted an astrologer about the sex of his second child), Henry could not afford to ignore Elizabeth Barton—who was known as "The Nun of Kent," "The Holy Maid of Kent" and later "The Mad Maid of Kent." She claimed to have had divine revelations and prophesied that "in a short time this king would not only lose his kingdom, but that he should be damned, and that she had seen the place and seat prepared for him in Hell." Henry had her imprisoned and, later on, in 1534, she was executed. Her supporters claimed that she was "a good, simple, and saintly woman," but for Henry, this was the worst kind of rumor-mongering popular political agitation.[22] Already paranoid, he would not stand for this.

Barton's prophecies had reached as far as the court of London, and it was hardly surprising that Catherine of Aragon's friends welcomed them. Indeed, Gertrude Courtenay, Marchioness of Exeter, helped spread Barton's revelations. In late November, however, the marchioness was forced to apologize profusely to the king, and beg for mercy "concerning my abuse, lightness, and indiscreet offenses committed in frequenting the conversation and company of that most unworthy, subtle, and deceivable woman called the Holy Maid of Kent, and in giving too much credence to the malicious and detestable proceedings of her and her adherents." Gertrude reminded the king, "I am a woman, whose fragility and brittleness is easily seduced and brought to abusion and light belief." She promised that "I have never acted from any male opinion, malice, or grudge against the King, the Queen, or their prosperity."[23]

Although it was commonly known that the marchioness was an adherent of Catherine and Princess Mary, her willingness to repent prevented any serious punishment from the king this time. Nevertheless, the internal coherence of the Tudor court was becoming fractured, and perhaps neither Henry nor Anne could have predicted quite how far-reaching the consequences of their marriage would be.

Henry's anger and impatience with the French had only intensified. In mid-November, the new French ambassador, Louis de Perreau, Sieur de Castillon, had landed in England to replace Jean of Dinteville, Bailiff of Troyes. For his part, Troyes could not have welcomed this replacement more. His last audience with Henry had been a series of recriminations that Troyes did not believe were fair.

"The king, my good brother [Francis], lied to me and promised that he would not marry his son, the duke of Orléans, to the Pope's niece unless the Pope changed his policy toward me," Henry had barked at Troyes, who, less than impressed by the king's behavior, had complained profusely to the Duke of Norfolk, who agreed that this was indeed inappropriate.[24]

"I would rather be the poorest gentleman in France than have to relate such conversations to the king of France," Troyes admitted.[25]

The Boleyn faction, it seemed, was starting to shed its natural allies—and yet no rapprochement was possible with the Habsburgs, leaving them in a difficult position when it came to political games and pursuits.

Troyes was vexed, and several councillors—including Thomas Boleyn and Norfolk—tried to appease him. It is believed that Anne was also frustrated by the situation. Troyes's trust was not to be regained and, upon his return to France, he wrote a damning report to be read by everyone at the French court. He could not continue to bear the insults he had suffered at the hands of Henry and the message was clear: Henry could no longer be trusted as an ally to the French. Worse, the devout Catholic ambassador was certain that Henry "would completely and irrevocably remove himself and his country from the authority of the Pope [...] which is setting a bad example for any other princes."[26]

Jean du Bellay convinced Francis to send him as a special envoy to the English court before the relationship broke down entirely. He believed he could find a remedy to the situation, and that he could convince Henry—probably through Anne—to remain an ally of France, under the Pope's authority.

Du Bellay arrived in London on December 17, 1533, and, as predicted, found a furious Henry who had publicly rejected papal supremacy and was now making preparations for the schism. Du Bellay was granted an audience with the king, during which Henry demonstrated his hot temper and continued to reprimand Francis's actions. "All Christian princes think that the friendship between myself and Francis is not sincere as it was at the beginning. My honor is injured and the promises made by your master are broken," Henry declared.[27]

"Such complaints against my master, the king of France, are utterly unacceptable," du Bellay replied.[28] He then carefully continued with the audience, reminding Henry that conflict was in no one's best interests.

Henry could at least agree on this point, and a grudging compromise was found. "I agree to not separate from Rome if, within nine weeks, without further proceedings and before Easter-day, the Pope would issue a statement that annuls his sentence of the 11th of July, declaring that my marriage to Catherine of Aragon is null and void and that my marriage to Anne Boleyn is valid and legitimate."[29]

Alarmed but not panicked, though this was not the outcome Jean du Bellay or the French had hoped for, it was at least better than a declaration of war. He knew that his best ally at court was still Anne, and he believed he could obtain her support in his enterprise, but the situation was most delicate.

And du Bellay was also facing personal problems back in France. His brother René reported that his enemies at the French court were using his absence to link him and his brothers to Lutherans and evangelical thinkers—in other words, heretics. René warned Jean that "rumors were spreading at court that he [Jean] had been supporting Lutheran preachers" and that Francis had also heard the reports. This was highly problematic, as although Jean du Bellay was interested in reformed ideas—he was, after all, one of Marguerite of Navarre's protégés—his bishopric and status were founded on his Catholic faith. The little influence and power he had left remained intertwined with Catholicism. René revealed that, in order to defend his brother's name and honor, he had taken the blame "as I would rather have my ruin than yours."[30] Ultimately, René was forced to renounce his own bishopric because of the allegations made against his brother.

Jean du Bellay was incredibly grateful for his brother's sacrifice, but he also understood that he had now been left in a precarious position, where his support of the English king and queen was costing him and his brothers dearly. For now, however, he had to concentrate on what he'd been instructed to focus on:

he had been entrusted with important diplomatic missions by Francis I, and he needed to come to terms with those. Although he spent his time at the Tudor court to fulfill his obligations, he was also conscious of the need to not stay in England a moment too long. Yet this did not deprive him of one of his favorite pastimes, which was to enrage his imperial counterpart. For instance, in a discussion with Chapuys, du Bellay insisted on "the great affection that exists between my master and the king here," infuriating the imperial ambassador.

"It is a great necessity to have union among princes, and my master, the emperor, has always been a true friend to the king here, that sick men often hate their physicians because they prescribe bitter things to them, but when they are convalescent esteem them more highly than those who, contrary to the order of the physicians, would give them wine, fruit, and other objectional things," Chapuys responded.

The French ambassador ignored the insult. Instead, he decided to show off about having just met Queen Anne, as he had letters that "the king, his master, has written her and she received me so well that she even kissed me."

There was nothing like the mention of "Anne" to enrage Chapuys. He would still not recognize her title nor position. Du Bellay was still seen by Anne and remained at Greenwich with her until his departure on December 29, despite the tensions. Anne remained keen to keep the French on good terms, even if it was proving more difficult.

The strain between Henry and the French representatives certainly remained. In a private audience with Castillon, the resident ambassador at the English court, Henry boldly declared that he recognized the Pope "as bishop of Rome, or as Pope, as he wished to be named; not that the Pope has any superiority over him or his subjects."[31]

The forthcoming negotiations were clearly set to fail, but that didn't stop du Bellay and other partisans of the Boleyn faction endeavoring to try to hold things together. In the months to come, Rome and the Pope's authority would be undermined—at every possible opportunity.

In late 1533, Cranmer made a speech in favor of the convocation of a "General Council." Here he claimed that "the court of Rome, like rich men flying from an enemy, has destroyed many ancient writings and hid the rest so that it is difficult to discover the truth about all things."[32] The aim of this council was to restore clarity and significance to English laws.

Henry's own aims were simple. If his marriage to Anne was not finally acknowledged by the Pope, he would separate from Rome and seek spiritual supremacy in his country.

Anne, now with a daughter to consider, needed her marriage and her daughter's legitimacy to be uncontested. Her own personal religious beliefs were hard to determine. Being interested in reformed ideas, she had obtained books that were censored on the continent, but she was also a woman of more conventional religiosity. She treasured her Book of Hours, which was bound and printed in Paris by Germain Hardouyn in the late 1520s, proving that asserting the exact nature of someone's faith at the beginning of the sixteenth century was a difficult task indeed.[33]

And while this should have been a happy time for her, records cease to record much sign of affection between her and the king, as there had been in previous years. For New Year, as custom dictated, Anne nevertheless offered the king a gift: "a goodly bason [basin in modern English], having a rail or board of gold in the midst of the brim, garnished with rubies and pearls, wherein standeth a fountain, also having a rail of gold about it garnished with diamonds; out thereof issueth water, at the teat of three naked women standing at the foot of the same fountain."[34] But such a gift was a formality, and there were signs that their passion was dwindling. Anne knew that a male heir was the solution to these problems, and the pressure to produce one must have been overwhelming. All she could do was hope for a better future.

10

An Impossible Mission

One must preserve one's authority at all costs.

By January 3, 1534, Chapuys had become alarmed by what he had seen and heard at the English court. Consequently, he warned the Holy Roman Emperor, Charles, of the atrocities that were being committed against the Roman Catholic Church.

"The little pamphlet composed by the Council, which I lately sent to your Majesty, is only a preamble and prologue of others more important, which are now being printed," he stated.

> One is called *Defensor Pacis* [...] Formerly no one dared read it, for fear of being burnt, but now it is translated into English so that all the people may see and understand it. The other is entitled *Concerning Royal and Priestly Authority* and proves that bishops ought to be equal to other priests, except in precedence and in the honor showed them in church, and that kings and princes ought to be sovereign over churchmen, according to the ancient law, which is the point most agreeable to the King.[1]

For Chapuys, there was only one person to blame. The enemy behind all of this, he said, was neither Henry nor Cromwell, but Anne Boleyn. In his eyes, she was the true reason behind the schism with Rome. He utterly despised her and blamed her—for everything, stirring up further ill sentiment. It was clear that the court worried about this, as, in early 1534, parliament passed an act that made it "treason to impugn the King's marriage with Anne Boleyn."[2] For now, Anne remained protected by the court.

However, there were signs of distance between the two lovers. For one thing, Princess Mary—Henry's older daughter—was angering Anne by refusing to give up her title of princess and by refusing to acknowledge her as queen of England, defying Anne's authority and position. This clear lack of respect made Anne irritable, even in the presence of the king.

Anne was of the opinion that the princess "was badly advised and that her answers could not have been made without the suggestion of others."[3] One way or another, she felt that Mary had to comply and obey. On top of all this, rumors were spread by Chapuys, who claimed that Anne was "determined to poison" the princess—further vilifying her.[4] His constant unfounded allegations must have angered Anne more than once, and this unfolded into a narrative at court that she had a bad temper and was far from the docile wife she was expected to be.

The truth was, Anne was and always had been her own free woman.

*

As du Bellay made his way to Rome on an impossible mission, his detractors started colluding against him. In Paris, rumors of his religious nonconformity put his reputation at risk. If it hadn't been for his brother's sacrifice, he would have lost favor with Francis I. Abroad, the du Bellays were equally despised as they were known for being protégés of the Queen of Navarre, sister to the king. This was a protection that was, at times, helpful but, more often than not, quite feeble. By now, the du Bellay brothers had enemies all around Europe. Jean's support of the Boleyn faction, and especially Anne, had made him a particular enemy of the Habsburgs and the Holy Roman Empire.

The imperial ambassador in Rome, the Count of Cifuentes, was poisoning the Pope's ears with lies about him.

"It is outrageous that the bishop of Paris [Jean du Bellay] has congratulated the king of England for leaving the obedience of the Church," the Pope snapped after hearing Cifuentes's report on the matter.[5] With such a revelation, the imperial ambassador was hoping to make du Bellay's mission more complicated than he hoped.

Just before Easter, Henry had given du Bellay nine weeks to resolve the matter—or, he said, he would break with Rome officially. This deadline met one obstacle after another. First, du Bellay became unwell on his way to Rome and had to be carried in a chair—it is thought he may have had some sort of sciatica. He finally arrived in Rome in early 1534.

Charles de Hémard de Denonville, Bishop of Mâcon, was the resident French ambassador in Rome who worked with du Bellay on his delicate mission. They both knew the support Catherine of Aragon received at the Vatican; they were now, undeniably, in enemy territory.

The Duke of Norfolk—Anne's uncle—was pleased that the mission was underway. He believed that if Clement VII would persist "in favoring the Emperor more than the two kings, and through favor or fear, acts unjustly in the king's cause, he will give occasion to his loyal subjects to take every opportunity to impugn the authority he [the Pope] unjustly usurps."[6] For him, the hope of a schism with Rome was high.

However, du Bellay was determined to avoid such a disaster. After all, his brother had just lost his bishopric so he could continue to work as a diplomatic agent of the French crown, and du Bellay felt the pressure not to fail. Here, he had a perfect opportunity to prove to his detractors that—despite his inclination for evangelical ideas—he remained a staunch supporter of the

Roman Catholic Church, and that wanting to reform the Church did not equal wanting to separate from it.

Du Bellay had a plan for continuing negotiations with the Pope: he believed that if Clement agreed to a divorce, Henry would then concede much more than he had ever offered to in the past. A chief aim of this mission, then, was to get the Pope to agree to revoke the papal bull that refused to recognize the union between Henry and Anne, as well as granting Henry a divorce from Catherine. For this, a new council of only two cardinals, both in France—Antoine Duprat and Niccolò Gaddi—had to be approved to judge Henry's case. For Francis, this was the only way to ensure France's influence and guarantee the most suitable result.

A marriage proposal was also being discussed between Clement's nephew—the illegitimate son of Lorenzo II of Medici, half-brother to Catherine de Medici and Alessandro de Medici, Duke of Florence—and King Henry's daughter, Princess Mary. She would have to renounce her rights to the English throne and, in exchange, she would be given a dowry. The plan would have highly benefited the French as they would have isolated Charles V of Spain and his influence over the Pope while maintaining an even stronger alliance with England. And this would also be good news for Anne, who would be rid of the princess.

Jean du Bellay and Hémard tried to obtain a secret audience with the Pope, but they were denied it.

"We will continue to try," they promised in their dispatches.[7]

They were, however, granted public audiences, but these often featured agents of Charles V, making it impossible to make their case. Du Bellay, considering the best solution, decided to frighten the Pope: a separation of England from Rome would mean an even further spread of heresy over all Christendom.

"The situation is dire," warned the French special envoy. "If you do not find a way to settle the king of England's case, his country will be lost, but not only it: other lands will be lost to the church."[8]

"I have not found a way to settle it," said the Pope.⁹

Du Bellay paused before replying, "Rome might no longer be safe."¹⁰

Instilling fear was one way of putting more pressure on Clement VII, but would it be enough, given the circumstances?

★

Cifuentes sent Dr. Ortiz, an imperial agent in Rome at the time, to learn more about England's situation and the true purposes of du Bellay's mission. Upon his arrival at the house of Hémard, tensions rose almost immediately.

"How is the queen of England's health?" Ortiz inquired, referring to rumors that Catherine of Aragon had been unwell for quite some time.

"Which queen?" du Bellay replied.

"You know well that I am asking after the true queen," Ortiz barked.

"Anne is the queen of England and she is well and triumphant," said du Bellay.

The atmosphere was brittle, and du Bellay eventually revealed that Catherine had indeed been unwell, trying to make Ortiz believe the illness had been worse than it actually was so that he might highlight Anne's superiority. The conversation then moved on to the situation that was preoccupying their minds the most: Henry's potential break with Rome.

"Cranmer is to blame for what is happening in England," Ortiz said.

"He is considered a saint in the country and the Flemish have been the cause of the disregard of the censures in England, for they had pulled them down from the doors where they were fixed and trampled them in the mud, to the great joy of the English."¹¹ Du Bellay was now teasing his imperial counterpart—trying to get a rise out of him.

The meeting was abruptly cut short.

Du Bellay was proud that he had stood up to an imperial agent. It was also his hope that his words would be reported to Charles V, so he would know that France was still a great ally to England—and his wish soon became a reality. Ortiz reported every single word of their conversation, which had been such an insult to his master.

Du Bellay's mission seemed compromised, as Ortiz was clearly no ally, but he was determined to make it a success as he desperately tried to obtain an extension from Henry through Castillon.

The French ambassador in England received his letter at the beginning of March 1534. He was fortunate, as things had progressed slowly but surely. The House of Lords had been summoned on January 31, 1534, at which point they were invited to accept a treaty with France—with the promise that the Holy Roman Emperor would not invade England—as well as passing a bill that revoked the king's marriage to Catherine of Aragon.

Ten days later, it was proposed that Catherine be officially made "Princess Dowager of Wales." Several voices loudly contested this new bill, including Henry's close friend and former chancellor, Sir Thomas More, who saw it as heresy. At the end of February, the Boleyn faction still persisted with trying to pass the bill, but the opposition they faced was even louder now. The fear was that Spain would retaliate and that commerce with Spanish Flanders would grind to a halt, causing an economic crisis that England could simply not afford.

Anne's patience was running thin; Chapuys recalled that "if the lady wants something, no one dares upsetting her, not even the king."[12] She was counting on du Bellay for a positive resolution, but the truth was that her enemies were becoming more powerful, and while her allies may have felt affection for her, their best interests no longer matched.

Anne's letters were destroyed after her death, so her distress cannot be fully assessed but one can assume that this situation must have caused her great anxiety. But, maintaining her composure, she would not give her enemies the satisfaction of showing it publicly.

On March 4, Castillon was received in a private audience with Henry, where he explained the situation in Rome and asked for a delay, as well as the dispatch of a special envoy with increased decision-making powers who would help progress the matter with greater authority, from England to Rome. Henry received him well but did not give a clear answer.

"I wish to consult my council first," the king said.

The next day, Castillon was summoned to discuss the situation with Henry's council. They were not receptive to the Frenchman's promises and instead advised Henry that it was a waste of time to give the French any more time in their endeavors.

"The king seemed colder to me than he was in private," Castillon reported to Montmorency.[13]

The French ambassador was not, however, going to give up so easily.

"I beg you to listen to me. Convince the Pope to revoke his papal bull so the marriage to Queen Anne is recognized by all. The way to do so is to maintain the peace and amity with him, and to convince him to declare the first union to be invalid." He paused. "This is the only one to ensure the queen's safety as well as her children's legitimacy. Furthermore, by seeking an alliance with the Pope, the Holy Roman Emperor will be weakened, which will greatly benefit England. The king of France, my master, has been but only a great supporter of your Majesty and has worked relentlessly to ensure a good resolution of your matter. More time is, however, needed."

Castillon tried his best, but the councillors did not seem to agree that France knew the best way forward and, instead, felt that Henry should break with Rome and take charge of his own laws. For France, and particularly Francis, a separation from

Rome was unimaginable and would certainly put an end to their support of the English cause—and of Anne herself.

Henry must have felt obliged to give more reassurance to Castillon, so he took him to a garden to have a heartfelt conversation in private. During their talk, he promised: "I will make no haste to have anything published against the authority of the Holy See and I will wait to hear from the agents in Rome. However, the money that used to go to Rome will no longer do so."[14]

This was good enough for Castillon, at least for now. The French had not been granted an extension, but at least Henry was not pushing for an official rupture, which they wanted to avoid at all costs. Or at least, he wasn't yet.

*

In Rome, du Bellay continued putting his plan into action. He continued to be received by Clement VII, but it seemed that he had underestimated not only the Pope's will, and the egotism of his papal authority, but also how frightened Clement was of Charles V. He clearly feared the consequences for Rome if he did not side with him. For du Bellay, it was becoming clear: the only real obstacle to Henry's wish was Charles, as the Pope surely had no other reason not to grant Henry's request for a divorce and remarriage now that the situation had progressed this far.

"I am not too much of a papist, but I do feel bad for seeing him [the Pope] in such a difficult position," du Bellay confessed.[15] His evangelical views were personal, and he was determined to continue his career as a bishop; after his efforts to resolve the greatest European diplomatic matter of the first half of the sixteenth century, he hoped to be made cardinal. And the repercussions of separating from Rome would cause great damage to France's political position in Europe.

"If Henry separated from Rome, the King [Francis] will not be able to remain friends and allies with both the king of England

and the Pope. A decision will have to be made and I fear that, given the situation in Italy, the alliance with Rome will prevail," du Bellay admitted.[16]

Clement had still not received the council of two cardinals in Cambray, nor the marriage proposal between his nephew and Henry's daughter, Mary. Du Bellay was adamant that if Henry agreed to send a special adviser, he would be able to convince the Pope of this new intimate council. The French government, namely Francis and Montmorency, were pleased with du Bellay's handling of the affair.

"The King [Francis] is extremely pleased with you and the negotiations you have undertaken in his name. Do not worry about the Imperialists and continue your efforts," Montmorency wrote to the French ambassador in March 1534.[17]

Unfortunately, the French were counting their chickens before they had hatched. Influenced by his ministers, Henry had no intention of making the negotiations easy for the French. His royal authority would suffice in this matter and, if separation from Rome should occur, he believed his country would be prepared for it.

On March 7, 1534, Chapuys was shocked to hear the news that "the divorce has been pronounced by the Archbishop of Canterbury, and the Queen [Catherine] therefore is deprived of her title, she could neither enjoy the name of queen, nor the good given her on her marriage." He continued,

> Some who have not dared expressly to oppose the Queen's affair as much as they can be proposal against the Pope, considering that the said affair depends upon his authority, but I believe the King will obtain his wishes in the end. There are also many of the party against the Queen who are displeased that the King wishes to renounce his obedience to the Roman Church, as the duke of Norfolk, who said to the French ambassador that neither he nor his friends would consent to it.[18]

Henry's will would not be bent or changed.

This disobedience did not please the French, who felt particularly betrayed by Henry given they had been supporters of his second marriage. Never did they imagine that things would go so far as to create a split between England and the rest of Christendom. They simply could not support it.

In an audience granted in mid-March to Castillon, Henry was less agreeable to the French party in Rome. "I will send an adviser, but will not grant him power to appear in my name," Henry said. "As of your master [Francis I], I will continue the session of parliament until after Easter, which falls on April 5, and will delay publishing my separation from Rome."

"This will make the negotiations impossible, your Majesty," Castillon muttered, completely baffled by Henry's line of thinking.

"If as you and du Bellay keep promising is true, which is that the Pope is in good disposition toward me and my cause, this should not create any difficulty and he should grant me my desired sentence. Then, I will recognize once more the papal jurisdiction," Henry told him.

Castillon tried to change his mind, begging for more time. He was refused.

"I believe it to be just and reasonable," Henry said definitively.[19]

The next day, Castillon—who had received further instructions from Francis I—asked once again for an audience. This time the French ambassador was to ensure that Henry would agree to a marriage between his daughter, Mary, and the Pope's nephew, Alexander of Medici.

"I am afraid that though my daughter has lost her rank, she is still superior to a duke for being the daughter of a king, and as such I will not have her married to a Duke of Florence, which would be beneath her and my dignity," Henry exclaimed.

"But your Majesty, you need to consider that with such an alliance, you would become the Pope's closest ally, which would put the emperor in a difficult position," Castillon retorted.

While Henry seemed receptive to the idea of creating a rift between the Pope and the emperor, he did not reply and instead invited Castillon for dinner, where they would be joined by Queen Anne and several councillors. After these festivities, Castillon was received alone again by the king, who claimed to have had time to think about the proposal.

"While I refuse a marriage proposal between the duke and my daughter, I am happy to provide alternatives such as my nieces: Lady Margaret Douglas or Lady Mary Brandon," the king offered. "However, I fear that these discussions on marriage proposals are only a pretext to delay a conclusion to my matter, and if I do not have real proof of the Pope's willingness to make a swift decision in my favor, I will put my anti-papal measures forward without any further delay."

"I assure you, my lord, that this marriage proposal is not a pretext to delay anything. In fact, it is to ensure the good resolution of your matter," Castillon protested.

"Let the Pope pronounce sentence in my favor and I will admit his authority," Henry said.[20]

It was another stalemate and Anne's fate was caught once more in the middle of political games.

*

In Rome, the situation wasn't much better. Du Bellay realized that the Pope had superior intelligence regarding what was happening in England than he did—making negotiations almost impossible, as he rightly felt his authority was being contested.

By now, du Bellay's patience was running out; he complained openly to Francis I and Montmorency of Henry's behavior: "It would be good if the king of England would moderate his actions. [...] He needs to be reasoned [with]."[21]

During his audiences with the Pope, du Bellay employed all his diplomatic wiles to see the matter through. Finally, he discovered that a consistory of cardinals would be held on March 23 to make a final decision on the matter. Feeling hopeful, the French ambassador saw this as a sign that the Pope would concede at last to the French and the English, and that soon the matter would be resolved once and for all. Du Bellay would be the reason for this union between England, France and Rome. He would obtain a cardinal's hat and ensure his future, as well as his brother's. He was sure of it.

He did think that the proceedings would need more time, but because it had been agreed that they would start before Easter, he believed Henry would surely grant an extension. He felt triumphant, confident that the papal dispensation granted in 1509 for the marriage of Henry VIII to Catherine of Aragon would be dismissed by the cardinals and therefore, with Henry's marriage being annulled, he would have the right to remarry whomever he pleased.

All would be well, and the path to glory was to be secured.

Or, at least, so he thought.

In July 1533, a commission had already declared that the papal dispensation was valid, and du Bellay was unaware that one French cardinal—the Cardinal of Tournon—had, after being pressured by his peers, agreed to it. Francis I and du Bellay had not known about this vote, and they were about to find out that they had been duped. Furthermore, no French cardinal, except Trivultio (Agostino Trivulzio), appeared at the commission, which should have been an immediate concern for du Bellay. The reason was simple: the French cardinals each refused to vote against their conscience and they had decided that they no longer supported the English king, whom they regarded as insolent and arrogant. Henry's behavior in the recent months certainly didn't help that case. Cardinal Trivultio turned up and fought for the English cause, but this was in vain.

Then, on March 23, came the final blow, and the consistory made the decision in only one sitting. This was very rare indeed, and du Bellay would never have expected it. The verdict was clear. They refused to recognize Henry's right to either an annulment or a divorce, and they continued to declare his union to Anne Boleyn invalid—and their child and future children to be illegitimate.

Du Bellay felt humiliated; he did not understand how such a judgment could have prevailed. Determined to leave at once, at the end of March he received packets of letters from Montmorency and Castillon. In that of the former, he found his safe conduct to leave without any further delay. In the other dispatch, Castillon was pleased to report that Henry had granted an extension and had agreed to send an executor who would represent him in Cambray.

This announcement rekindled some hope in du Bellay—who had never worked so hard, probably more so than Anne Boleyn herself, for a happy ending. He believed he could attempt to change the cardinals' minds or at least obtain a delay in the publication of the new papal decision. So, once more du Bellay met with the Count of Cifuentes, the cunning imperial ambassador in Rome.

"I promise that I have not come here to oppose the good right of Catherine nor to act in favor of the king of England," du Bellay confessed.

"Why be here, then?" Cifuentes asked.

"I am here to avoid the risk that the Pope would lose the obedience of England by giving sentence against the king," du Bellay replied. "I have just received a letter from my opposite number in England who promised that Henry would recognize the authority of the Pope if the judgment takes place in Cambray," he assured him.

"These are only tricks to delay the publication of the sentence," the imperial ambassador coldly rebuked. "If, when you were in England, you were unable to obtain any concessions from the king, what makes you think that he would accept a judgment that he has always refused?"

Du Bellay had no convincing answer. Instead, he just muttered, "The Holy Spirit has enlightened the king."

"In that case, the Holy Spirit will move him still further to submit to the sentence." Cifuentes paused. "You know, the Cardinal of Santa Croce predicted at the end of the session that the French would now claim that they have received further powers from England to make more concessions and agree to a compromise. But this is all too little too late."[22]

Du Bellay was crushed.

*

The matter worsened. Henry VIII had lied to the French. He had no intention of sending an executor with representative powers to make decisions on his behalf, and even if he had, it would have had little consequence. Furthermore, Henry betrayed Castillon—and, therefore, he betrayed Francis. He did not wait until after Easter; instead, he prorogued parliament on March 20. The House of Lords passed a bill that not only ratified Henry's marriage to Anne Boleyn but also recognized Elizabeth as the only heir to the English throne.

The authority of the Pope was rejected; he no longer had any jurisdiction in England. It was unprecedented for a major Christian country to break with Rome, not on religious grounds but on a political one, and even more so, on such a personal one.

While this must have been a major relief for Anne, it also came at a great cost to her relationship with France. Her former allies felt cheated. They had supported the new couple for years and had fought hard for their union to be recognized by all of Christendom. They had put all their efforts and all their hearts into a case that would eventually go against their own best interests.

In April, John Wallop—the resident ambassador in France—was granted an audience with Francis I, who had received a letter from Henry, inviting him to join the English king in revolting more, with how he had negotiated the matter, even if the man himself felt the mission had failed. But he had proven to be a loyal agent to the French crown, despite the rumors of his evangelical inclinations. His brother's sacrifice seemed not to have been in vain after all.

The Anglo-French alliance remained uncertain.

Henry, probably with Anne's counsel, sent Anne's brother, George Boleyn, Lord Rochford, to France, accompanied by Sir William Fitzwilliam. The aim was still to convince Francis to abandon his alliance with the Pope, but this was in vain. While they were pleasantly received and entertained, however, Francis made clear that he did not wish to be drawn on the matter of the English. For the Boleyns, including George, the break with Rome was the path for glory for Anne and they continued to support her fully.

"Our master [Henry VIII] expects you to revoke your alliance with the bishop of Rome [the Pope] given the insult he has caused our king," the ambassadors claimed.

"I have no alliance with the Pope," Francis replied. "However, while I do not blame your master's decision, I do not see why France should follow the same path. I have no objection for another meeting with my good brother, but I would also like to know what about Charles V? Now that the sentence has been given, anyone who supports Henry is threatened to be excommunicated themselves. I, therefore, do not see how I can continue to do so."[25]

These were not encouraging words. The only positive outcome was that Francis agreed to a meeting with Henry in person—probably over the following summer.

Meanwhile, Henry's enemies seemed to be multiplying. Thomas More and John Fisher had publicly opposed the break with Rome; they were arrested after refusing to recognize the new status quo in its entirety. More made the concession of recognizing the new line of succession but, as a pious Catholic, he

AN IMPOSSIBLE MISSION

against the Pope's authority. Wallop read the letter out lo[ud to] Francis:

> And you shall say to our said good brother that we send not th[ese] messages and requests unto him [Francis] only for displeas[ure] that the said bishop has lately pronounced a sentence against [us] contrary to the law and will of God, but you shall assure our s[aid] good brother upon our honor that in case he had given senten[ce] with us, we would have labored as diligently and as studiou[sly] for his reformation as we will now.²³

This was an outrage. If Henry thought that Francis w[ould] follow the path of reforming the Church, he had not rea[lized] what a staunch Catholic the French king truly was.

The audience was adjourned quickly—leaving Wallop [with] very little to report back to England.

Henry had also sent a letter to Jean du Bellay, who had b[een] relentlessly fighting for England's interests for the past [few] months—if not years: "I thank you for your dexterity and per[pet]ual good service toward us. [...] I command your mas[ter's] honor and yours, as you have taken so much trouble and for [the] good friendship that bonds us."²⁴

For du Bellay, the humiliation was insufferable. He felt betra[yed] by Henry, and he could not be sure that his former ally Anne [had] not helped to drive this choice. After all, she had shown gr[eat] interest in evangelical ideals and she cared very little now ab[out] papal authority. Anne's true religious beliefs were mysterio[us]. What Jean du Bellay could be sure of, however, was Ann[e's] determination to be respected as queen of England. In this c[on]text, it was perhaps understandable that she would support h[er] husband's choices.

Upon his return to Paris, du Bellay was well received by Mo[nt]morency and the French king himself. They knew that he'd h[ad] an impossible mission to accomplish and were content, on[ce] simply had to recognize the authority of the Pope. Henry was not prepared to have his authority contested and, on April 16, 1534, Thomas More was arrested and sent to the Tower of London followed by Fisher—though Henry was not yet prepared to make a decision regarding their fates.

Catherine of Aragon, his former wife, faced the same dilemma. She had to accept the new state of affairs and recognize her marriage as illegitimate. The bishops of Durham and Chester showed no mercy when they discussed the matter with her.

"You have to comply and accept the new law, Madam."

"I will not," Catherine replied.

"If you refuse to comply, you will be put to death," they said.

"Which one of you will be my executioner?" Catherine asked, defiant.

Her courage and dignity moved them.

"I am saddened by the king's weakness and the cowardice of not telling me in person," she continued. "All of this because of this woman who has poisoned his ears and thoughts!"

Catherine still felt Anne had stolen everything from her.

Weak and tired, Catherine was confined to her apartments with her ladies.[26]

Plans were being made for Francis and Henry to meet. For Anne, this would offer her the chance to act as regent during Henry's absence. And there was other good news.

Anne was full of hope again as she told Henry that she believed she was pregnant once more. With this in mind, the meeting was postponed until the following spring.

Henry was delighted and full of affection for his wife, whom he believed this time would be the mother of his so-longed-for male heir.

During the summer, they tried to ingratiate themselves with the people who still remained hostile to their union, and to Anne herself. She was clearly feeling the strain. Her detractors, including Chapuys, reported her bad temper on every possible occasion. It seemed as if she had no control over herself, though it's hard to know how true this was, given the control she had shown in her five years of ascent. It was true, however, that she would speak her mind without fear. For this she had been vilified when, in fact, her true crime was not giving Henry the son he wanted.

By the summer, Anne had suffered a tragedy: a miscarriage at three and a half months. The pain, given such desperate expectation, must have been immense. Even worse, some reported that the baby had been a boy. As such, Anne must have feared Henry's reaction, and she was right to do so. He was furious, showing no care for Anne's health, nor any tenderness. After the short burst of affection in her pregnancy, a rift was growing between them, much to the satisfaction of Chapuys—who had happily witnessed their quarrels at court and reported them to Charles V.

Anne's position at the English court was undeniably weakened, and she had precious few allies left to count on. France was now her last hope for support—but what if the recent fiasco had undermined those relationships, built and sustained since her time as lady-in-waiting in their court?

What would become of her?

II

The Tide Has Turned

The pursuit of glory had come at a far greater price than she expected.

Anne Boleyn had now been queen of England for over a year. The title should have only brought triumph, but the reality was very different. Her enemies were vultures, waiting for her to be stripped of everything she had obtained so that they might feast on the spoils. Henry was growing more and more distant, and the pressure to give him a male heir was only increasing. Now, she also carried the burden of responsibility for the break with Rome and its resultant turmoil. She was quickly becoming public enemy number one in England, her own beloved country.

Rumors of Anne's bad temper continued to circulate, along with the belief that she was no better than a "harlot." Chapuys, her greatest enemy, accused Anne of plotting Catherine of Aragon and her daughter's, Mary's, deaths. There is no evidence, however, to corroborate such a claim. If Anne had wanted their deaths, she surely would have sought this end long before rather than waiting years to obtain the crown in increasingly fractious circumstances.

For Anne, there was another shock: Chapuys was now reporting that Henry was openly showing affection to other women at court. Anne was becoming more and more jealous and enraged.

She was not the type to turn a blind eye to extramarital affairs—even if her husband was the king. But unlike Catherine of Aragon—who had walked this path before her—Anne felt her marriage to Henry was based on genuine passion, not just dynastic grounds, and that made this development even more troubling. In other words, if Henry were to fall out of love with her, she did not have the protection of a powerful European house. Her last throw of the dice was to give the king a son.

The French attempt to intervene at Rome had manifestly failed. What an irony, considering that Anne had tried so hard to perform the role of an alternative French princess for years.

★

In April 1534, Charles de Solier, Count of Morette, who was accustomed to the ways of the English court, was dispatched to replace Castillon, who had been sent to Rome with other missions—including helping Jean du Bellay secure a cardinal's hat. Morette's reception at the English court, however, had been cooler than anticipated. The fracture between France and England was now becoming very real.

Then, on September 25, 1534—having complained of stomach problems for some time—Pope Clement VII died. His death marked another shift in European politics as his successor, Paul III, had always been a good friend of Henry VIII, and he truly hoped to repair the damage caused by Henry's divorce. Francis I—who had just ensured a dynastic alliance with Clement through the marriage of the future Henry II to his niece, Catherine de Medici—knew that he needed to create new dynastic alliances if he wished to maintain his current political advantage.

Furthermore, the French king was once again obsessed with regaining territories in Italy. By sending envoys to the respective German princes' court, Francis I was trying to undermine Charles V's authority, ensuring that if—as he expected it to—his alliance with Henry VIII were to turn sour, he would still have the upper hand against his mortal enemy: the Holy Roman Emperor.

Amid the bigger political landscape, Anne Boleyn was now an afterthought, and, irrespective of any personal goodwill, political support for her seemed to have ceased. At court, friendships could not exist that were at odds with political games of power.

Worse for Anne, rumors were circulating that the French would now pivot to support Princess Mary in response to the new political shifts in Europe.

In October 1534, Philippe de Chabot, Admiral of France—and no friend of the Boleyn faction—was sent to England as a special envoy. His instructions were clear: he had to make Henry believe that Charles V had proposed two new marriages—one between his son Philip and Francis I's youngest daughter, and one between Princess Mary and Francis's youngest son, Charles, Duke of Angoulême, as a way to ensure peace in the whole of Christendom.

The first marriage proposal was real enough: discussions were indeed taking place. The second was less well established, as Charles V never suggested that his cousin, Princess Mary, should be married to a French prince, even if it was Francis's desire. It was, however, a betrayal from Anne's perspective. By trying to arrange a marriage between Princess Mary and Angoulême, the French were disavowing Anne and suggesting that her union with Henry was not legitimate—and, therefore, that their daughter, Elizabeth, was of less importance than Henry's firstborn by seeming to honor instead his union with Catherine of Aragon. Anne Boleyn was "very angry."[1] With Henry, they continued to pressure the French Admiral to accept their view that Elizabeth was the legitimate princess of England.

The French defended their proposal by reminding Henry that Mary had been betrothed to the dauphin in 1518 and, as this had not been pursued, it was only fair that another arrangement should be made for her. If Henry acknowledged the previous treaty, Francis would still be victorious, as one of his sons would marry the person whom he believed to be the heir to the throne. All around Europe, Chapuys now asserted mysteriously, discussions were taking place regarding deposing Henry and putting Mary on the throne instead, which would—without a doubt—result in a reversal of the parliamentary statutes that had broken the nation's jurisdictional links with Rome.

If Henry accepted a marriage between Angoulême and Mary, the dauphin would be free to marry another European princess and, therefore, Francis would potentially make two dynastic alliances that would benefit his political agenda instead of one.

Chabot arrived at the English court, after a tumultuous journey, in mid-November 1534. His instructions were to convince Henry to reconsider his decision to break with Rome, and to reopen negotiations on the potential marriage between Princess Mary and the Duke of Angoulême. Upon his arrival, however, Chabot rapidly understood that this was going to be impossible. The English government seemed to have no interest whatsoever in reconciling with Rome. Worse still, the Act of Supremacy—further rejecting the authority of the Pope—had been passed on November 4, 1534. Paul III, however, would not be so easily defeated. Public opinion should matter, and not all English people were ready to part ways with the rest of Christendom, such as Thomas More and Thomas Fisher and their supporters. Moreover, two years later, the Pilgrimage of Grace, fighting against the dissolution of the monasteries, would shake the country. This Act could be overturned, and hope still existed for England's salvation.

Chapuys reported the dissent among those at court and beyond, with people promising they "would raise the banner of the Crucifix together with yours [Charles V], and among the first things he [Henry] would do would be to seize some lords who favored these follies."[2]

Chabot was, on a personal level, appalled by the Act of

Supremacy, and—like many other men—he attributed it to Queen Anne. He believed she had been influencing Henry to cause a schism with Rome in order to protect her status as queen, which may have been the case, though it was hardly the case that the break with Rome was entirely her responsibility, as he liked to suggest.

Chapuys reported his meeting with the French admiral to Charles: "I promise you, my lord, the agent of France is devoted to your cause and kept praising you in abundance." Chapuys continued his gossip: "I am told he has not made much account of the Lady [Anne Boleyn], and when the King asked him the first time if he would not like to see her, he replied very coldly that he would do so if it pleased the King."[3]

This apparent new tension between an ambassador of France and Anne was surprising—even shocking—given Anne had always enjoyed cordial relationships with French ambassadors irrespective of any political challenges at play. She was clearly losing her most powerful allies. If she did not provide Henry with a male heir, she would be left with no friends at all. Chabot spent more and more time with Chapuys, showing that the tide had, indeed, turned.

He was also determined to make his mission successful. Jehan du Moucheau, Chabot's secretary, wrote a letter to Honor Grenville, Viscountess Lisle—the wife of Arthur Plantagenet, who was the illegitimate son of King Edward IV and uncle to Henry VIII. The viscountess had been in service of Queen Anne's household when the English royal couple went to Calais and Boulogne to visit Francis I in 1532. Since 1533, she had been living in Calais, as her husband had been made lord deputy of the city.

A fervent Catholic, Jehan wrote on behalf of his master, assuring the lady that Chabot was "more bound to you and my lord [Lord Lisle] than to any man." Furthermore, Chabot was giving exotic gifts to the couple in Calais, such as "small animals" from Brazil: "These animals only eat apples, small nuts and almonds, and they must not be given anything to drink but a little milk, warmed up. [...] I sent you the said animals by the bearer, a merchant of Rouen."[4]

The fact that these esteemed diplomatic gifts were given to the Lisles—rather than to the king and queen of England, as would normally be the case—further proved the discontent of Chabot, and in turn this embodied the new French attitude toward the English royal couple.

Further insults would soon be added to injury.

★

Chabot carried out his mission in secrecy, to avoid any rumors that Anglo-French relations were in trouble. While it might have been true, it was not something the French wished to broadcast.

Chapuys noted that neither Chabot nor Henry seemed satisfied with the outcome of their audience in early December, and that Chabot had left England weeks later without obtaining any resolution, suggesting that his mission must have been a failure.

The marriage proposal between Angoulême and Mary made no sense to Henry, who could not agree to something that would seem to render his other daughter illegitimate. Instead, he made a counteroffer for a union between Francis I's son and Elizabeth. While Chabot was careful not to reject the proposal outright, he began avoiding Henry, as Chapuys recalled: "The Admiral declined to go to Windsor and other places, as the King desired, though he had promised to do so beforehand."[5] Instead, Chapuys and Chabot met in private on two occasions where they discussed the admiral's frustration.

"I am much vexed that I have not been able to see Princess Mary despite me trying many times to organize a meeting," Chabot complained.

"Have you not been allowed to see her?" Chapuys inquired.

"I have not asked directly but my intentions were clear enough and the king never came to the point." The French admiral then paused. "I have never heard of a lady so praised as the Princess, even by those who have been giving her trouble, and I am her devoted servant, both on account of her great virtues, and because she is related to the queen [Catherine] my mistress, and that I hope for certain soon to do her good service."[6]

Chabot also revealed to Chapuys that Henry had doubted his intentions and confirmed that he was working on the orders of Francis I.

"My good brother, the king of France, must have spoken of the affair to you in jest," Henry had declared to Chabot.

Inevitably, the French admiral felt compelled to show proof that this was not the case, and that the alliance Francis sought would indeed happen through Princess Mary and not Princess Elizabeth. "I am charged to urge the said marriage as stated in this instruction letter," Chabot said while handing over Francis's letter to Henry. "I also exhort your Majesty [Henry] to resume your obedience to the Church of Rome and to acknowledge your daughter's [Mary's] legitimacy."[7]

According to Chapuys, Henry might make some concessions on the marriage and would consider it if both Angoulême and Mary would renounce all rights in his own kingdom. The other consideration was dismissed out of hand, as Henry had no intention of a reconciliation with the Church of Rome.

> The King, besides the 30,000 crowns which he has newly obtained from the clergy, and an ordinary fifteenth from the laity which was granted him last year, and which may amount to 28,000 crowns, has just imposed a tax by authority of Parliament of the 20th penny of all the goods of his subjects, and that foreigners shall pay double, which will amount to a great sum. These are devices of Cromwell, who boasts that he will make his master more wealthy than all the other princes of Christendom.[8]

The break with Rome was evidently a lucrative decision, too, and one that would not be reversed now that the opportunity had been seized.

On the evening before Chabot's departure, Henry VIII organized a feast for the admiral—hoping, presumably, that it would make him more favorable to the English court and ease any of the ill will that might have lately developed. The French ambassador was seated next to Anne, who tried to engage him in conversation. Her efforts, however, were in vain, as Chabot showed no interest in talking to her. As they were enjoying the meal and the entertainment, which consisted of dancers and music, Henry saw one of Chabot's secretaries, Palamède Gontier, in the crowd.

"I will fetch him to introduce him to you," Henry told Anne.

As he walked into the crowd, Anne stared at him for a moment and then burst into laughter. Puzzled, and mostly annoyed, Chabot frowned as he bluntly asked her: "What, madam, do you laugh at me?"

Trying to regain control of herself, Anne apologized. "Not at all, my lord. I'm laughing because the king who said he would fetch your secretary to introduce him to me, has just met a lady on his way who apparently made him forget the matter."[9]

It was clear that Anne no longer held Henry's attention, which must by now have been deeply unsettling. Chabot did not seem impressed with Anne's reaction, nor the reason behind it, and he became silent, ignoring her.

The feast ended and so, too, did Chabot's mission, which had proven unsuccessful. Henry still refused to promise Princess Mary to Angoulême, instead, offering Princess Elizabeth—who, he reminded Chabot, was the only legitimate heir to the English throne according to current English laws.

Now Anne's situation was even more precarious than it had been before her marriage to Henry. With the break with Rome, the French no longer supporting her and her enemies circling, it seemed she had also lost the attentions of her husband. Anne had to find a way to intervene.

*

Palamède Gontier was sent back to England in January 1535 in order to assist Morette, who was still resident ambassador at the English court. Chabot and Gontier had left for France in December 1534, and Gontier had been sent back with an answer from Chabot to the counteroffer Henry had made to Francis of a prospective marriage between Elizabeth and Angoulême.

For Anne, if the offer was accepted, it would mean that not all hope was lost, indicating that Francis remained an ally. If it was declined, however, Anne's position would be worse than she had anticipated.

Morette took Gontier to the Palace of Whitehall to see the English king, who was pacing up and down as he awaited the news.

"I assure you, your Majesty, that my master, your good brother and cousin, honors and desires nothing more than a strong alliance between your two realms," Gontier began. "As to the proposed marriage between Princess Elizabeth and Angoulême, the king of France does not doubt that having given her that name, your Majesty [Henry] will assure it to her and treat her as his only heiress, so that the Crown of England may come to her on his death. However, an issue remains, as some means ought to be found to deprive Lady Mary of any occasion or means of claiming the Crown."

"The Parliament has proclaimed Princess Elizabeth as my only heir," Henry replied. "An oath has been taken throughout the kingdom stating that Lady Mary is a bastard and that I will have no other heir but the Princess. There is no chance of Mary becoming queen or claiming any right to the Crown. It now only requires for Francis to convince the Pope to annul the invalid dispensation given for my first marriage, and then all doubts will cease."[10]

The conversation moved on to dowries, and former payments linked to past peace treaties that were unresolved between the two realms.

Henry soon requested another meeting with Francis, to which Gontier, too, happily agreed. The audience was then dismissed before it could take place, and Gontier was summoned to court the next day. While a dynastic alliance with France was key to Henry's political machinations, Cromwell reminded him that Francis was only offering his third son and not the dauphin—whom he had promised to Charles V's daughter instead. The situation, therefore, was difficult. After so many years of wars and animosity, could Francis and Charles truly make peace and become allies? This was a terrifying thought for Henry, given in his break from Rome he had just turned his back on the whole of Christendom.

Yet again he found himself in a precarious position. Simply put, the dynastic alliance between England and France was once more not meant to be.

A few days later, Cromwell agreed to accompany Gontier to meet with Anne, who had expressed her desire to see him in person.

"You might leave us, my lord," Anne told Cromwell, who would certainly have liked to stay and witness their conversation.

As soon as he left the room, Anne turned to Gontier. She had no time to waste. "I have been waiting for your return for so long. It has caused my husband many doubts regarding your intentions," she said, seeming troubled.

"This was not our intention, my lady. Such decision must be dealt with great care, and it took us longer to come back with agreeable terms for both England and France," Gontier explained.

Anne nodded but could not hide her unease. "Would you share with your master, the Admiral, my desire that he applies some remedy to my situation and acts toward the king so I may not be ruined and lost?" she asked, her throat tightening. "As I see myself very near that and in more grief and trouble than before my marriage," she confessed.

Gontier was disarmed. Anne was known for her fiery temperament but very rarely did she show her vulnerability. And yet here she was, wearing her heart on her sleeve.

"I beg the Admiral to consider my affairs of which I cannot speak as fully as I wish, partly because of my fears, but mostly because of the eyes that are all looking at me and my husband. I cannot write nor see you again nor stay any longer, but please I beg you to act on my behalf."[11]

Anne then abruptly left the room and attended the feast Henry had organized for the French ambassadors, Gontier and Morette. Her fate remained, once more, in French hands.

*

Meanwhile, the animosity between Charles V and Francis I continued to grow. Their rivalry knew no bounds and, with the Ottomans once more threatening the borders of Europe with the attacks led by their admiral Hayreddin Barbarossa, Francis saw an opportunity to do more damage to his enemy. An alliance between Suleiman and Francis had been on the cards since 1534 and, to justify his heathen alliance, Francis allegedly said, "When wolves fall on my flock, it is necessary to call upon dogs for help."[12] However, a problem had arisen, making it more difficult, though not impossible, for Francis to pursue this bold alliance.

In October 1534, a series of anti-Catholic placards was nailed on doors all over Paris. They denounced the abuses of the Roman Catholic Church and criticized papal authority. This incident, known as the Affair of the Placards, put Francis in a thorny situation and brought into question his own authority.

It is believed that one such placard was found on the king's own door and, furious and enraged by such a bold display, he vouched to "exterminate everyone" responsible.[13] Having once supported the woman who, it was said, caused England's break with Rome, and now engaging in an alliance with the "Infidels," Francis needed to be careful not to alienate Rome, even though he was a flexible thinker whose political decisions were rarely made on religious grounds.

On January 13, 1535, another set of placards was found in Paris. This was the last straw for Francis, who ordered the arrest and execution of several people who were deemed responsible. No mercy would be granted as:

> the law courts of Paris have been occupied with the trial of those wicked heretics [...] The King caused a procession to be made at Paris on Thursday 21 January, the finest ever seen, in which he bore a torch, and all the princes and all the colleges of Paris and the churches [...] and at the end of the procession was made a sacrifice to our Lord Jesus Christ of six wicked heretics, who were burned. One was the treasurer of Nantes in Brittany, a very rich man.[14]

Rumors were spreading that the King of France was also a heretic and that, although these prosecutions should, in theory, prove Francis's Catholicism, his diplomacy with the Ottomans had undeniably tarnished his reputation—even within his own country. Yet, it did not prevent him from burning more heretics in the capital, or from making the following declaration:

> Our fathers have shown us how to live according to the doctrine of God and of the Holy Mother Church, in which I hope to live and die... I would see these errors chased out of my kingdom and no one excused, in such sort that if one of my arms were infected by this corruption, I would cut it off. And were my children stained by it, I myself would burn them.[15]

The persecution continued all over the summer as Francis sought to underline his religious authority, and, although he never earned, as he might have done, the title of "Bloody Francis," the violence with which he reacted to these events showed that the King of France would have had little to learn from Henry's eldest daughter—who, decades later, would be named "Bloody Mary" for taking similar action.

In February 1535, Francis sent a special envoy—Jean de la Forest—to Suleiman's court. While the persecution of Protestants continued in France, the French king did not deviate when it came to his own alliance with the infidels. A king in his position needed to be strategic about his allies, and, it was clear, Francis no longer had any need of England and its queen.

Instead, his eyes turned once more toward the Italian territories and the destruction of his ultimate enemy, Charles V.

★

For Anne, the situation in England was dire. Chapuys observed that Henry did not even try to hide his interest in other women, including "a first cousin of the concubine [Anne], daughter of the new governess of the princess."[16] This was a reference to Mary Shelton, who now became mistress to the king and who was a first cousin of Anne's on her father's side.

The affair did not last, but it was a warning to Anne that Henry was no longer interested in her. If she completely lost his love, what would become of her? What chance would she have of remaining queen? And, more importantly, what chance would her daughter have of remaining legitimate?

The latest rumor at court was that Henry was already looking into getting another divorce. Luckily for Anne, this would not be easily achieved—particularly not with Catherine of Aragon still alive. The only two choices Henry had in 1535 were Catherine or Anne. His people—and surely even his ministers, who had sought to appease him on so many controversial decisions so far—would not accept yet another wife.

Anne's detractors were becoming more vocal, and absurd claims were made that Anne had bribed a man to declare to the king and Cromwell that he'd had "psychic" revelations regarding the queen's infertility: "She will never conceive children as long as the Queen [Catherine] and Princess are alive."[17]

Furthermore, there were other tensions for Henry to contend with. There was discontent from some quarters about his treatment of his opponents, especially John Fisher and Thomas More, who had been imprisoned in the Tower since mid-1534. The two men were given six weeks to recognize the Act of Supremacy of 1534 and to take the oath to enforce it. They could not, in their good conscience, recognize Henry's break with Rome, which meant that they did not recognize Anne Boleyn as the legitimate queen of England. They were publicly defying Henry's authority. As a result, they would remain imprisoned, but this only brought them more support from those who shared their cause.

Chapuys claimed that Anne was the mastermind behind all this and that she was now

> fiercer and haughtier than ever she was, and has been bold enough to tell the king, as I hear, that he is as much indebted to her as ever man was to woman, for she has been the cause of his being cleansed from sin in which he was living; and, moreover, that by marrying her as he had done, he had become the richest monarch that ever was in England, inasmuch as without her he would never have been able to reform the affairs of the Church in his kingdom, to his very great personal profit and that of his kingdom.[18]

There are no other reports of Anne making such bold statements, and so perhaps Chapuys's claim was invented. It certainly seems, given her vulnerable position, that it would have been difficult for her to control the situation at court so entirely, and her meeting with Gontier had proved she knew this only too well.

John Fisher's and Thomas More's situation would only aggravate Anne's reputation; there was nothing to gain for her by making such a drastic decision.

But Anne was not the one in power, and she could do nothing as events unfolded before her eyes.

*

In April 1535, members of the London Charterhouse who signaled their opposition to the king's policy were arrested and sent to the Tower of London. On April 29, they were taken to the Guildhall and declared guilty: they would suffer the traitor's punishment. So, on May 4, at Tyburn, they "were hanged, cut down alive, disemboweled, beheaded, and quartered."[19] The news soon reached the continent, horrifying everyone, including Francis I and Chabot, the admiral. Henry's cruelty was denounced and the chances of an Anglo-French alliance continued to diminish. Meanwhile, the threat to Fisher's and More's lives had never been so real.

More was summoned by the privy council to recognize the new statutes of the country but, once more, he courageously refused. A few weeks later, he, along with Fisher, the former chaplain of Catherine of Aragon, Dr. Abel, and Mary's former schoolmaster were given six weeks to submit—or their own trial for treason would start.

In the meantime, word had reached Pope Paul III that Henry's infatuation with Anne was on the wane. He thought, therefore, it was the right time to convince the English king to rejoin the rest of Christendom. To show his readiness to favor the English once more by giving them representation at the Vatican, the Pope made John Fisher a cardinal, in a bid to convince Henry to rejoin the Catholic Church as well as potentially secure his release—though this appointment didn't exactly have the effect he'd wished for. Henry VIII was furious, seeing it as another means of contesting his royal authority, and sent Gregorio Casali as his special envoy to protest against it. How dare the Pope raise a traitor in Henry's own realm to the status of a cardinal?

"I will give him another hat, for I will send the bishop's head to Rome for that purpose!" Henry screamed violently for everyone to hear.[20]

Paul III urged the French king to intervene as he feared this would not bode well for John Fisher. However, Francis could do very little in the matter. Charles de Hémard de Denonville, Bishop of Mâcon, Jean du Bellay and Nicolas Raince, the French secretary, urged the Pope to admit that he was never asked by Francis to "confer the cardinal hat's on the Bishop of Rochester [Fisher]."[21]

Casali made a proposal: Fisher could promise that, if his life was spared, he would recognize the new statutes of the realm and would then be granted a safe passage to Rome, where he would receive his new ordinance. This compromise would help both the Pope and Henry save face. The French and their king also reached out to Henry—begging him to spare Fisher's life. He was, after all, a highly esteemed bishop of the Roman Catholic Church.

Henry was not, however, in a merciful mood. His distrust of the French—particularly du Bellay, who had just accepted a cardinalship himself—made him even more resentful of their attempt to intervene.

"I considered him before his creation as a very bad Papist!" Henry yelled.

To remedy his bad temper, Anne organized a feast—including great entertainment—and did not invite the French ambassador, Morette, as a deliberate insult. Chapuys was convinced of that.[22] It seemed that Anne and Henry's relationship was strongest when it united them against the rest of the world, and perhaps Anne would have felt relieved even if it meant anti-English sentiment was growing abroad.

Henry, who now believed that Fisher had been plotting against him with the French and the Pope, was more determined than ever to put an end to his treachery.

So, on June 14, 1535, in one last attempt to prove that he could be the bigger man, Henry ordered the assembling of the prisoners. Fisher and More were asked, once again, to accept the Acts of Succession and Supremacy. They both refused. That was it. Now, Henry would show no mercy.

Three days later, Fisher's trial began.

He was accused of declaring, contrary to the new law, that "the King our sovereign lord is not Supreme Head on Earth of the Church of England" and insisted "I cannot nor will consent to be obedient to the King's Highness as a true, lawful, and obedient subject, to take and repute him to be Supreme Head on Earth of the Church of England under Christ."

Fisher was not tried by his peers, but instead by a common jury, composed of commoners rather than clergy, and although he pleaded "not guilty," the jury found him guilty of treason.[23]

On June 22, John Fisher was decapitated on Tower Hill. According to Chapuys, he died with dignity and bravery.

Henry's fury, however, would not stop with Fisher.

★

Eyes were now turned to Thomas More, who—like Fisher—had continued to refuse to recognize the new statutes; his conscience made it impossible for him to accept the new Church of England. So, on July 1, More was summoned to Westminster Hall to be tried before a special commission. He did his best to defend his honor and, although he was eloquent and articulate, he did not have any influence on the jury, who had no doubt already been ordered to find him guilty. A few days later, Thomas More was also beheaded—his head placed on a spike next to John Fisher's on Tower Hill.

The news of more executions in England shook the rest of Europe. Imperialists and the French alike were outraged by Henry's cruelty. England became isolated as, while other German princes had embraced Protestantism in their differences on the scripture, they would not dare engage in royal supremacy and make themselves head of their Church. Henry's break with Rome went further than anyone else was ready to imagine, let alone execute, and everyone knew it had nothing to do with theology and everything to do with Henry's own ego—and his pursuit of a dynasty.

Now, Henry was with no ally, no male heir and, in some regions, a discontented population. A flood of printed material admiring the men who had dared stand up to Henry's tyranny was spreading all over Europe, and many of England's Catholics must surely have agreed.[24]

In many ways, his tyranny had made the path clearer for his former allies, and the French were now resolute in their opposition to Henry's political course. Paul III issued a brief to all Christian princes, requiring them to sever their diplomatic ties with the English court. Francis took this opportunity to send a special envoy to support his resident ambassador in London, Antoine de Castelnau, who had been dispatched a month or so before alongside his secretary, Lancelot de Carle, to inform Henry of the brief, and that France would no longer side with England.

The special envoy was none other than the experienced former resident ambassador, Jean de Dinteville, Bailiff of Troyes, who abhorred the English king for his recent actions. Castelnau had already received a chilly reception on his arrival in England, where access to Bridewell Palace, which was a semi-official residence for French ambassadors, was denied him.

Francis I would end his alliance with England, but not without holding Henry to account for all their past agreements, particularly the payments of armies and promises of goods and weapons for a war against Charles. He was determined to collect what he was owed while the extent of Henry's ruthlessness was clear for all to see.

Anne, however, had little choice but to remain loyal to her husband, and was more determined than ever to bear him a son.

*

The Bailiff of Troyes had arrived earlier, in September 1535, and was meant to meet the English royal couple at Winchester, where they had just finished their summer progress to rekindle their relationship—but also to prevent any further discord after the terrible events of June and July 1535.

Troyes's task was not a pleasant one, though he was certainly the best person for it: as an experienced diplomat who was well connected all around Europe, he was a man of great stature who commanded respect. He was easily impressed and was perfectly positioned to embody Francis's own grandeur. Wealthy and resourceful, he was also determined to make his master's desire known to Henry.

A record of his exact instructions have since been lost, but we know he had two main objectives. The first was to ensure that Henry would pay his debt to Francis for all the assistance he had provided with his "great matter" over the years. The Anglo-French alliance had been essential for Francis's quest of reestablishing himself as a powerful political player after his humiliating defeat against Charles V in 1525. The money was essential as it would ensure that Francis would not lose the funding for his army, which he needed in order to regain crucial territories in Italy. It was unlikely that Henry would respond to this request enthusiastically.

The second goal was equally difficult to achieve. Pope Paul III had issued a statement prohibiting any alliance with Henry since the execution of Cardinal Fisher. More than that, he had declared that the English king should be "deprived of his kingdom and royal dignity."[25] He ordered Francis I to be "his messenger" in conveying this to Henry.[26] Even a man as esteemed as Troyes might find this hard to accomplish, but he was confident that this was the moral position.

Chapuys reported that Troyes was received by the king and queen upon his arrival in Winchester. There was no word of Castelnau being present—another insult to the resident ambassador.

Troyes handed over the letters he had brought from his master. Henry "appeared sad and melancholy when he had read the letters" that the ambassador presented.[27] He did not offer an immediate answer and instead ordered a meeting with his most trusted advisers, notably Thomas Cranmer and Stephen Gardiner. He also summoned other lords, including the Duke of Norfolk and the Duke of Suffolk. They needed to present a united front on the matter as the threat of excommunication was looming.

Anne, meanwhile, was now resolute in her support for her husband, her feelings of loyalty to France now much diminished. Chabot's arrogance toward her had been the final straw.

These external threats had reunited Henry and Anne, who, after having previously grown apart, now seemed to be more in love with each other than ever. The brutal events of the summer—and the deaths of Fisher and More, two voices against their union—as well as new laws regarding Henry's supremacy and line of succession, had all reinforced Henry and Anne's desire to have their union prevail. Without a male heir, however, this intimacy would unfortunately not last.

However, Anne did not entirely give up on her ties with the French. In a private audience given to an unknown man who was in the service of Troyes, she confessed wholeheartedly: "All I pray for is to give the king, my husband, a son, and one day to see again my dear friend, Marguerite, queen of Navarre."[28]

The mysterious Frenchman reported these exact words back to Marguerite, but there is no evidence that she responded directly to the English queen. Whatever Anne might have felt for her former mentor, it did not seem to have been reciprocal, and if she hoped for an influence over Francis through Marguerite, she was only going to find disappointment. Anne was on her own.

★

At the beginning of October 1535, Anne and Henry rode to Southampton—the last stop of their royal progress. They had been spending their time hunting, hawking and feasting. In all, it had been exactly what they needed: an opportunity to relax away from the political chaos, and to rediscover their love for each other.

All evidence suggested that "the King's Grace and the Queen's Grace were very merry in Hampshire."[29] Their happiness shone through, and hopes that Anne might be pregnant again started to spread.

By now, she must surely have been consumed by this mission. The longer it took, the more pressure she felt, but in the summer and early autumn of 1535, her renewed connection with her husband must have given her some hope.

Alongside the royal couple, many courtiers took part in the summer tour, including one particular young and dashing musician. He had first been hired as a groom of Henry's privy chamber and, since around 1529, had become favored by the king. His name was Mark Smeaton.

He became known as a fixture of the king and the queen's close circle and his talent was highly praised.

Yet, while the jovial atmosphere seemed to predict better months to come, Smeaton's name would soon come to haunt Anne.

12

The Inconceivable

Their summer season may have brought the king and queen closer, but now it was over, and there still remained the pressure on Anne to produce a male heir. But their recent reconciliation had brought Anne hope—and she would always choose hope over fear.

Upon his return to Windsor, Henry decided to send Stephen Gardiner, one of his most trusted advisers, to the French court. Securing his alliance with the King of France was at the forefront of his preoccupations.

"You will negotiate the articles sent by my dear good brother, Francis, and ensure they serve the interest of the two crowns," Henry instructed him. "Remind the king of France that when we met in Boulogne he thought that the claims made by the Bishop of Rome [the Pope] to be false, untrue, and malicious."[1]

In other words, Henry needed Francis to remember that they had once been united and that a reconciliation of that union would be beneficial for both of them. For Francis, however, the only way for Henry to prove it remained the dynastic marriage between his eldest daughter, Princess Mary, and Francis's son, the dauphin—and this continued to be an insult to Anne from her former strongest ally and, at times, even protector.

In his reports and letters, Castelnau could not help but note that Anne's list of supporters was diminishing. Even the people of the realm—what should have been *her* realm—still seemed to favor the former queen, Catherine of Aragon, over her. He wrote: "This is common opinion, among noblemen, the lower people, and the King's own servants."

Beyond the court, ordinary people blamed Anne for the uncertainty her marriage to the king had induced, as well as for the prospect of a war with the Catholic European powers. Princess Mary, on the other hand, was more beloved than ever, which irritated Henry VIII more than he could have imagined.

"Lately, when she [Mary] was removed from Greenwich, a great troop of citizens' wives and others, unknown to their husbands, presented themselves before her, weeping and crying that she was Princess, notwithstanding all that had been done."

Castelnau also claimed that the English people were in favor of their proposal for "the marriage between the Dauphin and her [Mary]." He also complained that access to her had not been granted to him and his agents. Francis pursued this alliance vigorously, knowing it offered a chance at stability, but once again Anne was an obstacle.

"If the king of England does not approve because his wife persuades him to the contrary, he will fear to set Francis and the Emperor against himself solely through his affection for his wife, which is less than it has been, and diminished day by day, because he has new amours."[2]

Troyes's diplomatic mission was a failure and he returned to France in the middle of October, without having progressed negotiations for a marriage between Princess Mary and the dauphin and without any further payments from the English. Francis was furious at this lack of progress. Did he blame Anne for it? It is hard to determine his feelings on this particular matter, but Castelnau's letters showed that the popular conception was that the English queen might have been the reason behind the failure to secure a dynastic marriage between her stepdaughter and the

French prince. In her mind, it was said, if they wanted a princess, they should have betrothed her daughter, Elizabeth, instead—the only rightful heir to the English throne.

By now, however, the fear of a full-scale invasion by Charles V and other European powers was very much on Henry's mind. Despite their differences, he knew that a dynastic alliance with Francis could strengthen his position in Europe, if he could just overcome his fear that his French counterpart might betray him by trying to put his daughter, Mary, on the throne with the dauphin—a fear that was not unfounded.

Antoine Perrenot de Granvelle was the Spanish imperial ambassador to France. His correspondence with his master, Charles V, revealed that in a union between Princess Mary and the dauphin the Holy Roman Emperor saw a potential benefit for the whole of Christendom, one that would "prevent further evil, both as regards of the Faith and the Church."[3]

Soon, there was another twist in the tale. In November 1535, dreadful news reached England: Francis I was "ill with flux and tertian fever and more likely to die than be cured."[4] Although we have no evidence of the private responses of Henry and Anne to this, they did show great public concern: when news arrived that Francis was over the worst, Henry ordered a great procession in London in honor of his recovery.

Chapuys reported to Charles V that "the crowd was enormous, and there were a number of musical instruments; the Sacrament of the Altar was carried almost the whole length of the town by the bishop of London." However, some people were conspicuous in their absence. None of the official French representatives, including Castelnau and his secretaries, were in attendance. For Henry, it was an opportunity to prove that "there was most fraternal love between the two Kings" when in fact they were, once again, on opposing paths that would inevitably collide once more.[5]

And someone else was missing. Anne Boleyn, Francis's former staunch supporter, did not attend the procession either.

★

During his recovery, Francis I had some time to ponder his alliance with Henry. He was rather stuck, particularly as his support of the King of England was now causing him greater grief with the Pope than he had ever anticipated. He had to obey Paul III's orders if he were to maintain the peace, and yet he was still trying to negotiate between the two parties to ensure that all of his own interests, in both Italy and Flanders, remained protected. He needed some assistance.

The man Francis chose to help him find a compromise between Paul III and Henry was the once-staunch supporter of Anne Boleyn and protégé of Marguerite of Navarre: Jean du Bellay. Having recently been made cardinal, du Bellay had consolidated his power and influence, and had been serving for some months as an ambassador to Rome. He was also very familiar with English affairs.

Paul III was determined to make Henry's case a cautionary tale. He ensured that a draft of his excommunication and deprivation was approved by his council, and was ready to use it. Du Bellay was alarmed at the news and warned Francis that this decree also had the purpose "to compel you to lose either the pope or the king of England."[6]

Francis had to choose a side, and the safer bet would be the Pope.

Yet du Bellay was not ready to give up. He tried to delay the Pope's decision as long as he could, arguing the case for the king. He was, however, outnumbered once more at the papal court, with other cardinals—such as Campeggio—claiming that "the French king has great friendship and treaties with the king of England still, which are secret, as usual, which leave us to suspect that there is something between them to the prejudice of the Church."⁷ Du Bellay assured them that there was never any secret in this alliance and that his master, Francis I, was not hiding his desire to marry his son to Princess Mary, for a single purpose: to bring England back under the control of the papal authority.

This claim was not believed by his peers, nor by the Pope, and the pressure on Francis to cease all alliance with Henry continued to increase. Du Bellay was once more defeated in his diplomatic endeavors as Francis instructed him to stop interfering in favor of Henry and Anne.

The sentence of excommunication for Henry was deemed too severe by other cardinals, though they all agreed that he should be punished for the execution of Cardinal Fisher earlier that year. Paul III was outraged at the cardinals' pusillanimous approach to such an important matter.

"God has placed me above emperor, kings, and princes, and I intend to make use of his power!" he burst out in anger. "Being excommunicated for the execution of a cardinal is entirely appropriate."

The cardinals did not dare reply.

Du Bellay risked his own reputation when he remarked: "Surely both the emperor and the king of France should be consulted first on the sentence."

"They were consulted long ago. It is time to pass the bull," the Pope replied, taking du Bellay aback with his certainty.⁸ However, since he was in the service of Francis I, not the Pope, he would continue to defend his master's interests.

"My master has withdrawn from negotiations between the duke of Angoulême, his son, and Princess Elizabeth, and instead pursued a dynastic match with Princess Mary, showing his allegiance to the Pope," Du Bellay said.

"This is untrue. Your master stopped the negotiations because the king of England asked for the duke to be kept in England during his betrothed time to his second daughter. It has nothing to do with his allegiance to me or the Roman Catholic Church."[9]

This was an outrage. Du Bellay knew full well that his master, Francis, would not accept Paul III's interpretation of his own authority. Unfortunately for the ambassador, the Pope was not in the mood to change his mind; he continued to advance his decision for the excommunication of Henry VIII.

Back in England, once again Anne was losing influence over Henry, as Chapuys explained in a letter to his counterpart in France, who showed a cunning interest in Thomas Cromwell, Henry's man:

> He is the son of a poor farrier, who lived in a little village a league and a half from here and is buried in the parish graveyard. His uncle, father of the cousin whom he has already made rich, was cook of the late archbishop of Canterbury. Cromwell was ill-behaved when young, and after an imprisonment, was forced to leave the country. He went to Flanders, Rome, and elsewhere in Italy. When he returned he married the daughter of a shearman, and served in his house; he then became a solicitor [before entering into the service of the former cardinal of York, Thomas Wolsey]. "Now he stands above everyone but the Lady, and everyone considers he has more credit with his master than Wolsey had."[10]

Thomas Cromwell was indeed a man of wit and raw ambition. Well traveled and experienced, nothing was handed to him on a platter. He had risen among a court of wolves. He had learned how to be patient and that the most important rule at Henry's court was simple: please the king in all you do.

Cromwell was, for now, still standing by Henry and Anne, but more out of necessity than any loyalty to the queen, and most of all because of his disdain for the French, whom he felt were untrustworthy. He also realized that Henry's patience with his former wife, Catherine, and eldest daughter, Mary, was running out.

*

On November 6, 1535, Gertrude Courtenay, Marchioness of Exeter and loyal friend and supporter of Catherine of Aragon, warned Chapuys of what she had heard:

> The king had lately told his most trusted counselors that he would no longer remain in trouble, fear, and suspense in which he had so long endured on account of the queen [Catherine] and the princess [Mary], and that they should see, at the coming parliament, to get him released therefrom, swearing most obstinately that he would wait no longer.[11]

Henry had now made a bold decision. He wanted to take everything from the queen and his firstborn daughter: their status, their titles, and any other sort of powers they might have had.

Catherine's constant appeals to Rome and her nephew, Charles V, had caused much torment for Anne. But Catherine's life and continued high status were more problematic for Henry than they were for her. As long as Catherine lived, Henry had only two options: remaining with Anne or going back to Catherine. And now, with no heir, what he really wanted was the freedom to explore a third option: a third spouse. Suddenly, the fates of Anne and Catherine depended on each other.

Putting his demands before his parliament, Henry insisted that if his wishes were not granted, he would fulfill the prophecy regarding his rulership, in which he had stated: "At the beginning of my reign I would be gentle as a lamb, and at the end worse than a lion."[12]

He was right. A shift in his character was occurring. He showed cruelty over mercy; ruthlessness over compassion; defiance over compromise. Henry was no longer the man for whom Anne had fallen.

Meanwhile, Chapuys continued to claim that Anne had, for some time, "conspired and wished for the death of the said ladies [Catherine and Mary]."[13] While of course the rivalry was undeniable, there is no evidence of any murder plot by Anne in any other contemporary sources.

In 1535, Catherine was about to turn 50—a great age at the time, since the average life expectancy was around 35 to 40—and her health seemed unstable. In early December, a fortnight before her fiftieth birthday, Catherine started suffering from violent pains in her stomach, which led to awful vomiting. According to her physician, de Lasco, she recovered within a week but still showed signs of weakness. The episode had been horrendous for the poor woman.

Then residing at Kimbolton Castle, close to Cambridge, a weakened Catherine expressed her wish to her nephew, Charles, to be moved somewhere else; she instructed him to do anything in his power to make it happen but, more importantly, she insisted on "the necessity of remedying the affairs of the king, my lord, on my behalf and my daughter. I am forced to write again by what I am daily told will be attempted in this Parliament against the Church [Roman Catholic Church] and our own persons."[14]

Instructed by the emperor, Chapuys did all he could "about changing the said Queen's lodging, and advancing her for these feasts the small remainder of her arrears. Cromwell gave me good words and good hope."[15] But Cromwell did not follow through; the true decision-maker here was Henry, and Henry alone. And, of course, he had no intention of moving Catherine anywhere. She had been his prisoner for years and only death could set her free.

*

In late December, Chapuys was informed that Catherine was ill again, and that "she could not retain any food nor liquid."[16]

Catherine was getting weaker by the day. Alarmed, Chapuys asked for permission to see the former queen, but Henry and Cromwell kept delaying their approval.

Charles was disgusted with Henry's lack of compassion: "The ill will of the king of England to the Queen and Princess is cruel and horrible. It is impossible to believe that he would be so unnatural as to put them to death, considering his ties to them, their descent, their virtues and long sufferings. He probably intends by threats to make them swear to and approve his statutes."[17]

On December 30, Chapuys was finally granted an audience with the king, though he still had not been granted a safe conduct to see Catherine. The conversation, initiated by Henry, was about Charles V's intentions regarding England, which surprised Chapuys at first.

"What makes you think that my master wants to launch a war against you?" he asked.

Puzzled by this question, Henry became defensive. "I have to protect my kingdom and not allow your master to grow so powerful," he said. "The Emperor has shown me the greatest ingratitude, procuring so many things against me at the desire of a woman, which has involved me in many troubles, and that the Emperor has by threats and force obtained a sentence against him, as the Bishop of Rome [the Pope] himself confessed."

"My master, the Emperor, has set off to much prosperity, and the complaint you are making is because of what has been undertaken against the righteous cause of the Queen."

In an effort to appease Henry, Chapuys asked, "What would you have the Emperor do?"

"Simply that he cease to favor these good ladies [Catherine and Mary]," he replied, "but also that he gets the sentence given in Madame's [Catherine's] favor revoked."

"He cannot do that. There is no good reason for this. It is not in his power," Chapuys insisted.

Henry was enraged, once more blaming the Pope and his

influence. "Madame [Catherine] will not live long now," he burst out in rage, "and when she dies, your master will have no cause to trouble himself about the affairs of this kingdom."

"The death of the queen could not possibly be good for anyone," Chapuys replied indignantly before taking his leave. He didn't know how right he was about this—especially when it came to Anne. Without a male heir, Catherine was the only obstacle that prevented Henry from discarding her.

As Chapuys made his way to the door, the Duke of Norfolk rushed in and whispered something in the ear of the king. Smirking, Henry made a sign to Norfolk to repeat it loudly so that Chapuys could hear.

"Madame [Catherine] is in extremis. You will not find her alive."

Chapuys left in a hurry to confirm this with Catherine's physician, who replied that he did not see the case "as so urgent."[18] Nevertheless, the imperial ambassador begged for Princess Mary to be granted a last audience with her mother. This wish was denied.

With great frustration and anguish, Chapuys mounted his horse and headed straight to Kimbolton Castle. When he finally arrived, after two days of travel, he did not find hostility. The gates were open and it was agreed that he could see Catherine in the presence of royal officers.

As he entered her private chamber, he kneeled and kissed Catherine's hand. Chapuys had always been a fervent admirer and supporter of hers—and remained so, right until the end.

For the next few days, Catherine seemed to retain food, and her physician was hopeful that her condition would improve. Chapuys let her rest as much as she needed, but he also had long conversations with her, at her own request.

"I hope my nephew, the Emperor, is keeping well. He could not have done better for me, given the state of his affairs," Catherine told him, smiling.

Chapuys reassured her that she was his constant priority. She knew this was not entirely true, but she could not really fault him for what had happened to her.

Feeling saddened by her fate, Chapuys tried to cheer her up. "The king has promised me that you will be permitted to choose another house where to reside and that he will pay you what you are due," Chapuys whispered kindly. He added another little white lie: "He is very sorry about your illness."[19]

For Catherine, the man who had been her husband for over 25 years was now only a distant memory. Her last wish, her only wish, was to see her daughter but, once again, this was not granted. Chapuys knew that Catherine's death would be Mary's greatest grief, one that would darken her heart forever. And who could blame her for it?

Things took a final, definitive turn for the worse on January 6, 1536. Catherine was once again in abominable pain, her body weaker than ever. Then, in the early hours of January 7, she died, leaving her daughter to fight relentlessly for their honor—a mission Mary would never stop pursuing.

In truth, the only one who really benefited from Catherine's death was Henry. Now that his former wife was dead, a new door was opened and, if Anne could not provide his heir, perhaps he could look elsewhere. But there was news: Anne was now pregnant again. Could this at last be an opportunity to give Henry what he most desired?

*

Henry did not even try to conceal his joy at the news of Catherine's passing.

"God has liberated us from any threats of war!" he exulted.[20]

Both Sir Thomas Boleyn and his son, George, also showed their pleasure at the news, delighted to see Henry in good spirits. Anne, too, must have also felt some relief, no longer having to dispute her title and crown anymore. But the truth was, things were far more complicated than that. A significant part of the population was still loyal to the late Catherine and her daughter, and the queen's death had only reinforced their support for Mary, who was of course crushed by the loss of her mother.

Meanwhile, Henry was wearing yellow and "a white feather in his cap," and he ensured that Princess Elizabeth was taken to mass "with trumpets blowing before her."[21] At dinner, he carried Elizabeth in his arms and showed his happiness for everyone to see. At such a moment, Anne must have felt that her marriage was still strong and that Henry's love remained with her and their daughter.

Such public rejoicings were badly received by some, who were spreading rumors that Catherine might have been poisoned. Chapuys himself wanted to know for certain whether this had been her cause of death. He believed that during the embalming of her body by the chandler of the house, traces of poison would no doubt be found, but Catherine's physician, de Lasco, was refused access. The next day, the chandler confirmed that she had died of natural causes. He did, however, reveal that her heart was "all black and hideous to look at." He also reported that he found "a black round body attached to the outside of the heart."[22]

Though suspicions that her death was not natural persisted, without any evidence, her supporters were left with no real recourse of action. These suspicions, however, would soon be used against Anne herself—who, by this point, had been vilified by Catherine's supporters for almost a decade. Catherine's death certainly marked a shift in Anne's fate—but not the one she was hoping for.

★

Anne's eyes were now turning to Princess Mary. She believed that without the presence of her mother, the princess would be more easily convinced to accept Anne's union with the king as well as the new Acts that were being passed—declaring Henry head of the Church of England. Anne instructed one of her closest allies, Lady Shelton, to persuade Mary that if she obeyed her father, all past insults would be forgotten and Anne would become "her best friend in the world and a second mother."

"I wish nothing more but to obey my father, but I can't do it against my honor and conscience," Mary replied, standing her ground when it came to defending her mother's memory and her own legitimacy to a throne she wished to sit on one day.[23]

This was Anne's last attempt to make things right with Mary. After this, all her focus turned to her unborn baby, which by this point she had been carrying for three to four months. She had never prayed so hard for a boy.

On January 29, Catherine of Aragon was buried at Peterborough Cathedral. Chapuys complained that it was not a fitting location, and "the place where she is buried in the church is far removed from the high altar, and much less honorable than that of certain bishops buried there." He was appalled at the way, even in death, she had been treated, but then a piece of news reached him that gave him immense pleasure: "The concubine [Anne] has had a miscarriage, which seemed to be a male child which she has not born three and a half months, at which the king has shown great distress."

The baby, which was her only source of hope, had been lost. Chapuys reported that Anne, distraught, was blaming her uncle, the Duke of Norfolk, for distressing her, giving her news of a serious accident Henry had suffered at a tournament six days before. He had fallen from his horse, and some believed he had suffered serious brain injuries.[24] But Henry was fine. Learning of Anne's miscarriage, however, drew a line under his former affections for his wife. As far as he was concerned, the union was over.

Henry confided in one of his courtiers "in great secrecy" that: "I have been seduced and forced into this second marriage by means of sortilege and charms, and that, owing to that, I hold it as null. God had well shown me displeasure at it by denying me male children." He paused for a moment before adding, "I can take a third wife, as it is what I wish much to do."[25]

While Anne was still grieving her miscarried child, Henry withdrew all compassion and was already determined to discard her. He had pursued her all those years ago, and now here they were. After a decade of their toxic passion, he now planned to leave her. Her friends and allies, including those in France, had long since deserted her to protect their own political interests and agendas, and now her husband was looking for a new wife— and he would not have to look for long.

The French, upon hearing the news, were the first to think of an alternative for Henry. Nicolas Raince—one of Francis's trusted secretaries—was sent to Rome, and du Bellay, believed to be too much of a supporter of Anne Boleyn, was recalled. Raince suggested to the Pope that Madeleine, Francis's sixteen-year-old daughter, would be a good option for Henry's third marriage. Such a union would once more strengthen the Anglo-French alliance, would avoid Paul III having to excommunicate Henry, and would make England "return to communion with Rome."[26] Anne Boleyn, it seemed, was already forgotten.

However, Henry already had his eyes on a new bride: Jane Seymour. As Cromwell made clear to Chapuys, "should the King, my master, want another wife, it is certainly not among the French that he will look for one."[27]

Henry had tired of Anne's French connections, and he certainly didn't want to risk having a real French princess, not to mention one under Francis's influence. He had certainly learned his lesson there.

*

Chapuys wrote to the French ambassador, Castelnau, about what he had discovered regarding Henry's new lover:

She is the sister of a certain Edward Semel [Seymour], who has been in the service of his majesty; she is of middle height, and nobody thinks that she has much beauty. Her complexion is so whitish that she may be called rather pale [a clear contrast with Anne's olive skin]. She is a little over twenty-five. You may imagine whether, being an Englishwoman and having been so long at court, she would not hold it a sin to be still a maid. At which this king will perhaps be rather pleased for he may marry her on condition that she is a virgin and when he wants a divorce he will find plenty of witnesses to the contrary.

Chapuys was certainly a man who could hold a grudge.

"The said Semel [Jane Seymour] is not very intelligent," he continued, "and is said to be rather haughty. She was formerly in the service of the good queen [Catherine] and seems to bear great good-will and respect to the princess [Mary]."[28]

Indeed, Jane Seymour was a staunch Catholic, and now she was an enemy of Anne herself.

After Anne had recovered from the physical trauma of her miscarriage, she hoped to be reunited with her husband and busied herself with looking after her and her daughter's needs. She bought many gowns in silk cloth and satin—promoting their royal status for everyone to see; a fashion taste that Elizabeth would continue later on during her reign.[29] Henry, however, no longer wished to be in Anne's presence and she was instructed to remain at Greenwich. Instead, he spent more and more time with his new mistress, making his intentions very clear to all, including Anne.

By the end of February 1536, Edward Seymour had been made a gentleman of the king's privy council. The Boleyn faction was crumbling away, losing influence in the privy council while the Seymours were on the rise, and Anne was absolutely powerless.

But she would not go down without a fight. She was Anne Boleyn, the woman for whom Henry had moved heaven and earth to marry, making her his queen. She was convinced that she could turn the tide in her favor once more.

★

In late March 1536, Anne Boleyn and Thomas Cromwell were clearly fighting the ultimate power struggle to determine which of them would remain in favor. Anne was sure that, if she could overcome Cromwell, she would find herself back in Henry's affections, and she believed that her intellect could help her in this. Anne was convinced that the religious reforms needed to be more moderate if they were not to alienate the people, as well as England's European neighbors, entirely, and she used her almoner, John Skipp, to preach her ideas on her behalf. This was also a welcome opportunity to challenge Cromwell's authority in the matter.

More specifically, Anne was against the "program of suppression which would see her husband's coffers filled with the wealth of the dissolved monasteries."[30] She believed that this money should serve the people instead and would ensure her husband, and also herself, remained more popular. In proposing this Anne was taking a stand against Cromwell and also her own husband, who did not see the benefit of the ideas she was putting forward, particularly now that he was preoccupied with a new mistress. Abandoned after the loss of her child, Anne was seeing her husband in all his unpredictable cruelty.

In late March, Chapuys received the Marchioness of Exeter, a fervent supporter of Catherine, who reported that "the concubine [Anne] and Cromwell were not on good terms."[31] The imperial ambassador felt that the tide had turned and that an alliance between Charles V and Henry VIII was now attainable. This was not good news for Anne.

Chapuys and Cromwell met a few times in secret to discuss the terms that might be agreeable to Henry. They knew that such an alliance would put Anne in an even more difficult position, as she had been a Francophile all her life and a supporter of an Anglo-French alliance for almost the entirety of her reign. Already isolated at court, she would be even more so if matters progressed in this way. But Anne also knew that an Anglo-French alliance would no longer serve her interests and that, ultimately, the French had turned their backs on her, with the exception, perhaps, of Jean du Bellay.

The French were no longer in favor at Henry's court, and Castelnau tried to use his own relationship with Chapuys to obtain audiences with either Cromwell or Henry. After being invited to meet the king at Greenwich, Castelnau ended up meeting the Duke of Norfolk instead, who promised him that "the friendship between the kings [Francis and Henry] cannot be affected by any practice or overture of the Emperor." This was a lie.

Henry showed great coldness toward the French ambassador, blaming Francis for "making war on the duke of Savoy" over Nice, and for once again trying to fight against Charles V over Milan.

Castelnau asked for Henry's aid.

"I have received letters from the Emperor himself that I need to scrutinize before giving anyone an answer," Henry replied.[32] After all the turmoil and the break with Rome, England still seemed to be a powerful influencer, especially when it came to the rivalry that raged between Francis and Charles.

On the Tuesday after Easter, Chapuys was summoned to court; he was to meet with the king for a private audience. Upon his arrival, he was greeted by George Boleyn, who was still attempting to mingle in state affairs, and other lords. When asked if he would meet with Anne, Chapuys politely refused: "For a long time, my will has been slave to this king [Henry] and that to serve him it is enough to command me; but I think, for several reasons, which I will tell the king another time, such a visit would not be advisable."[33]

He then accompanied the king to mass and noticed that "there was a great concourse of people, partly to see how the concubine and I behaved to each other. She was courteous enough, for when I was behind the door by which she entered, she returned, merely to do me reverence as I did to her."

After dinner, Chapuys reported that Anne made a bold statement against the French: "It is a great shame the way in which the king of France treats his uncle, the duke of Savoy, and to make war against Milan so as to break the enterprise against the Turks. It seems that the king of France, weary of his life on account of his illnesses, wishes by war to put an end to his days."[34]

Anne was playing the games set up by the men of the court, and said what she needed to say to retain her influence on Henry. This would not, however, be enough to protect her from what was to come.

Despite these clear attempts at reassuring Chapuys regarding England's position toward France, the imperial ambassador felt it was just another stratagem from the English, and therefore proceeded with caution when it came to discussing peace treaties with the Holy Roman Empire. He noticed that, at the end of April, the privy council was meeting for long hours—something he believed was related to European political affairs.

It was not. Instead, the council was discussing Anne. The men who, it was said, had been close to her were to be interrogated. A violent storm was brewing.

*

On April 26, 1536, Anne met with her chaplain, Matthew Parker. The details of the conversation were not recorded but, later in his life, Parker recalled the queen making him promise to "watch over her daughter" if anything happened to her.[35] This was a promise he kept, as he served Elizabeth as Archbishop of Canterbury from 1559 until his death in 1575. Anne knew that something was building against her but, as yet, she had no idea of its true scale.

On April 27, parliament was summoned unexpectedly. This would only happen in some kind of emergency, and rumors spread that the meeting concerned Anne's removal as queen of England. For now, Anne was oblivious to this. She had been told by Henry that they would travel together to Dover, stopping at "Rochester" on their way down to the coast.[36]

However, Anne must have known her influence, and that of her family, was on the wane when Nicholas Carew received the Order of the Garter over the expected appointment, her brother George. Chapuys rejoiced that "the concubine has not had sufficient influence to get it for her brother" and Carew was certainly no supporter of Anne or her faction.[37] Chapuys continued, gleefully, that "the king is already sick and tired of the concubine... he could abandon the said concubine."[38]

Next, on Saturday, April 29, Anne had an altercation with Henry Norris, who had been promised to her cousin, Mary Shelton, though the union had been delayed.

"You look for dead men's shoes for it aught came to the king but good, you would look to have me!" she barked at him.[39]

Suddenly realizing what she had said, and how it could be interpreted—as the new Treason Act of 1534 forbade even imagining the king's death—Anne tried to take back her words, but it was too late. Her sentiments of anger and frustration, spoken metaphorically rather than literally, would soon be used against her.

Anne's planned journey to Dover was abruptly canceled as rumors that her marriage would soon be ended now spread like wildfire. Henry, for his part, had no interest in seeing her. On May 2, Chapuys reported the scandalous news to Charles:

> The great disgrace of the concubine who by the judgment of God has been brought in full daylight from Greenwich to the Tower of London conducted by the duke of Norfolk, the two Chamberlains of the realm and of the chamber, and only four women have been left to her. The report is that it is for adultery, in which she has long continued, with a player on the spinet of her chamber, who has been this morning lodged in the Tower, and Mr. Norris [...] the concubine's brother, named Rocheford, has also been lodged in the Tower, but more than six hours after the others, and three or four before his sister, and even if the said crime of adultery had not been discovered, this king as I have for some days been informed by good authority, has been determined to abandon her.

Chapuys ended his letter with a comment that characterized the sheer surprise of such a shift of events: "These news are indeed new, but it is still more wonderful to think of the sudden change from yesterday to today."[40] It was a huge and horrifying shift, Anne now accused unfounded of adultery and imprisoned in the Tower of London so abruptly.

Thomas Cranmer sent a letter to the king, showing his support to the sovereign—but also his surprise at hearing such news: "If the reports of the queen be true, they are only to her dishonor, not yours. I am clean amazed, for, I had never better opinion of a woman. [...] I was most bound to her of all creatures living, and therefore beg that I may, with your Grace's favor, wish and pray that she may declare herself innocent."[41]

So this was what had been happening behind closed doors of the privy council: they were finding a way to discard Anne for good. The first accusation was that she had bedded Henry Percy, Earl of Northumberland, who swore that no "pre-contract between the queen" and him ever happened. "I intend to receive that the same may be to my damnation if ever there were any contract or promise of marriage between her and me."[42]

Anne had never agreed to marry any other man than Henry.

These false accusations of adultery were simply Henry's way of removing her from the equation, for good.

*

At the Tower of London, Anne felt lost and surely devastated; she probably could not believe that such charges would be brought upon her. She had been nothing but a loyal servant to her husband, the king. For all the savvy maneuvers she had made, it is likely that she truly loved him, having put herself through so much to be with him and to become his queen. Surely, a politically astute woman with no family lineage to fall back on could not be foolish enough to make the repeated mistake of taking lovers at court for everyone to see?

Sir William Kingston, the constable of the Tower, visited Anne upon her arrival.

"Shall I go into a dungeon?" she asked, trembling with fear.

"No, Madam. You shall go into the lodging you lay in at your coronation," the constable replied.

"It is too good for me," she whimpered before pausing for a moment. "Jesus have mercy on me!" she added, kneeling down and weeping.

As she calmed down, she inquired about when he would see the king, but he told her he would not. She also asked about her "sweet brother" and the men who had also been brought to the Tower, and she continued by weeping, "My mother will die with sorrow. Will I die without justice?" she trembled.

"I'm afraid the king has justice," he replied.[43]

A few days passed and Kingston made another visit to Anne, who had rallied, and was now "merry," insisting that she "shall have justice."

"I have done nothing. They cannot bring witnesses as there are none," she told him.[44]

Anne was resolute and would not let her spirit be destroyed.

With this in mind, she wrote to Henry:

> Your grace's displeasure and my imprisonment are things so strange unto me as what to write or what to excuse, I am altogether ignorant. [...] But do not imagine that your poor wife will ever confess a fault which she never even imagined. Never had prince a more dutiful wife than you have in me, Anne Boleyn. [...] You chose me from a low estate, and I beg you not to let an unworthy stain of disloyalty blot me and the infant Princess, your daughter. Let me have a lawful trial and let not my enemies be my judges. Let it be an open trial, I fear no open shame and you will see my innocence cleared or my guilt openly proved.

She knew that the claims against her had no grounds. She was not afraid of defending herself publicly, and she was not afraid to be outspoken as she added: "But if you have already determined that my death and an infamous slander will bring you the enjoyment of your desired happiness, then I pray God he will pardon your great sin. My innocence will be known at the Day of Judgment."

Before signing her missive, she begged for the lives of the men falsely accused of having had sexual relationships with her: "My last request is that I alone may bear the burden of your displeasure, and not those poor gentlemen, who, I understand, are likewise imprisoned for my sake."[45]

She maintained her innocence, but Henry was unmoved.

*

Cromwell, seizing his moment to rid himself of a rival, instructed the English ambassadors at the French court to make Anne's guilt as clear as possible to Francis, claiming that even "the ladies of her privy chamber could not conceal it" and that there had been a "certain conspiracy of the king's death."[46] Yet, these ladies, whatever confessions they might have made, must have been coerced to do so. No one would risk going against the king's will once it had been made so clear.

On May 15, 1536, Anne was tried alongside her brother, George. The members of the trial commission, sitting in judgment, included many former allies and supporters, including Henry Percy and Charles Brandon, Duke of Suffolk. The accusations were vile:

"Queen Anne has been the wife of Henry VIII for three years and more. She, despising her marriage and entertaining malice against the king, and following daily her frail and carnal lust, did falsely and traitorously procure by base conversations and kisses, touching, gifts, and other infamous incitations, divers of the king's daily and familiar servants to be her adulterers and concubines."

It was claimed that, on October 12, 1533, she'd had intercourse with Henry Norris, only a month after giving birth to Elizabeth, and that in November of the same year, they again had sexual intercourse at court. Many more such accusations were made against her, with different men, and at times and places including those where Anne could not have been physically present. In November 1535, it was said that she had "incited her own brother, George Boleyn, to violate her," alluring him with her tongue in his mouth. She then apparently pursued and convinced William Brereton to engage with her in sexual intercourse, and again with Sir Francis Weston, and then again with Mark Smeaton, the musician who had entertained them. These men were all accused of having met and "conspired the death and destruction of the king."

After such accusations, Anne stood firm and pleaded "not guilty."

The verdicts were, however, not long delayed. The prisoners were "to be taken to prison in the Tower, and then, at the king's command, to the Green within the Tower, and there to be burned or beheaded as shall please the king."[47]

Lancelot de Carle, Castelnau's secretary, reported that Anne remained composed when receiving the sentence. Upon hearing of her terrible fate, she prayed to God: "O Father of humankind, wherein is the life, way, and truth?" she asked. "You know if I deserve this death." She then turned to the judges. "I believe you know full well the reason why you have condemned me, which is other than the one you have deduced from this trial, for I am clear of all of it. And I have no need for God to pardon me for it, nor ever grant me any grace for it: for I have always been faithful to the king."

Anne made her innocence as clear as she could without offending the men who had clearly been instructed to find her guilty.

"And for this reason, I wish that this last speech serve only to give solace to my sense of honor, and that of my brother and of those men whom you have judged to die and have estranged from their good reputation, such that I wish that I had the ability to defend and deliver them and take on for myself a thousand deaths."[48]

She remained dignified and eloquent even in those frightening moments. And her spirit continued to be strong. A day later, she told Kingston that she would have dinner with the nuns and that she was "in hope of life." Cranmer also potentially met with her at that dinner to "confess to an impediment to her marriage."[49]

Maybe there was hope after all, and that, even if her marriage was not spared, her life might yet be....

★

On May 17, George Boleyn, Henry Norris, Francis Weston, William Brereton and Mark Smeaton were executed on Tower Hill for crimes they had not committed. They were beheaded by ax.

Anne learned she was to be executed the next day.

Heartbroken, she still hoped for mercy. She would find none, however, from her husband—though he clearly believed he was acting with benevolence. He issued a writ declaring that he would spare Anne being burned by fire and that, instead: "we, however, command that immediately after receipt of these presents, upon the Green within our Tower of London aforesaid, the head of the same Anne shall be caused to be cut off."[50] As another gesture, he ordered that the decapitation should be with a sword and not with an ax.

A French swordsman was due to arrive to perform his duty, though to this day his identity remains unknown; executioners' names were often kept secret to avoid retaliations against their families.

Perhaps because this swordsman had been delayed, Anne's execution was postponed by one more day, prolonging her agonies.

"I hear say that I shall not die afore noon, and I am very sorry therefore; for I thought to be dead and past my pain," Anne replied to Kingston, who had informed her of the situation.[51]

What if Henry had changed his mind? What if he had had a change of heart and had decided to send her to a convent instead? She must have considered such possibilities and, although she had lost so much already, they must have given her a hint of hope that this nightmare would end—a hint of life to which she held on to, maybe until the very last minute. The next day, however, on May 19, 1536, Kingston came to Anne's apartment to inform her of her imminent execution.

As she walked out of her apartments and over to the scaffold that had been erected between the White Tower and the Green, Anne showed her composure and looked bravely forward. She saw the faces of many people she knew, including Charles Brandon, Henry Fitzroy (Henry VIII's illegitimate son), Thomas Cromwell and Lancelot de Carle, who would immortalize her final moments in writing. Her former French allies had eventually abandoned her, but they would certainly not forget her.

If Anne had hoped that Henry was hidden somewhere among the crowd, and that he was waiting until the very last moment to show her mercy, she was mistaken. He was miles away, hunting with his new mistress, Jane Seymour—to whom he would be betrothed the next day, and he would marry ten days later.

As she stood on the scaffold, Anne made her last speech, one that would resonate through the centuries, in which she showed the courage that ran through her blood—courage that would ultimately have the aim of protecting her daughter from their detractors.

"Good Christian people," she announced, looking out at the gathered crowd, "I am come hither to die, for according to the law and by the law I am judged to die, and therefore I will speak nothing against it. I am come hither to accuse no man, nor to speak anything of that whereof I am accused and condemned to die, but I pray God to save the king and send him long to reign over you [...] And thus I take my leave of the world and of you all, and I heartily desire you all to pray for me."[52]

Anne was a pious woman for whom religion remained an important, if ambiguous, part of her identity—as she wished it in her book of prayers, where she wrote, "remember me when you do pray / that hope doth lead from day to day / Anne Boleyn."[53]

After her last speech, all shred of hope she might have held on to slowly left her body and soul as she kneeled down and prayed to God one last time.

The act itself by the swordsman was swift and smooth—God did take mercy on her after all.

Anne Boleyn, the woman who had changed the course of history, was now dead. Despite Henry's efforts to destroy her reputation, she would be forever immortalized, in all her intelligence and strength, in the injustice of her death.

Epilogue

À Jamais *Remembered*

"I am becoming more and more French, my dear Anne [Savage]. After two years at this court, it is said that I have changed greatly. [...] They laugh a lot here, and when it comes to the sense of humor, I am quite *Gauloise* [French]. They call me Mademoiselle de Boulen here, as a councilor to the king said: it is the real name of my family before they established themselves in England," Anne Boleyn allegedly wrote to her friend, Anne Savage, during her time in France.[1]

In 1837, the author and noble Paul de Musset—brother of the famous French poet Alfred de Musset—who was fascinated by the life and memory of Anne Boleyn, decided to write a historical novel based on her life, achievements and tragic end. He claimed that "four letters to Anne Savage" from Anne Boleyn was all we had left of her during her stay at the French court. The above excerpt is taken from one of them.

In another letter, Anne wrote: "I have left the service of the queen to serve Princess Marguerite, the king's sister, who has befriended me"—corroborating many accounts of the nineteenth century, albeit based on no hard evidence, that stated Anne must have been in service of Marguerite, which is why she would later in life call her "a friend."[2] This claim is obviously hard to maintain because of the lack of sources, but it cannot be completely dismissed as not all of Marguerite's household records have been kept.

Musset, who felt confident in using these letters in his work, was a writer whose historical novels were colorful and vivid. He had to make them so in order to differentiate himself from what he saw as boring, plain history. It is no surprise, therefore, that he chose to romanticize these letters, taking many liberties when conveying them to the readers: vocabulary, grammatical and linguistic changes were evidently made. He also did not provide any footnotes or bibliography, and seemed to refer to manuscripts to which he supposedly had personal access. Their veracity, then, can definitely be called into question, which is why I have not cited them in this book, but two important points deserve to be taken into account.

First, given his own status as a nobleman during the French revolutions, as well as his affiliation with his brother who was acclaimed and respected, it is not impossible to imagine that, given the controversies of Anne's life, such a lie would have damaged his own reputation.

Second, and perhaps more crucially, the noble family of the de Mussets were cousins of the noble family of the du Bellays.[3] Could it be possible that Jean du Bellay—fervent supporter of Anne Boleyn during his lifetime, and someone who was close to her—had acquired these letters from her or one of her friends and passed them down to his descendants or cousins? This idea cannot be too easily discarded as, if real, these letters are everything we have left of Anne during her time in France.

Regardless of their veracity, Paul de Musset's work proves that Anne's memory and legacy continued in France even centuries after her death.

Lancelot de Carle, who witnessed the queen's execution and who was a friend of Joachim du Bellay, a cousin of Jean du Bellay, ensured that his pamphlet *The Story of the Death of Anne Boleyn*,

Queen of England was printed and circulated at the French court. Who read it, no one will truly ever know for sure, but it would be fair to assume that Francis and the French royals read it, as well as Jean du Bellay—who must have felt terrible about Anne's tragic end. De Carle's long narrative poem was printed in 1545 when he was a renowned poet of the French court and chaplain to Henry, Dauphin of France, the future Henry III—showing that the ghost of Anne Boleyn never truly left the French court.

De Carle hoped that God "should wish to have mercy on this queen and also on these gentlemen, and that they may be with Him in glory and honor."[4] This "glory and honor" might have been found in Heaven but has also certainly been found on Earth, with so many authors, playwrights and screenwriters paying tribute to the queen who unjustly lost her head.

In 1854, French playwright Adolphe-Simonis Empis wished to show Anne's vulnerability to the public, especially after her miscarriage in January 1536, and the terrible events that would eventually unfold for her:

> Anne: When I think of what Elizabeth Barton and Anne Askew [this is a mistake made by the author, as Askew, who was executed in 1546, would have been just 15 years old in 1536] predicted for me...All these horrible accidents...So many foes...The loss of this baby, of this son that I have so wished for...Stillborn... He was so strong and beautiful...(*she wipes her tears away*). And the king's fall...What would have happened to me if he had died that day? And now...now...What is he going to do with me? Is he going to repudiate me like he repudiated Catherine of Aragon?

Anne's tragic end has inspired many authors to imagine and reimagine her life, but also the words she said. She sparked interest and fascination to the point where, even today, she continues to be remembered and adored by "fans" all around the world, with many societies bearing her name, many of whom focus on the injustices meted out to women by men.

Later in his play, Empis created an iconic scene between the toddler Elizabeth—who seemed very mature and articulate for her young age—and her mother, Anne.

> Elizabeth: Mother, do you think that one day I will be queen myself?
> Anne: Why? Have you been thinking about it, Elizabeth?
> Elizabeth: I am not sure... I always think about it.
> Anne: Maybe, my daughter...
> Elizabeth: Queen... possessing a realm? Ruling a state?... Or only queen, like you are, Mother? Like you, wife of a king?
> Anne: My daughter, no one can predict fate!
> Elizabeth: Last night, Lord Wriothesley came to me to compliment me.
> Anne: About what?
> Elizabeth: He told me a big secret... that the son of the king of France wants to marry me. At my age, wouldn't it be too early? Mother, is it true? Lord Wriothesley is so fake and such a liar...
> Anne: Wouldn't you be proud to be one day queen of France? Like your aunt, Mary?
> Elizabeth: Ah! That would be something... but no... I do not wish to marry... I want to stay a girl...
> Anne: Why?
> Elizabeth: Mother... I've seen you cry so many times...
> Anne: My daughter, there are queens much happier than I am...
> Elizabeth: Anyway, I do not wish to marry as I do not wish to obey...
> Anne: Elizabeth! (*with a tone of disapproval*)
> Elizabeth: Except for God and for you, Mother.
> Anne: That is my girl.[5]

In many ways, this scene, though fanciful, shows that Anne's legacy would live on through her daughter, Queen Elizabeth I, who would ultimately avenge Anne's mistreatment by her enemies—even Henry VIII.

Anne might not have given Henry a son—the crime of which, ultimately, cost her life—but in Elizabeth she gave England a ruler who refused to marry, and so became its first female "king," a monarch who challenged patriarchal society and defied the greatest European power at that time: Spain.

Elizabeth is often remembered for her fierce and fiery temperament, qualities that were often attributed to her father, but, in my view, she inherited these qualities from her mother. After all, like Elizabeth, Anne was "a rock who will not bend in any direction."[6]

Even centuries later, Anne Boleyn continues to fascinate not just historians, but novelists, playwrights and librettists. The truth is, she will always be an intriguing royal icon: the woman whose influence helped shape the future of Anglo-French relations, but who, in the end, could not rely on her French allies to protect either her status as Henry's queen, or her life. Anne's tragic end—and France's involvement in her story—explains why her memory has lived on there as well as in England, and, I believe, will continue to live on, forever.

Notes

Prologue: A Rose Between a Lion and a Salamander, Calais, October 25–27, 1532

1 *Entrevue de François Ier avec Henry VIII à Boulogne-sur-Mer en 1532*, ed. Alfred Hamy (Paris: L. Gougy, 1898), 74.
2 Ibid., 76.
3 Ibid., 244.

1: Games of Court

1 Jacques Santrot, *Les doubles funérailles d'Anne de Bretagne: Le corps et le coeur (Janvier–mars 1514)* (Paris: Librairie Droz, 2017), 62.
2 *Le Trespas de l'Hermine regrettée*, Musée des Beaux-arts, Paris, LDUT665, fol. 10v.
3 Desmond Seward, *Prince of the Renaissance: The Life of François I* (London: Constable, 1973), 34.
4 Ibid.
5 Leonie Frieda, *Francis I: The Maker of Modern France* (London: Weidenfeld & Nicolson, 2021), 37–8.
6 Pierre de Bourdeille, Brantôme, *Œuvres complètes*, ed. Ludovic Lalanne, vol. 3 (1848, repr., New York: Johnson Reprint, 1968), 242–3.
7 Lauren Mackay, *Among the Wolves of Court: The Untold Story of Thomas and George Boleyn* (London: Bloomsbury Academic, 2020), 55.
8 For more on the important role of ladies-in-waiting, see Nadine Akkerman and Birgit Houben (eds.), *The Politics of Female Household: Ladies-in-Waiting Across Early Modern Europe* (Leiden: Brill, 2014).
9 *Correspondance de l'empereur Maximilien Ier et de Marguerite d'Autriche, sa fille, Gouvernante des Pays-Bas, de 1507 à 1519*, vol. 2 (Paris: Imprimerie de Crapelet, 1839), 461, n. 2, translation by Eric Ives, *The Life and Death of Anne Boleyn* (Oxford: Blackwell, 2004), 19.

10 Margaret of Savoy, April 24, 1514, *Letters and Papers, Foreign and Domestic, Henry VIII, Vol. 1, Part 1. 1513–1514*, 1242.
11 *Letters and Papers, Foreign and Domestic, Henry VIII (L&P)*, vol. 1, 1250.
12 Ibid., 1271.
13 Ibid., 1275.
14 Gérard de Plaines to Margaret of Savoy, June 30, 1514, *Lettres de Louis XII*, vol. 4 (Brussels: François Foppens, 1759), 335.
15 L&P, vol. 1, 1344.
16 British Library, Harley MS 3642, f. 142.
17 BL, Cotton MS Caligula D. VI, f. 143.
18 L&P, vol. 1, 1421.
19 *The Manuscripts of J. Eliot Hodgkin*, Fifteenth Report, Appendix, Part II (London: Her Majesty's Stationery Office, 1897), 30.
20 BL, Cotton MS Caligula D. VII, f. 253.
21 L&P, vol. 1, 1413.
22 Bibliothèque Nationale de Coeur, NAF 9175, f. 365.
23 For a thorough discussion on who was the eldest daughter, Anne or Mary (still disputed among historians), see Alison Weir, *Mary Boleyn* (London: Vintage, 2012), 17–20.
24 BL, Cotton MS Caligula D. VI, f. 203.
25 L&P, vol. 1, 1433–6.
26 Ibid., 1438.
27 Dorset to Wolsey, November 22, 1514, BL, Cotton MS Caligula D. VI, f. 192.

2: The Rise of a Magnificent King and His Ladies

1 R. E. Giesey, *The Funeral Ceremony in Renaissance France* (Geneva: Librairie Droz, 1960), 39.
2 Lancelot de Carle, *The Story of the Death of Anne Boleyn, Queen of England*, transcribed from the seventeen versions of that text in JoAnn DellaNeva, *The Story of the Death of Anne Boleyn, a Poem by Lancelot de Carle* (Tempe: ACMRS Press, 2021), 155.
3 Frieda, *Francis I*, 45.
4 BL, Cotton MS Caligula D. VI, f. 268.
5 Ibid., f. 179.
6 Ibid., f. 165.
7 Ibid., f. 206.
8 Ibid., f. 176.
9 Ibid., f. 242.
10 Paget, "The Youth of Anne Boleyn," 166. Also see Lauren Mackay's PhD dissertation, which came to the same conclusion when it comes to which queen Anne is referring to, *Among the Wolves of Court*, 32.
11 Carle in DellaNeva, *Story of the Death of Anne Boleyn*, 157.

12 Archives de Tarascon, BB 12, f. 353, délib, January 16, 1516.
13 Émile Baux, Victor-Louis Bourrilly, Philippe Mabilly, "Le voyage des reines et de François 1er en Provence et dans la vallée du Rhône (décembre 1515–février 1516)," *Annales du Midi*, vol. 16, no. 61 (1904), 48.
14 Ibid., 49–50.
15 BNF, MS Fr 14116, f. 11v.
16 BNF, MS Fr 5750, f. 17r.
17 Antonio de Beatis, *The Travel Journal of Antonio de Beatis: Germany, Switzerland, the Low Countries, France and Italy, 1517–1518* (London: Hakluyt Society, 1979), 107.
18 Seward, *Prince of the Renaissance*, 70.
19 Cynthia J. Brown, ed., *Pierre Gringore, Les entrées royales à Paris de Marie d'Angleterre (1514) et Claude de France (1517)* (Geneva: Librairie Droz, 2005), 44.
20 Ibid., 45.
21 Ibid., 73.
22 BL, Cotton MS Caligula D. VII, f. 7.
23 L&P, vol. 2, 4336.
24 BL, Cotton MS Caligula E. I. II, f. 17.
25 L&P, vol. 2, 4475.
26 Ibid., 4480.
27 Ibid., 4504.
28 Ibid., 4626.
29 BNF, MS Fr 5761, f. 13.
30 BL, Cotton MS Caligula D. VII, f. 167.
31 Ibid., f. 57.
32 L&P, vol. 2, 4661.
33 Ibid.
34 BL, Cotton MS Caligula D. VII, f. 58.
35 L&P, vol. 2, 4661.
36 Ibid., 4674.
37 Report of Antonion Giustinian, Venetian ambassador in France, ibid., 4675.

3: Witnessing the Pursuit of Grandeur

1 BL, Cotton MS Caligula D. VII, f. 90.
2 Ibid., f. 91.
3 Ibid., f. 98.
4 L&P, vol. 3, 84.
5 BL, Cotton MS Caligula D. VII, f. 99.
6 Ibid., f. 101.
7 Ibid.
8 L&P, vol. 3, 137.
9 Ibid., 142.

10 Bibliothèque Sainte-Geneviève, MS 848, ff. 150–5.
11 L&P, vol. 3, 748.
12 BNF, MS Fr 10383, f. 27.
13 For a full description, see B. De Montfaucon, *Les Monuments de la monarchie française*, vol. 4 (Paris: Gandouin et Giffart, 1732), 164–81.
14 BNF, MS Fr 10383, f. 20.
15 Bodleian Library, MS Ashmole, 1116, f. 100.
16 L&P, vol. 3, 869.
17 Bodleian Library, MS Ashmole, 1116, f. 97.
18 Ibid., f. 101.

4: Troubled Waters

1 L&P, vol. 3, 1736.
2 Ibid., 1762.
3 Ibid., 1994.
4 Edward Hall, *Hall's Chronicles* (London: Johnson, 1809), 631.
5 Weir, *Mary Boleyn*, 145.
6 BL, Cotton MS Caligula D. VIII, f. 219.
7 L&P, vol. 4, 420.
8 Frieda, *Francis I*, 158.
9 Ibid., 159.
10 Ibid., 171.
11 BNF, Fonds Béthumes 8471, f. 137.
12 Ibid., f. 28.
13 DellaNeva, *Story of the Death of Anne Boleyn*, 159.
14 Ibid., 67.
15 Ives, *Life and Death of Anne Boleyn*, 63.

5: Struggle to Power

1 L&P, vol. 4, 3105.
2 Ibid.
3 On a discussion of when the divorce discussions might have started and other historiographical debates on the topic, see Ives, *Life and Death of Anne Boleyn*, 86–90.
4 L&P, vol. 4, 3140.
5 *Calendar of State Papers, Spain* (CSPS), vol. 3, 113.
6 Ibid., 118.
7 "Love Letters from King Henry VIII to Anne Boleyn" (LLHAB), Biblioteca Apostolica Vaticana, Vat.lat.3731, Letter 1, 3.
8 LLHAB, Letter 16, 29–30.

9 Ives, *Life and Death of Anne Boleyn*, 87.
10 LLHAB, Letter 5, 13–14.
11 CSPS, vol. 3, 152.
12 LLHAB, Letter 2, 5.
13 BNF, MS Fr 3079, f. 24.
14 BNF, MS Fr 3076, f. 2.
15 For more on this, see Owen Emmerson, Kate McCaffrey and Alison Palmer, *Catherine and Anne: Queens, Mothers, Rivals* (Hever Castle: Jigsaw Publishing, 2023).
16 BNF, MS Fr 5499, f. 51.
17 BNF, MS Fr 3021, f. 105.
18 BNF, MS Fr 5499, f. 61.
19 BNF, MS Fr 3080, f. 117.
20 L&P, vol. 4, 4360.
21 BNF, MS Fr 3077, f. 75.
22 Ibid., 76.
23 Ibid., 77.
24 L&P, vol. 4, 4383.
25 BNF, MS Fr 3078, f. 62.
26 BNF, MS Fr 3080, f. 41.
27 Ibid., f. 42.
28 BNF, MS Fr 3079, f. 1.

6: *Ainsi Sera, Groigne qui Groigne*

1 CSPS, vol. 3, 621.
2 BNF, MS Fr 3076, f. 58.
3 BNF, MS Fr 2974, f. 85.
4 L&P, vol. 4, 5675.
5 BNF, MS Fr 3078, f. 34.
6 L&P, vol. 4, 5681.
7 Ibid., 5687.
8 Ibid., 5695.
9 BNF, MS Fr 5499, f. 135.
10 Ibid., f. 136.
11 L&P, vol. 4, 5422.
12 BNF, MS Fr 3040, f. 69.
13 L&P, vol. 4, 6016.
14 Ibid., 5999.
15 BNF, Clairambault 329, f. 10.
16 CSPS, vol. 4, part 1, 194.
17 BNF, MS Fr 3005, f. 165–6.

18 L&P, vol. 4, 6075.
19 *Calendar of State Papers relating to English Affairs in the Archives of Venice, Vol. 4, 1527–1533* (London: Her Majesty's Stationery Office, 1871) (CSPV), 559.
20 CSPS, vol. 4, part 1, 232.
21 CSPV, 560.
22 Ibid., 561.
23 CSPS, vol. 4, part 1, 245.
24 Ibid., 250.
25 BNF, MS Fr 3012, f. 79.
26 BNF, MS Fr 3014, f. 78.
27 BNF, MS Fr 3078, f. 103.
28 BNF, MS Fr 3077, ff. 93–8.
29 Ibid., f. 107.
30 CSPS, vol. 4, part 1, 354.
31 Ibid., 373.
32 Ibid., 372.
33 Ibid., 509.
34 Ives, *Life and Death of Anne Boleyn*, 141.

7: Every Rose Has Its Thorn

1 CSPS, vol. 4, part 1, 555.
2 Paul Friedmann, *Anne Boleyn, 1527–1536* (London: Macmillan and Co., 1884), vol. 1, 128.
3 CSPS, vol. 4, part 2, 584.
4 L&P, vol. 5, 27.
5 Ibid., 64.
6 Ibid., 216.
7 Friedmann, *Anne Boleyn*, vol. 1, 142.
8 L&P, vol. 5, 251.
9 CSPS, vol. 4, part 2, 739.
10 Ibid.
11 Ibid., 802.
12 Ibid.
13 Ibid.
14 CSPV, 701.
15 CSPS, vol. 4, part 2, 880.
16 BNF, MS Fr 15970, f. 8.
17 Nicolas Camusat, *Meslanges historiques* (Troyes, 1644), 171.
18 L&P, vol. 5, 706.
19 Ibid., 750.
20 BNF, MS Fr 4126, f. 5.

21 Friedmann, *Anne Boleyn*, vol. 1, 156.
22 CSPS, vol. 4, part 2, 934.
23 Friedmann, *Anne Boleyn*, vol. 1, 158.
24 L&P, vol. 5, 1247.
25 BNF, MS Fr 15970, f. 5.
26 CSPS, vol 4, part 2, 1256.
27 *Entrevue*, x.
28 Jean-Luc Déjean, *Marguerite de Navarre* (Paris: Fayard, 1987), 156.
29 L&P, vol. 5, 1187.
30 BL, Add. MS 6113, f. 70.
31 L&P, vol. 5, 1316.

8: "The Most Happy"

1 Camusat, *Meslanges*, 109.
2 Ives, *Life and Death of Anne Boleyn*, 161.
3 L&P, vol. 5, 1541.
4 BNF, Dupuy 260, f. 411.
5 Camusat, *Meslanges*, ii.
6 CSPS, vol. 4, part 2, 1043.
7 Thomas Cranmer, *Letters* (Cambridge: Cambridge University Press, 1746), 246.
8 L&P, vol. 6, 230.
9 Franny Moyle speculates that the portrait was commissioned by Anne Boleyn but I have not found sustainable evidence to corroborate this.
10 L&P, vol. 6, 254.
11 Ibid., 255.
12 Camusat, *Meslanges*, 82.
13 Ibid., 83.
14 L&P, vol. 6, 296.
15 BNF, Dupuy 547, f. 218.
16 L&P, vol. 6, 311.
17 Ibid., 324.
18 Ibid., 341.
19 Ibid., 351.
20 Ibid.
21 Ibid., 391.
22 BL, Harley MS 283, f. 96.
23 BL, Add. MS 6113, f. 33.
24 L&P, vol. 6, 424.
25 Camusat, *Meslanges*, 128.
26 L&P, vol. 6, 585.

27 CPSV, vol. 4, 893.
28 Carle in DellaNeva, *Story of the Death of Anne Boleyn*, 164–5.
29 Ives, *Life and Death of Anne Boleyn*, 184.
30 Friedmann, *Anne Boleyn*, vol. 1, 220.

9: A Tudor Rose Cannot Replace a Lion Cub

1 L&P, vol. 6, 1069.
2 Camusat, *Meslanges*, 139.
3 Ibid., 11.
4 Ibid., 140–1.
5 L&P, vol. 6, 1111.
6 Ibid., 918.
7 Ibid., 1164.
8 Camusat, *Meslanges*, 12.
9 BNF, Dupuy 33, f. 52.
10 L&P, vol. 6, 1301.
11 Ibid., 1330.
12 BNF, Dupuy 33, f. 62.
13 L&P, vol. 6, 1392.
14 Camusat, *Meslanges*, 142.
15 Ibid., 143.
16 Friedmann, *Anne Boleyn*, vol. 1, 253.
17 BNF, Dupuy 33, f. 56.
18 Ibid., f. 60.
19 L&P, vol. 6, 1425.
20 Ibid.
21 Ibid., 1426.
22 Ibid., 1419.
23 Ibid., 1464.
24 BNF, Dupuy 547, f. 276.
25 Camusat, *Meslanges*, 19.
26 BNF, Dupuy 33, f. 19.
27 Camusat, *Meslanges*, 19.
28 BNF, Dupuy 33, f. 52.
29 BNF, MS Fr 5499, f. 197.
30 BNF, Dupuy 269, f. 82–3.
31 Camusat, *Meslanges*, 19.
32 L&P, vol. 6, 1488.
33 Emmerson, McCaffrey, Palmer, *Catherine and Anne*.
34 L&P, vol. 7, 9.

10: An Impossible Mission

1. L&P, vol. 7, 14.
2. Ibid., 61.
3. Ibid., 83.
4. Ibid., 171.
5. BL, Add. MS 28,586, f. 117.
6. L&P, vol. 7, 111.
7. BNF, MS Fr 5499, f. 189.
8. Ibid., f. 191.
9. BL, Add. MS 28,586, f. 129.
10. BNF, MS Fr 5499, f. 191.
11. BL, Add. MS 28,586, f. 125.
12. Friedmann, *Anne Boleyn*, vol. 1, 285.
13. BNF, Dupuy 33, f. 46.
14. Ibid.
15. BNF, MS Fr 5499, f. 195.
16. Ibid., f. 192.
17. BNF, Dupuy 265, f. 230.
18. L&P, vol. 7, 296.
19. BNF, MS Fr 5499, f. 197.
20. Ibid., f. 198.
21. Ibid., ff. 193–5.
22. BL, Add. MS 28,586, f. 213.
23. Friedmann, *Anne Boleyn*, vol. 1, 308.
24. L&P, vol. 7, 519.
25. BNF, MS Fr 3005, f. 129.
26. L&P, vol. 7, 726.

11: The Tide Has Turned

1. L&P, vol. 7, 1482.
2. Ibid., 1208.
3. Ibid., 1482.
4. Ibid., 1489.
5. Ibid., 1507.
6. Ibid.
7. Ibid.
8. Ibid.
9. L&P, vol. 8, 48.
10. Jean Le Laboureur, *Les Mémoires de Messire Michel de Castelnau*, vol. 1 (Paris: Pierre Lamy, 1659), 405.

11 L&P, vol. 8, 174.
12 Frieda, *Francis I*, 246.
13 Ibid.
14 L&P, vol. 8, 185.
15 Frieda, *Francis I*, 248.
16 L&P, vol. 8, 263.
17 CSPS, vol. 5, part 1, 144.
18 Ibid., 156.
19 Friedmann, *Anne Boleyn*, vol. 2, 64.
20 CSPS, vol. 5, part 1, 174.
21 BNF Dupuy 265, f. 138.
22 CSPS, vol. 5, part 1, 174.
23 L&P, vol. 8, 886.
24 Friedmann, *Anne Boleyn*, vol. 2, 85–7.
25 L&P, vol. 8, 1117.
26 BNF, Dupuy 547, f. 293.
27 L&P, vol. 9, 434.
28 BNF, MS Fr 3014, f. 98.
29 *The Lisle Letters*, eds. Muriel St. Clare Byrne and Bridget Boland (Chicago: Chicago University Press, 1981), vol. 2, 459.

12: *The Inconceivable*

1 BL, Add. MS 25,114, f. 96.
2 L&P, vol. 9, 566.
3 Ibid., 674.
4 Ibid., 819.
5 Ibid., 861.
6 BNF, MS Fr 5499, f. 246.
7 Ibid., f. 275.
8 Ibid., f. 276.
9 Ibid.
10 L&P, vol. 9, 862.
11 Ibid., 776.
12 Ibid., 862.
13 Ibid., 861.
14 Ibid., 966.
15 Ibid., 987.
16 BL, Add. MS 25,114, f. 117.
17 L&P, vol. 9, 1035.
18 Ibid., 1036.
19 L&P, vol. 10, 59.

20 Ibid., 141.
21 Ibid.
22 Ibid.
23 Ibid.
24 Ibid. For discussion on Henry VIII's fall and how it impacted his life, see Suzannah Lipscomb, *1536: The Year That Changed Henry VIII* (London: Lyon Books, 2006), and Natalie Grueninger, *The Final Year of Anne Boleyn* (Barnsley: Pen & Sword, 2022), 132–3.
25 L&P, vol. 10, 282.
26 Friedmann, *Anne Boleyn*, vol. 2, 209.
27 CSPS, vol. 5, part 2, 43.
28 Friedmann, *Anne Boleyn*, vol. 2, 200; and L&P, vol. 10, 901.
29 See Grueninger, *Final Year*, 158; and Tracy Borman, *Elizabeth and Anne Boleyn: The Mother and Daughter Who Changed History* (London: Hodder & Stoughton, 2023).
30 Grueninger, *Final Year*, 146. Also see M. Dowling, ed., *William Latymer's Chronickille of Anne Boleyn* (London: Camden Society London, 1990), 57.
31 L&P, vol. 10, 601.
32 Camusat, *Meslanges*, 155.
33 L&P, vol. 10, 699.
34 Ibid.
35 *Correspondence of Matthew Parker* (Cambridge: Cambridge University Press, 1753), 59 and 400.
36 L&P, vol. 10, 748.
37 Ibid., 752.
38 Ibid.
39 Ibid., 793.
40 Ibid., 782.
41 Ibid., 792.
42 Ibid., 864.
43 Ibid., 793.
44 Ibid., 797.
45 Ibid., 808.
46 Ibid., 873.
47 Ibid.
48 DellaNeva, *Story of the Death of Anne Boleyn*, 261–7.
49 L&P, vol. 10, 890.
50 Ibid., 902.
51 Grueninger, *Final Year*, 179.
52 *Hall's Chronicles*, 819.
53 Anne Boleyn's *Book of Prayers*.

Epilogue: À Jamais *Remembered*

1 Paul de Musset, *Anne Boleyn* (Bruxelles: Wahlen et cie, 1837), 21 and 23.
2 Ibid., 22.
3 Nicolas Vilton de Saint-Allais, *Nobiliaire universel de Coeur* (Paris: Bureau du Nobiliaire universel de Coeur, 1815).
4 DellaNeva, *Story of the Death of Anne Boleyn*, 303.
5 Adolphe-Simonis Empis, *Les six femmes de Henri VIII*, vol. 1 (Paris: A. Bertrand, 1854), 361–3.
6 Estelle Paranque, *Elizabeth I of England Through Valois Eyes* (New York: Palgrave Macmillan, 2019), 73.

Bibliography

Manuscript sources

Archives de Tarascon

BB 12

Biblioteca Apostolica Vaticana

Vat.lat.3731

Bibliothèque Nationale de Cœur (BNF)

Clairambault 329
Dupuy 33
Dupuy 260
Dupuy 265
Dupuy 269
Dupuy 547
Fonds Béthumes 8471
Fonds Béthumes 8651
MS Fr 2974
MS Fr 4126
MS Fr 3005
MS Fr 3012
MS Fr 3014
MS Fr 3021
MS Fr 3040
MS Fr 3076
MS Fr 3077

MS Fr 3078
MS Fr 3079
MS Fr 3080
MS Fr 4126
MS Fr 5499
MS Fr 5750
MS Fr 5761
MS Fr 10383
MS Fr 14116
MS Fr 15970
NAF 9175

Bibliothèque Sainte-Geneviève

MS 848

Bodleian Library

MS Ashmole, 1116

Musée des Beaux-arts, Paris

Le Trespas de l'Hermine regrettée, LDUT 665

The British Library (BL)

Add. MS 6113
Add. MS 25,114
Add. MS 28,586
Cotton MS Caligula D. VI
Cotton MS Caligula D. VII
Cotton MS Caligula D. VIII
Cotton MS Caligula E. I. II
Harley MS 283
Harley MS 3642

Printed primary sources

Abbreviations

CSPS: *Calendar of State Papers, Spain*, all volumes
CSPV: *Calendar of State Papers relating to English Affairs in the Archives of Venice*

Entrevue: Entrevue de François Ier avec Henry VIII à Boulogne-sur-Mer en 1532
L&P: *Letters and Papers, Foreign and Domestic, Henry VIII*, all volumes

Sources

Baux, Émile, Bourrilly, Victor-Louis and Mabilly, Philippe, "Le voyage des reines et de François I en Provence et dans la vallée du Rhône (décembre 1515–février 1516)," *Annales du Midi*, vol. 16, no. 61 (1904)

Brantôme, Pierre de Bourteuille, *Œuvres complètes*, ed. Ludovic Lalanne, vol. 3 (1848, repr., New York: Johnson Reprint, 1968)

Brown, Cynthia J., ed., *Pierre Gringore, Les entrées royales à Paris de Marie d'Angleterre (1514) et Claude de Cœur (1517)* (Geneva: Librairie Droz, 2005)

Calendar of State Papers relating to English Affairs in the Archives of Venice, Vol. 4, 1527–1533 (London: Her Majesty's Stationery Office, 1871)

Calendar of State Papers, Spain, Vol. 3, Part 1, 1525–1526, ed. Pascual de Gayangos (London: Her Majesty's Stationery Office, 1873)

Calendar of State Papers, Spain, Vol. 4, Part 1, 1529–1530, ed. Pascual de Gayangos (London: Her Majesty's Stationery Office, 1879)

Calendar of State Papers, Spain, Vol. 4, Part 2, 1531–1533, ed. Pascual de Gayangos (London: Her Majesty's Stationery Office, 1882)

Calendar of State Papers, Spain, Vol. 5, Part 1, 1534–1535, ed. Pascual de Gayangos (London: Her Majesty's Stationery Office, 1886)

Camusat, Nicolas, *Meslanges historiques* (Troyes, 1644)

Correspondence de l'empereur Maximilien Ier et de Marguerite d'cœur, sa fille, Gouvernante des Pays-Bas, de 1507 à 1519, vol. 2 (Paris: Imprimerie de Crapelet, 1839)

Correspondence of Matthew Parker (Cambridge: Cambridge University Press, 1753)

Cranmer, Thomas, *Letters* (Cambridge: Cambridge University Press, 1746)

De Beatis, Antonio, *The Travel Journal of Antonio de Beatis: Germany, Switzerland, the Low Countries, France and Italy, 1517–1518* (London: Hakluyt Society, 1979)

De Montfaucon, B., *Les Monuments de la monarchie française*, vol. 4 (Paris: Gandouin et Giffart, 1732)

De Musset, Paul, *Anne Boleyn* (Bruxelles: Wahlen et cie, 1837)

DellaNeva, JoAnn, *The Story of the Death of Anne Boleyn, a Poem by Lancelot de Carle* (Tempe: ACMRS Press, 2021)

Dowling, M., ed., *William Latymer's Chronickille of Anne Boleyn* (London: Camden Society London, 1990)

Entrevue de François Ier avec Henry VIII à Boulogne-sur-Mer en 1532, ed. Alfred Hamy (Paris: L. Gougy, 1898)

Friedmann, Paul, *Anne Boleyn, 1527–1536*, vols. 1 and 2 (London: Macmillan and Co., 1884)

Hall, Edward, *Hall's Chronicles* (London: Johnson, 1809)

Le Laboureur, Jean, *Les Mémoires de Messire Michel de Castelnau*, vol. 1 (Paris: Pierre Lamy, 1659)
Letters and Papers, Foreign and Domestic, Henry VIII, Vol. 1, 1509–1514, ed. J. S. Brewer (London: His Majesty's Stationery Office, 1920)
Letters and Papers, Foreign and Domestic, Henry VIII, Vol. 2, 1515–1518, ed. J. S. Brewer (London: Her Majesty's Stationery Office, 1864)
Letters and Papers, Foreign and Domestic, Henry VIII, Vol. 3, 1519–1523, ed. J. S. Brewer (London: Her Majesty's Stationery Office, 1867)
Letters and Papers, Foreign and Domestic, Henry VIII, Vol. 4, 1524–1530, ed. J. S. Brewer (London: Her Majesty's Stationery Office, 1875)
Letters and Papers, Foreign and Domestic, Henry VIII, Vol. 5, 1531–1532, ed. James Gairdner (London: Her Majesty's Stationery Office, 1880)
Letters and Papers, Foreign and Domestic, Henry VIII, Vol. 6, 1533, ed. James Gairdner (London: Her Majesty's Stationery Office, 1882)
Letters and Papers, Foreign and Domestic, Henry VIII, Vol. 7, 1534, ed. James Gairdner (London: Her Majesty's Stationery Office, 1883)
Letters and Papers, Foreign and Domestic, Henry VIII, Vol. 8, January–July 1535, ed. James Gairdner (London: Her Majesty's Stationery Office, 1885)
Letters and Papers, Foreign and Domestic, Henry VIII, Vol. 9, August–December 1535, ed. James Gairdner (London: Her Majesty's Stationery Office, 1886)
Letters and Papers, Foreign and Domestic, Henry VIII, Vol. 10, January–June 1536, ed. James Gairdner (London: Her Majesty's Stationery Office, 1887)
Lettres de Louis XII, vol. 4 (Brussels: François Foppens, 1759)
The Lisle Letters, eds. Muriel St. Clare Byrne and Bridget Boland (Chicago: Chicago University Press, 1981)
The Manuscripts of J. Eliot Hodgkin, Fifteenth Report, Appendix, Part II (London: Her Majesty's Stationery Office, 1897)
Vilton de Saint-Allais, Nicolas, *Nobiliaire universel de Cœur* (Paris: Bureau du Nobiliaire universel de Cœur, 1815)

Secondary works

Akkerman, Nadine and Houben, Birgit, eds., *The Politics of Female Household: Ladies-in-Waiting Across Early Modern Europe* (Leiden: Brill, 2014)
Borman, Tracy, *Elizabeth and Anne Boleyn: The Mother and Daughter Who Changed History* (London: Hodder & Stoughton, 2023)
Déjean, Jean-Luc, *Marguerite de Navarre* (Paris: Fayard, 1987)
Emmerson, Owen, McCaffrey, Kate and Palmer, Alison, *Catherine and Anne: Queens, Mothers, Rivals* (Hever Castle: Jigsaw Publishing, 2023)
Empis, Adolphe-Simonis, *Les six femmes de Henri VIII*, vol. 1 (Paris: A. Bertrand, 1854)
Frieda, Leonie, *Francis I: The Maker of Modern France* (London: Weidenfeld & Nicolson, 2021)

Giesey, R. E., *The Funeral Ceremony in Renaissance France* (Geneva: Librairie Droz, 1960)

Grueninger, Natalie, *The Final Year of Anne Boleyn* (Barnsley: Pen & Sword, 2022)

Ives, Eric, *The Life and Death of Anne Boleyn* (Oxford: Blackwell, 2004)

Lipscomb, Suzannah, *1536: The Year That Changed Henry VIII* (London: Lyon Books, 2006)

Mackay, Lauren, *Among the Wolves of Court: The Untold Story of Thomas and George Boleyn* (London: Bloomsbury Academic, 2020)

Paget, Hugh, "The Youth of Anne Boleyn," *Bulletin of the Institute of Historical Research*, 55 (1981), 162–70.

Paranque, Estelle, *Elizabeth I of England Through Valois Eyes* (New York: Palgrave Macmillan, 2019)

Santrot, Jacques, *Les doubles funérailles d'Anne de Bretagne: Le corps et le cœur (Janvier–Mars 1514)* (Paris: Librairie Droz, 2017)

Seward, Desmond, *Prince of the Renaissance: The Life of François I* (London: Constable, 1973)

Weir, Alison, *Mary Boleyn* (London: Vintage, 2012)

Acknowledgments

The more I write books, the more I find acknowledgments difficult to write. Not because I'm no longer grateful or appreciative of all the support I receive, but quite the opposite, because I find there are not enough words to express my profound gratitude to the people who support and nurture me.

To Anne Boleyn, first and foremost, thank you for being your own free woman, for your ambition, for breaking the expectations that a woman should be docile and quiet, for your fiery temperament, for your courage. I truly believe you were ahead of your time.

I am incredibly grateful to my wonderful agent, Rachel Conway, who believed in this book the moment I mentioned my desire to write it. Thank you for always championing me and my ideas.

Thank you, Robyn Drury, for being once more the best editor ever—always supporting my queens and ensuring that the right words are on the page (all errors obviously remain mine and mine only). My sincere gratitude to every team at Ebury, from marketing to foreign rights to copyediting and so on. You are all a delight to work with.

Many friends and colleagues have offered their support, knowledge and assistance. Thank you so much. I will never take your friendship for granted. Michael Questier (we barely agree on anything but it has never mattered—thank you for all you do for me), Olivette Otele, Eilish Gregory, Lauren Mackay, Joanne Paul, Owen Emmerson, Gareth Russell, James Michael, Nicola Tallis, Sandi Vasoli, Natalie Grueninger, Kat Marchant, Philippa Brewell, Jon Marshall, Suzannah Lipscomb, Lacey Noel, Renée Langlois, Ellie Woodacre, Kate McCaffrey, Edmund Neill, Mike Peacey, Leighan Renaud, Laetitia Calabrese, Marie Armilano, Justine Brun and Lizzie V. Merchant.

Many people keep asking me, "How do you juggle all your work commitments and your personal life?" The answer is simple: with the help and support of my family. First and foremost, my parents, Bernard and Joëlle Paranque. Despite the distance, they always offer support in any way they can and continue to believe in my dreams. My "in-laws" who take on childcare duties so I can pursue writing, especially Sally Gill and Mike Green, who go above and beyond. Thank you to everyone else for checking in on me and my well-being, my sister, Sandrine Doré, my niece and nephew Charlotte and Matthias Collomb, and all the rest of the Gill tribe, including its matriarch, the fabulous 100-year-old Dawn Gill, who will always be an inspiration to me and who always shows an interest in my writing, being a writer and painter herself. I could not do any of this without your love and support. Thank you for believing in me and my books.

To my readers, I would like to thank all of you who support my work and my passion for history. I could not write these books and do this research without you all, and for that you have my deepest gratitude. Always.

My last words are as usual for the ones with whom I share all my days: my funny, intelligent, brave, witty son to whom this book is dedicated. Zachary, you truly are the *lumière* of my life and I will always love you and cherish you. *"Je t'aime pour toujours."*

My daughter, the *joie* of my life, Zoë. I didn't know how much I wanted you until I was told I was going to have you. I finished this book with you inside and you have given me incredible strength and determination. *"Je t'aime pour toujours."*

Mes enfants, I can tell you that my love for you knows no bound and that I am truly privileged to be your mother.

Mon coeur, Nick St. John Gill, I am truly blessed to have you in my life. You are the best, and rest assured that I will say forever *"je t'aime le plus"* because it is simply the truth. Thank you for all you do for me and our family. Your efforts and sacrifices will never go unnoticed.

Index

Act of Succession (1534) 210
Act of Supremacy (1534) 198–9, 208, 210
Allement, Nicolas 52
Allen, John 85
Allington Castle 76
Amboise 23, 31
Anne of Brittany 3–4, 5
Ardres 51, 52

Barbarossa, Hayreddin 205
Barton, Elizabeth 170–1
Basilica of Saint-Denis 28–9
Beatis, Antonio de 29
Beaune-Semblançay, Jacques de 24
Bennet, William 85
Blount, Elizabeth xi–xii, 88
Boleyn, Anne 39–40, 133–4
  allies and supporters of 128–9, 137
  altercation with Henry Norris 235
  anointed Queen of England 152
    impatience and distress 182–3
    St. Edward's Crown 152
    unfavorable accounts of 152–3
    wedding gift from Francis 153
    welcoming reception 153
  anointing of Claude 29
  appeals to Gontier 205
  appearance 63–4
  attends pageant at York Place 64
  Catherine of Aragon
    animosity toward 124
    displaying disdain toward 124–5
  closeness to du Bellay brothers 116
  company of French ambassadors 136
  coronation
    arrives at Westminster Abbey 152
    ceremony 152
    preparation for 150, 152
    support from nobility 150
  critics xv, 125, 128–9, 131, 193, 208
    enragement of 149–50
  delayed in Mechelen 14, 17
  enemies 128, 131, 162–3, 193–4, 195
    conspiracy by 234–5
    threats by 130–1
  falsely accused of adultery 235–7, 239
  France
    angers allies in 190
    betrayal by 197
    French royal grandeur 24, 25–6
    intimacy with 138
    recall from 60, 61, 62
  Francis I
    audience with xv
    dances with xiv–xv
    diamond gift from xii–xiii, 139
  Henry VIII
    accepts marriage proposal from 89
    center of attention at court 99–100
    consummation of relationship 140
    gift to 89, 175
    jealousy toward 195–6
    keeps at a distance 90–1
    letter maintaining innocence 237–8
    love letters from 87–8, 88–90
    marriage ratified by law 190
    organizes feast for 210–11
    pressure to produce male heir 159–60, 175, 193, 195, 215, 217
    reunited in adversity 214
    royal progress with 215
    secret wedding ceremony 143

INDEX

Boleyn, Anne (*Cont.*)
  sitting by side of 114
  teases Henry 90–1, 99
  tension between 194, 195, 202
  wants marriage in England 130
 interpreter role 55
 isolation 233
 lady-in-waiting 35
  to Catherine of Aragon 76, 92
  to Claude of France 20, 22–30, 40, 41, 43, 44, 52–3, 54–5, 60
  to Margaret of Austria 6, 7, 12–13
  observing the French court 29–30, 35, 47
  royal procession 23–8
 letters to
  Anne Savage 243
  father 22
  Wolsey 96
 marchioness of Pembroke 137–8
 Marguerite of Angoulême
  betrayal by 136
  influence of 41–2, 48
  lady-in-waiting 48
  meeting 24
  reaches out to 214–15
 marriage match with James Butler 61
 Mary (Princess)
  angered by 178
  olive branch to 228–9
 meetings with
  Francis and Henry 135–7, 139–40
  Gontier 204–5
  Matthew Parker 234–5
 memory and legacy of 243–7
 murder attempt 130
 personality and character
  charisma 63–4
  confidence 120
  fortitude 121
  passion 126
  self-importance of 124–5
  temper 128, 193–4, 195
 political agenda 96, 112, 119, 234
 powerlessness 231
 power struggle with Cromwell 232
 pregnancies 193, 227, 229
  birth of Elizabeth 159
  confined to chamber 153–4, 155
  confirmation of 153
  difficulties during 153–4
  miscarriages 194, 229, 230
 rumors of 143, 145, 151
 protected by legislation 178
 referred to as "queen" 149
 relationship with Mary (sister) 66
 religious beliefs 175
  Catholicism 42
 shows favor to Jean of Dinteville 163
 spying for father 35, 40, 43–4
 status enhancement 137–8, 150
 sweating sickness 98
 tension with Wolsey 101–2, 109
 thoughts of marriage 76–7
 trial 239–40
  dignity and elegance 239–40
  execution 241–2
  final speech 242
  imprisonment 237–8
  sentence 239–40
Boleyn, Elizabeth 55
Boleyn, George, Lord Rochford 235
 ambassadorial role 111, 112, 117, 143, 192, 233
 execution 240
 trial 239
Boleyn, Mary 64, 65
 lady-in-waiting 14, 17
 marriage to William Carey 76
 relationship with Anne 66
Boleyn, Sir Thomas, Viscount of Rochford 7, 92, 138
 Anne
  offers services to Catherine of Aragon 63
  reunited with 62–3
  secures position for 6
 approaches du Bellay 111–12
 diplomatic incident 45–6
 feat of arms 55
 Francis I
  meetings with 40, 41
  relationship with 42–3
 Henry's papal aspirations 42
 Margaret of Austria
  friendship with 6
  request to 12–13
 pressure on clergy 134
 pursuing Wolsey's political agenda 44–5
 replaces George in Rome 117
 secures position for Mary 14
 sent to France 34–5
 special envoy 6

Boleyn, Sir William 123–4
Bonner, Edmund 167, 169
Books of Hours 92, 175
Bourdeille, Pierre de 5
Brandon, Charles, Duke of Suffolk 10, 11, 101, 138, 214, 241
   anger at Thomas Wolsey 109, 113
   Mary Tudor
      enamored with 20
      marriage to 21–2
      pleads to Henry for 20
   opposes ambitions of Boleyns 119
   opposes Henry's divorce 119
   responsibility for diplomatic relations 9
   trial commission of Anne 239
   Turkey's invasion of Hungary 103
Brandon, Lady Mary 187
Brandon Tudor, Mary *see* Tudor, Mary, Duchess of Suffolk
Brantôme, Seigneur de 5
Braye, Anne, Baroness Cobham 150
Brereton, William 239, 240
Brosse, Jean de 92
Browne, John 67
Bryan, Sir Francis 129
Budé, Guillaume 37, 48
Butler, Piers 60
Butler, Thomas, Earl of Ormonde 60

Calais 168, 169
Cambray 189
Campeggio, Cardinal Lorenzo 97, 99, 104, 105, 107, 111
Canal, Hironimo Da 35
Carew, Nicholas 235
Carey, William 76
Carle, Lancelot de 212, 239–40, 241, 244–5
Casali, Gregorio 210
Castelnau, Antoine de 212, 217–18, 233
Cathedral of Reims 28
Catherine of Aragon, Queen of England 11, 55
   animosity toward Anne 124, 193
   crown jewels 129
   death of 227
      burial 229
      poison rumor 228
   divorce from Henry
      begs to reconsider 107
      House of Lords bill 182
      legatine court 106–7
      resistance to 86, 99, 104–5, 193
      support from Charles V 131
   Field of the Cloth of Gold 54, 57
   humiliation 105, 128, 149
   illness 181, 224–5, 225–7
   isolation 128
   marriage to Arthur 85, 86
   meetings with
      Charles V 50
      French diplomats 84
   Princess Dowager of Wales 182
   visit from Chapuys 226–7
   see also Clement VII, Pope: Henry's divorce from Catherine; Henry VIII, King of England: divorce from Catherine
Chabot, Philippe de, Admiral of France 203
   Anne Boleyn
      blames 199
      ignores 202
   gifts 199–200
   Henry VIII
      avoids 200
      feast organized by 202
      meeting with Chapuys 200–1
   special envoy role 197, 198–9, 200, 202
Chapuys, Eustace xv, 112, 128
   alarm at Council pamphlet 177
   Anne Boleyn
      accuses of adultery 235–6
      accuses of murder plot 224
      accuses of plotting against Catherine 195
      blames for rift with Rome 177–8, 208
      on entertaining the du Bellays 116
      intimacy with France 138
      laments elevated position of 114
      preparation for coronation of 150
      refuses to meet 233–4
      rejoices in problems of 235
      separating from Henry 119
      spreading rumors about xv, 178
   birth of Elizabeth 161
   Catherine of Aragon
      assisting 224
      visits 226–7
   Charles V
      reporting to 199
      warns of atrocities 177
   encounters with La Pommeraie 130, 136

Chapuys, Eustace (*Cont.*)
  Henry VIII
    contempt for proclamation 146
    denied audience with 147, 148
    discussions to depose 198
    reconsidering break with Rome 198
    representing Charles at meeting 225–6
    shocked at proclamation 147–8
    speaks mind to 148–9
    unaware of marriage 145
  ill treatment 147, 148, 151–2
  insults du Bellay 174
  intelligence gathering 135–6
  on Jane Seymour 230–1
  meeting with Chabot 200–1
  powerlessness 151–2
  questions nomination for Archbishop of Canterbury 142
  reports of dissent 198
  seeking new alliances 161
  shocked at Cranmer's divorce announcement 185
  shocked at treatment of Wolsey 113–14
  Thomas Cromwell
    advises 161, 162
    interest in 222
    meetings with 232–3
Charles, Duke of Angoulême 197, 198, 200, 201, 203
Charles, Duke of Bourbon 53, 68–9, 71
Charles, Duke of Orléans 11
Charles IV, Duke of Alençon 47–8, 71
Charles of Orléans, Count of Angoulême 47
Charles V, King of Spain xv, xvi, 8, 10, 39
  claims Burgundy 69
  concerns about Tournay 32
  desire for power 59
  Francis I
    alliance with 169
    animosity toward 39, 40–1, 62, 66, 81, 205
    indirect peace with 110
  Henry VIII
    disgust at lack of compassion 225
    displeasure at divorce 146
    meetings with 49–50, 50–1
    pact against Francis I 62, 66
  Holy Roman Emperor
    candidacy for 39–40
    elected as 46
  humility in victory 72, 74
  invasion of Papal States 87
  marriage proposals of children 197
  peace treaty with Turkey 147
Château Vert pageant 63–5
Cheney, Sir Thomas 101–2
Chester, Bishop of 193
Christendom 10, 42, 103–4, 164, 180, 190, 219
Church of Notre-Dame xiii
Church of Observant Friars 160
Church of Rome *see* Rome (Catholic Church)
Church of Saint-Honorat 25
Cifuentes, Count of xvi, 169, 179, 181, 189, 190
Claiburgh, William 85
Claude of France, Queen xvii, 4, 22, 37
  anointing of 28–9
  coronation 29, 30
  pageants 30
  procession 23–8, 30
  appearance and qualities 29, 54–5, 56
  avoiding cities 23
  children 28, 30–1
  death of 70
  marriage to Francis I 4–5, 30–1
  nuns' prayers for fertility 27–8
  popularity of 29–30
  receives English ambassadors 36
  receives Henry VIII 53–4
  sickness 43–4
Clement VII, Pope 22
  authority undermined 175
  Charles V
    fear of 184
    under the control of 85, 93, 133
  death of 196
  Henry's divorce from Catherine
    refusal to recognize 85–6, 87, 102–3, 125, 189
    reply to 132–3
    response to proclamation 147
    settling matter in Rome 132–3
  Henry's marriage to Anne
    anger at 167–8
    annulment 154–5, 164–5
    letter to Henry 125
    papal bulls 142, 163, 164, 169, 180
    refusal to authorize 125
Jean du Bellay
  anger at 179
  denies audience with 180

INDEX

mediates between Charles and Francis 81
visits Francis I 164
see also Rome (Catholic Church)
Convocation of Canterbury 146
Cornish, William 65
Courtenay, Gertrude, Marchioness of
    Exeter 64, 171, 223, 232
Court of the Fleur-de-Lys 30
Cox, John 85
Cranmer, Thomas, Archbishop of
    Canterbury 151
  Anne Boleyn
    dinner with 240
    presents with crown 152
    surprise at accusations against 236
  beliefs and political views 142–3
  blamed by Ortiz 181
  godfather of Elizabeth 160
  nomination as Archbishop of
    Canterbury 142–3
  pronounces divorce of Henry and
    Catherine 185–6
  proposes General Council 175
Cromwell, Thomas 150, 204, 224, 241
  Anne Boleyn
    guilty slurs about 238–9
    power struggle with 232
  Chapuys
    advice from 161
    meetings with 232–3
  independent national Church 127
  opportunism 167
  political rise 127
  pressure on clergy 134
  prudence 161
  rapprochement with house of Austria
    162
  stature and ambition 222
  supporting Henry and Anne 222
Crown of Charlemagne 29

d'Albret, Henry, King of Navarre 75
d'Alençon, Françoise, Duchess of
    Vendôme 29
decretal 99
Denonville, Charles de Hémard de,
    Bishop of Mâcon 179, 180, 210
Derby, Lady xiv
Dinteville, Francis de, Bishop of Auxerre
    131–2, 135, 141, 145
Dinteville, Jean de, Bailiff of Troyes 152,
    159, 160

Anne Boleyn
  favoritism from 163
  pregnancy 151
  appearance and stature 144
  on Cranmer's pronouncement 151
  at English court 144, 145–6, 152
  failure of mission 218
  Henry VIII
    anger expressed by 166
    attempts to appease 166
    damning report of 172
    refused audience with 167
  meeting Henry and Anne
    letters from Francis 214
    objectives 213–14
  replacement and recriminations 171–2
  respect and stature 213
Dorothy, Countess of Sussex 137–8
Douglas, Lady Margaret 187
Du Bellay, Guillaume 91, 93, 135, 137, 166
  enemies 178–9
  welcomed at English Court 116
Du Bellay, Jean 94, 135, 154, 210, 245
  appearance 92
  delays Pope Paul's decision 220–1
  detractors 178, 179
  diplomatic mission to Rome 173–4,
    184–5, 188–9
    betrayed by Henry 191
    duping of 188
    humiliation 189, 191
    meets with Cifuentes 189
    optimism 188
  enemies 178–9
  envoy at English court 92, 116
  fears England's separation from Rome
    184–5
  financial struggles 95
France
  personal problems in 173
  welcomed on return to 191–2
friendship with Boleyns 93, 117
Henry VIII
  discarded by 112
  divorce from Catherine 93, 96–7,
    98–9, 104, 118, 131–2
  letter from 191
  marriage to Anne 102–3, 145–6
  meeting with 172–3
letter to Montmorency 108–9
meeting with Anne 174
meeting with Dr. Ortiz 181–2

Du Bellay, Jean (*Cont.*)
  Pope Clement VII
    denied audience with 180
    plan for negotiations with 179–80
    received by 184, 188–9
    warns against heresy 180–1
  praise from Francis I 185
  reconciling Henry and Clement 170
  religion
    accusations of Lutheranism 173
    ambitions 184
    Catholicism 173
  risks reputation 221–2
  Thomas Wolsey
    diplomatic discussions with 96–7
    reports on downfall of 112
    tension with Anne 101–2
  titles and career 91
Du Bellay, Louis, Sieur de Langley 91
Du Bellay, René 91, 173
Duprat, Cardinal Antoine 132, 165, 169, 180
dynastic alliances 9

Edward IV, King 199
Eleanor (sister of Charles V) 74, 83, 110, 137
Elizabeth, Countess of Rutland 137
Elizabeth, Princess (Henry's daughter) 66, 197, 227, 231, 246, 247
  birth of 159
  christening 160–1
  heir to throne 197, 203–4
  proposed marriage to Charles 200, 202, 203
Empis, Adolphe-Simonis 245, 246
England
  break from Rome 190
  expansion of navy 66–7
  France and
    alliance with 15–16, 32–3, 46, 51–7, 117, 133, 137, 139–40, 145
    compromise 49
    diplomatic incident 45–6
    ending of alliance with 212–13
    Field of the Cloth of Gold 51–7
    future war against 60, 66
    tournament 17
    treaty 133
    uneasy relations with 192
  mediator of European politics 59
Erasmus, Desiderius 7, 37, 48

Ferdinand of Aragon 8
Field of the Cloth of Gold xiv, 51–7
  feat of arms 52–5, 54, 57
  location 51–2
  prize-giving and gifts 57
Fisher, John, Bishop of Rochester 162, 192, 198
  beheaded 211
  imprisonment 193, 208
  mercy pleas rejected by Henry 210
  trial for treason 209, 210
Fitzroy, Henry xi–xii, 241
Fitzwater, Lady xiv
Fitzwilliam, Sir William 192
Foix, Françoise de, Countess of Châteaubriant 30, 88
Foix, Odet de, Vicomte de Lautrec 95
France
  Affair of the Placards 205–6
  diplomatic moves 130
  England and
    alliance with 15–16, 32–3, 46, 51–7, 117, 133, 137, 139–40, 145
    compromise 49
    diplomatic incident 45–6
    ending of alliance with 212–13
    Field of the Cloth of Gold 51–7
    tournament 17
    treaty 133
    uneasy relations with 192
  truce with Spanish Netherlands 96
Francis, dauphin
  birth of 31
  christening 31
  marriage to Mary
    discussions 81, 82–5
    Francis I's oath 33–4
    proposal 31–3, 36
Francis I, King of France xi–xiii
  alliance with Suleiman 205
  Anne Boleyn
    dances with xiv–xv
    gift for xii–xiii
  betrayed by Duke of Bourbon 68–9
  burning of heretics 206–7
  candidacy for Holy Roman Emperor 39, 40, 41
  Catholicism of 191
  Charles V
    alliance with 169
    animosity toward 39, 40–1, 62, 66, 81, 205

INDEX

fear of widening influence of 133
indirect peace with 110
insulted by 69
negotiates release from captivity 75
scheming against 196–7
children 144
  birth of Henry 46
  death of Charlotte 70
  imprisonment of sons xvi, 75, 83, 84, 93–4, 95, 103
  release of sons 110
Claude
  disrespect toward 5
  marriage to 4–5
  womanizing 5
concerns about treaty 34
conflict of aims 163
duping of 188
enemies on multiple fronts 68–9
Franco-Scottish "Auld Alliance" 67
funeral of Louis II 19–20
Henry VIII
  anger at broken promises 165–6
  balance of power between 116
  betrayed by 66, 190
  collecting dues from 213
  disappointment at birth of Elizabeth 159, 163
  friendship with xii, xiv
  meetings with 49, 50, 51–7, 193
  refuses to back break from Rome 192
  sides with Pope Paul against 220
  suspicious of 67
illness and recovery 219–20
marriage of Henry and Anne
  anger at Gardiner 165–6
  meeting with Henry and Anne 135–7, 139–40
  proposes council of legates 165–6
  rift 166–8
  support for xv–xvii, 132, 140–2, 144, 150–1, 163–4
military campaigns
  against Italy 67–8, 196
  captured and taken prisoner 71–5
  defeated by Charles's army 71
  release from prison 91
  siege of Pavia 70–1
  victories 23
mistresses 88
placards incident 205–6
political agenda 140
Pope Clement VII
  friendship required with 163
  letter to 132
  support for Henry VIII 140–2, 144, 150–1, 163–4
privileging Marguerite at dinner 37
pursuit of glory 22–3, 93–4
putting France's interests first 169
receives English commission 35–6
royal procession 26–7
theatrics 42–3
threatens England 61
Francis of Tournon, Cardinal 141, 155, 188

Gaddi, Niccolò 180
Gambara, Uberto 93
Gardiner, Stephen, Bishop of Winchester 10, 85, 129
  liaising with Anne 107–8
  rejects council of legate's proposal 165–6
  represents Henry at Marseille 164–5
  sent by Henry to French court 217
General Council 141, 169, 175
General of Normandy 9–10
Genouillac, Galiot de 52
George of Selve 144
Gontier, Palamède 202, 203–5
Gouffier, Guillaume, Lord of Bonnivet 32, 33, 53, 70, 71
Gramont, Gabriel de, Bishop of Tarbes 82–5, 103, 150–1, 155
Grampian Terrane 150–1
Granvelle, Antoine Perrenot de 219
Greenwich Palace 11, 84, 126
Grenville, Honor, Viscountess Lisle 199
Guildford, Lord 128
Guildford, Madame de 12, 13
Guildhall 209
Guînes 51, 52

Habsburgs 8–9, 10, 13, 146, 147
Hale, John 65
Hampton Court Palace 96, 128
Henry, Duke of Orléans xv, 144, 154, 163, 164
Henry, Duke of Richmond 88
Henry of Navarre 24

Henry VIII, King of England 6, 11
  alliance with France 8
  Anne Boleyn
    anger at council of legates 166
    clergy's opposition to marriage 133–4
    declares marriage finished 229–30
    discusses Castillon's proposal 183
    enjoying company of 109–10
    gifts 131
    interest in other women 207
    love interest in 80–1, 87–91, 126
    love letters to 87–8, 88–90, 98
    marriage proposal 89
    meeting with Casstillon 183–4
    notices 56
    postponement of wedding date 133–4
    primary adviser to Henry 126
    ratified by law 190
    reunited in adversity 214
    royal progress with 215
    secret wedding ceremony 143
    tension between 194, 195, 202
    threatens to bypass clergy 133–4
  attends pageant at York Place 64–5, 66
  candidacy for Holy Roman Emperor 39–40
  Charles V
    fear of invasion by 219
    meetings with 49–50, 50–1
    military threat from Spain 131
    pact against Francis I 62, 66
    power struggle with 115
  "Defender of the Faith" 125
  desires and aspirations 45
  divorce from Catherine xvi, 82, 93, 104
    annulment 85–6, 87, 114–15, 116, 127
    failure of Wolsey 108–9, 111
    House of Lords bill 182
    illegitimacy of marriage 85–6, 114–15, 118–19
    leaking of private conversation 86
    legates from Rome 127
    legatine court 106–7
    official proclamation 146–8
    Pope's refusal 85–6, 87, 102–3, 125
    support from Francis I 115, 116–17, 118, 123–4, 131–2
    support from scholars and theologians 115, 116–17, 117–18, 119
  Elizabeth (daughter)
    declares heir to the throne 197, 203
    devotion to 159
    marriage arrangement 200, 202, 203
  enemies 192
  festival for Chabot 202
  Francis I
    anger toward 170, 171, 172
    banquet for xiii–xiv
    friendship with xii, xiv, 95
    letters to 143, 191
    meetings with 49, 50, 51–7, 193
    procession in honor of 219–20
    rift 166–8
    suspicious of 67
    welcoming xi–xiii
  hunting 128
  isolation 212
  Jane Seymour 230–1, 232, 242
  Jean du Bellay
    letter to 191
    sets deadline 179
  joyous at Catherine's death 227, 228
  male heir 175, 193, 195, 215, 217
    disappointment at birth of Elizabeth 159–60
    naming his son 159
  Mary Boleyn 65
  Mary (daughter) 203
  meeting with Francis and Anne 135–7, 139–40
  meeting with Gontier 203–4
  mistresses 88, 207, 231, 232
  opponents
    cruelty toward 209, 212
    hangings and beheadings of 209, 211–12
    imprisonment of 192–3, 208, 209
    treatment of 208
  Pope Clement VII
    challenges superiority of 175
    legates from Rome 127–8
  Pope Paul III
    anger at 210, 225–6
    diplomatic ties severed by 212, 214
    excommunication threatened by 214, 220–1, 222
  search for new wife 207–8
  separation from Rome 127, 173, 175, 180, 181, 183–5, 186, 190, 212
    lucrative decision 202
    rejects reconciliation with 201
  shift in character 223–4
  superstitions 170

Hever Castle 7, 35
Holbein 144
Holy Roman Empire 39
House of Lords 182, 190
Howard, Elizabeth 6
Howard, Thomas, Duke of Norfolk 101,
    102, 112, 129, 138, 147, 233
  blamed by Anne 229
  Catherine's impending death 226
  consolidation of power 121
  dispatched to France 154
  entertained by French ambassadors 154
  entertained by Marguerite 154
  marriage of Henry and Anne 133, 134
  pleased with du Bellay mission 179
  pressurizes the clergy 134
  showing power at court 102
  uncovers Wolsey's treachery 120

Imperial Electoral College 39
Isabel of Castile 8
Italy 67–8

James V, King of Scotland 151
Julius II, Pope 85

Kimbolton Castle 224, 226
Kingston, Sir William 237, 240, 241

La Barre, Jean de xii–xiii
La Bastille banquet 36–7
ladies-in-waiting 6–7
La Forest, Jean de 207
La Pommeraie, Gilles de 123, 126, 130,
    131, 133–4, 135, 137
  letter to Francis de Dinteville 145
La Porte de Neuilly 44
La Sauche, Jean de 103
La Sauch, Jehan de 32
La Tour d'Auvergne, Madeleine de 31
La Tour-Landry, Marguerite de 91
Lautrec, Vicomte de 68
Lee, Dr. Edward 129
Leo X, Pope 10, 39
Lincoln, Bishop of 10
Lisle, Viscount 165
London Charterhouse 209
Lorenzo II of Medici 180
Louis I of Orléans, Duke of Longueville
    9–10, 11
Louis XII, King of France 3–4
  death of 19

Francis I
  agrees to marriage with Claude 4–5
  anger toward 5
  marriage to Mary 11–12
  letter to Cardinal Wolsey 11–12
  represented by the Duke of
    Longueville 11
  sends envoys to Henrician court 9–10
Louise of Savoy xvii, 4, 30, 37, 54, 136
  diplomatic incident 45–6
  Francis I
    advises against invasion 70
    negotiates release of 73
  meeting Margaret of Austria 110
  negotiating with England 72–3
  regent of the realm 72
  royal procession 23–8
  stateswoman qualities 73
  suspicious of Mary and Suffolk 20–1
  voracious reader 47
Lyon 23

Madeleine (daughter of Francis) 230
Magna Carta 134
Margaret of Austria, Duchess of Savoy 7,
    34, 50, 110
  agent of peace 94
  delays Anne's return to England 12–13
  friendship with Thomas Boleyn 6
  husbands 9
  marriage between Charles and Mary 8
Marguerite of Angoulême, Queen of
    Navarre xvii, 4, 54, 91
  Anne Boleyn
    declines invitation from 136
    ignores plea from 215
    influence on 41–2
    meeting 24
  early life 47
  evangelical beliefs 136–7, 154
  Francis I
    pleads for 73–4
    visits in captivity 73, 74
  humanist and reformist ideas 48
  influence of 29, 37, 47, 48
  marriages
    Charles IV of Alençon 47–8
    Henry d'Albret 75
  negotiator role 72, 73–5
  promotions and titles 47
Marignano, Battle of 23, 68
Marot, Clément 37

Marseille 25, 26–7
Mary, Lady xiv
Mary, Princess (Henry's daughter) 86, 149
  declared illegitimate by Henry 203–4
  defends legitimacy to throne 229
  denied visit to Catherine 226, 227
  deposing Henry 198
  French support for 197, 218
  lack of respect for Anne 178
  marriage to Alessandro de Medici
    dowry 180
    plans for 180, 185, 186, 203
    rejected by Henry 186–7
  marriage to Charles, Duke of
      Angoulême
    plans for 197, 198, 200, 201
    rejected by Henry 200
  marriage to Francis
    Henry's oath 33–4
    plans for 81, 82–5
    proposal 31–3, 36
    rejected by Henry VIII 84
Mary Rose 66–7
Maximilian, Holy Roman Emperor 6, 7, 39
Medici, Alessandro de, Duke of Florence 180, 185, 186–7, 203
Medici, Catherine de xv, 144, 154, 163, 164, 196
Medici, Lorenzo II de, Duke of Urbino 31
Mendoza 86, 87, 89–90, 101, 105–6
Montmorency, Anne de 91, 92, 95, 103, 108, 112, 131, 145, 169, 185
More, Sir Thomas 112, 113, 182, 198
  beheaded 212
  imprisonment 192–3, 208
  trial for treason 209, 211–12
More, the (house) 128
Moucheau, Jehan du 199–200
Musset, Alfred de 243
Musset, Paul de 243–4

Nicolas of Neufville, Lord of Villeroy 32
Norris, Henry 235, 239, 240
Notre-Dame de la Garde 26, 27–8

Ortiz, Dr. 181–2
Ottomans 73, 103–4, 205

Palace of Whitehall 203
Palais Royal 16
papacy *see* Rome (Catholic Church)

Paris 15
Parker, Jane 64
Parker, Matthew 234–5
Passaut, Jean Joachim de, Sieur de Vaux 82–3, 84–5, 116, 121, 123, 126, 129
Paul III, Pope 196, 198
  anoints Fisher as cardinal 209–10
  argues with du Bellay 221–2
  Henry VIII
    invitation to rejoin Christendom 209–10
    orders Francis to be messenger 214
    severing diplomatic ties with 212, 214
    threatens with excommunication 214, 220–1, 222
    urges Francis to intervene 210
Pavia 70–1
Percy, Henry, Earl of Northumberland 76–7, 236, 239
Perreau, Louis de, Sieur de Castillon 171, 174, 196
  Henry VIII
    baffled by thinking of 186
    marriage between Mary and Alexander 186–7
    private audiences with 183, 186–7
Peterborough Cathedral 229
Pilgrimage of Grace 198
Pisseleu-d'Heilly, Anne de, Duchess of Étampes 88
Plaines, Gérard de 10
Plantagenet, Arthur 199
Pole, Margaret, Countess of Salisbury 162
Pole, Reginald 162–3
Pompérant, Sieur de 71
Poncher, Stephen de, Bishop of Paris 31, 32
Porte of Saint-Denis 30
Provost of Paris 139

Queen Claude *see* Claude of France, Queen

Raince, Nicolas 210, 230
Rochecovard, Francis de, Seneschal of Toulouse 32
Rome (Catholic Church) 201
  consistory of cardinals 188–9
  judgments 189
  deteriorating relationship with Henry 115
  England's separation from 127, 173, 175, 179, 180, 181, 184–5

confirmation of 190
du Bellay's fears 184–5
Henry refuses reconciliation 201
factions 117
Henry's divorce from Catherine 114–15, 141
  papal dispensation 188
  settling matter in Rome 107–8, 132–3
Henry's marriage to Anne 126
see also Clement VII, Pope; Paul III, Pope

Sack of Rome 81, 85
Savage, Anne 243
Seigne, Guillaume de 52
Seymour, Edward 231
Seymour, Jane 230–1, 232, 242
Shelton, Lady Ann 229
Shelton, Mary 207, 235
Simonetta, Giacomo 165
Skipp, John 232
Smeaton, Mark 215, 239, 240
Solier, Charles de, Count of Morette 94, 154, 196, 203
Somerset, Charles, Earl of Worcester 34, 35
Spinelli, Thomas 43
Stewart, John, Duke of Albany 4, 67
Stokesley, John, Bishop of London 111, 128–9, 152, 160
Suleiman the Magnificent 73, 103–4, 147, 205
sweating sickness 97–8

Tarascon 24
"The Staple" xii
Thomas, Marquis of Dorset 17
Tournay 32–3, 34
Tower of London 152, 209, 237
Treason Act (1534) 235
Treaty of Cambray 110
Treaty of London 36
Treaty of Madrid 75
Treaty of the More 73
Treaty of Universal Peace 33–4
Trivulzio, Cardinal Agostino 188
Tudor, Mary, Duchess of Suffolk 8, 9, 10, 17, 54, 64
  appearance 14
  Charles Brandon
    enamored with 20
  marriage to 21–2
  coronation 14–15
    anointed Queen of France 14–15
    procession 15–16
  household arrangements 13
  marriage to Louis II 11
Tunstall, Cuthbert, Bishop of Durham 10, 33, 193
Turks 10, 32, 113, 139, 146, 147
see also Ottomans

Valois-Angoulême, house of 4

Wallop, John 190–1
Wallop, Lady xiv
Warham, William, Archbishop of Canterbury 11, 85, 134–5
West, Nicholas, Bishop of Ely 34, 35
Westminster Abbey 152
Westminster Hall 152, 211
Weston, Sir Francis 239, 240
Windsor Castle 128, 137
Wingfield, Sir Richard 21, 50, 53
Wolsey, Cardinal Thomas 8, 34–5
  distrust of du Bellay 92
  downfall 111, 112–13
    arrest and death 121
    articles against 113
    banishment 113–14
    enemies 113
    friendless 113
  Henry's divorce 93, 96–7, 98–9, 108–9
    failure to accomplish 111, 112
    letter to the Pope 93
    tension with Anne 101–2, 109
  instructions to Mary 20
  intelligence reports 59–60
  isolation of 109
  letter to Louis II 12
  marriage of Mary and Francis 83
  organizes dinner and pageant 63–5, 66
  organizes meeting of kings 49, 53, 56
  plots revenge 120–1
  powerlessness 108–9
  rebuffs French demands 83–4
  scheming 61
  secret meetings 85
Wyatt, Thomas 76

York Place (later Palace of Whitehall) 63, 64–5, 66

WITHDRAWN
from St. Joseph County Public Library
Excess ✓ Damaged
Date 2-19-25 Initials BL

M781.64 ABBA

ABBA (Musical group)

The New York times great songs of ABBA / 1980.